A souvenir guide

Wightwick Manor and Gardens

West Midlands

Stephen Ponder

🌳 **National Trust**

Cont[ents]

From P[...] 2
Varnish[...] 4
Theodo[...] 5
A country home on an ancient site 8
Making a home 10
Triumph and loss 12
Geoffrey and Florence Mander 14
Practical politics and good business 16
Politics and preservation 18
A Growing Collection 20
Collecting Morris 22
An Arts and Crafts house? 24
Wightwick and the Pre-Raphaelites 26
Collecting the Pre-Raphaelites 28
Collection highlights 30
Exploring the House 32
Rooms to enjoy 34
Drawing Room 1887 36
Great Parlour 1893 38
Billiard Room 1893 40
Dining Room 1893 42
Visitors' rooms 1893 44
Oak Room 1893 46
Visitors, family and servants 48
Making Wightwick work 50
An Underrated Garden? 52
An Edwardian garden 54
Change and revival 56
Formality around the house 58
The informal garden 60
Estates Old and New 62
Keeping Wightwick Alive 64

From Paint to Pre-Raphaelites

In 1887 Theodore Mander began building a new house in the country near Wolverhampton. He called it Wightwick Manor. Theodore was 34 and a partner in a successful family business making varnish and paint. He and his wife – aptly named Flora Paint – had two young children and a third on the way.

Wightwick still feels like the picturesque family home the Manders planned it to be. It's a house you can easily imagine living in – comfortable and inviting, full of interest, with every room different. You can picture curling up in one of its window seats or warming yourself by a log fire in one of the inglenook fireplaces. In the depths of the garden you easily forget you're on the outskirts of a Midlands city.

Making a new home

Theodore built Wightwick in two stages, although he hadn't planned it that way. He commissioned architect Edward Ould to design the house in the Old English style of timber framing, tile-hanging and bright red brick. In 1892–3 they added the east wing with elaborately patterned oak framing and brick chimneys. At first glance it looks like a carefully restored late medieval house – but it's just too good to be true.

The Manders wanted period details, fine craftsmanship and materials combined with artistic interest and modern comforts. They furnished their home comfortably but not ostentatiously. Quality was important, so the stained glass was by Charles Kempe, some wallpapers and fabrics by William Morris, and the house was filled with antique furniture, eastern rugs and Chinese porcelain.

The house's structure has changed little since then and many of Theodore and Flora's possessions are still here, making Wightwick an outstanding example of late Victorian taste. Sadly the Manders didn't live long to enjoy it. Theodore died in 1900; Flora, in 1905. As a widow Flora employed leading designer Thomas Mawson to create Wightwick's fine Edwardian garden. After her death her son Geoffrey commissioned Mawson to make further improvements.

Left The east wing is richly patterned and carved. The 1887 wing with its big brick chimneybreast is on the left

Right *Love Among the Ruins* by Edward Burne-Jones in the Great Parlour

Politics, preservation and Pre-Raphaelites

Geoffrey Mander and his second wife Rosalie Glynn Grylls took Wightwick in a new direction. He was an active Liberal member of parliament while Rosalie, a successful biographer, was selected as a Liberal candidate. Wightwick was a very political house. Geoffrey put his radical political convictions into practice by making Manders well known as a model employer – and by giving his home away. In 1937 he gave Wightwick and its contents to the National Trust. It was less than 50 years old, still a 'modern house'.

Geoffrey and Rosalie lived at Wightwick for the rest of their lives. Many of the things that you see today are due to their work as pioneering collectors. It was they who built up the outstanding collection of William Morris designs and Pre-Raphaelite art, in a unique partnership with the National Trust. Collecting was their passion, and we continue to collect in their spirit.

Varnish, Paint and Ink

Aged 16, Theodore Mander wrote to his mother from France where he was studying. 'My desire and I think my duty, is to prepare to enter Papa's business, as you say and I think I can be quite as useful in that way as being a minister.'

He stuck to his decision. Like previous generations of his family, Theodore's life was shaped by his Christian faith, business drive and a deep sense of public duty. The Manders were among the families who drove the industrial revolution that created much of Britain's wealth. They were prominent figures in Wolverhampton's development from a market town to a major industrial centre on the edge of the Black Country – 'the workshop of the world' – and the business they built up was one of the oldest varnish, paint and ink manufacturers in Britain.

Mander Brothers

Theodore's father Samuel Mander and his older brother Charles Benjamin took over their father Charles's successful varnish works established since about 1803. Still in their early twenties, they formed Mander Brothers in 1845. The business grew out of supplying materials for japanning tinplate (lacquerware) and the papier mâché trade, both specialities of Wolverhampton. Their grandfather, Benjamin, had opened his own japanning workshop in 1773.

Above The varnish vats at Mander Brothers' John Street Works

Left Colour sampling in the Mander Laboratory

A family and a firm

Mander Brothers diversified into paint and printing inks. The family were Nonconformist Protestants, like many industrialist families, but nevertheless Mander Brothers supplied varnish to the Vatican – business was business after all. The firm thrived to become a leading supplier to the British Empire and Europe. In the 1860s Samuel and Charles Benjamin moved their families to large houses near Wightwick, on the outskirts of Wolverhampton.

Like their Mander predecessors they were very active in Wolverhampton. As Sir Nicholas Mander, Bt (Charles Benjamin's great-great-grandson) writes, his family 'were grave and earnest, but always progressive and public spirited'. Samuel became a deacon of Queen Street Congregational Chapel, and Charles Benjamin was a town councillor.

Succeeding generations followed them into both the family business and public life. Theodore and cousin Charles Tertius Mander became partners. The firm was respected as a caring employer, offering its employees welfare provision and even a library. Charles was Conservative mayor of Wolverhampton from 1892 to 1896; Theodore, a Liberal, became mayor in 1899. Charles was the first chairman of Manders when it became a limited company in 1924; he was followed by Theodore's son Geoffrey. Over these successive generations, Manders continued to expand. In the Second World War the factory was a target for German bombers but escaped harm.

Geoffrey retired as chairman shortly before he died in 1962. In the late 1960s Manders redeveloped their town centre works site into shops and offices, still known as the Mander Centre. The family became less involved, and in the 1990s the company sold its paints division and the Mander Centre to concentrate on inks. The inks business was sold in 1997, ending Manders' two-hundred-year history.

Below The laboratory at Mander Brothers between the Wars. It was world-leading in the development of ink and paint technologies

Below left An early 20th-century advertisement for Manders' Varnishes

MANDER BROTHERS
WORLD RENOWNED
VARNISHES
LONDON · 17 GRACECHURCH Sᵀ EC
WORKS · WOLVERHAMPTON · ENGLAND

Theodore and Flora Mander

Writing in his notebook, Samuel Mander recorded, 'February 25th, 1853 This day we had the pleasure of embracing our first living child, a boy, to whom we gave the name of Samuel Theodore'.

Loving and deeply religious, Samuel and Mary Mander gave Theodore and his brothers and sisters secure and happy childhoods. When Theodore was eight Samuel noted 'he is naturally very shy' and he was to grow up reserved, serious and hard-working. Theodore was educated at Tettenhall College near his home, and he also studied in France. Christianity was central to his life; he noted chapels and churches visited, services attended and sermons heard, and at 20 was a lay preacher.

Theodore studied sciences, particularly chemistry, at London University and Clare College, Cambridge and travelled extensively. Whilst studying in Berlin he was constantly thinking about practical applications for Mander Brothers. His notebooks, diaries and letters are full of observations, experiences and facts that interested him, including visits to factories where he noted down the processes he saw. In his diary for 31 December 1876 Theodore wrote, 'have now finally settled down to business'.

Flora St Clair Paint

Aged 20 Theodore met the girl he would marry. His diary for December 1873 records 'Flora Paint of Halifax, Canada, very merry girl'. She was his sisters' school friend and almost 16. Her father Henry Paint was a merchant who became a member of the Canadian Parliament.

Left *Theodore Mander,* a watercolour portrait of about 1900 by an unknown artist

On 10 October 1877, while staying with the Paints in Canada, Theodore proposed to Flora. 'In the evening everyone went to a prayer meeting, everyone except Flora and myself… and something very important and agreeable occurred.' His family were delighted, and the wedding took place in Halifax, Nova Scotia in 1879. Flora's sister Mary later married Theodore's cousin Charles and lived at The Mount, near Wightwick.

Mornington Place

Theodore and Flora set up home at Mornington Place, a large semi-detached house in Wolverhampton. Life revolved around the business, chapel, family, local politics and public duties, with foreign travel for business and pleasure. In 1879 Theodore and Charles gave a dinner to celebrate becoming partners in Mander Brothers.

Theodore grew ever busier. He was elected as a Liberal town councillor in 1881, and played a leading role in building the new Wolverhampton School of Art. He became a governor of Tettenhall College, and a founding benefactor of Mansfield College – Oxford University's first Nonconformist college.

But their early married life was marked by grief. Their first child Gladys died soon after birth in 1880, and in 1881 Theodore's father died. Happily, their son Geoffrey Le Mesurier (after Flora's Guernsey ancestors) was born in 1882, followed by daughter Marjorie in 1883. Theodore kept a notebook of the children's early development. In February 1884 he wrote about Geoffrey, 'Very kind to his sister whom he calls "Mar" '.

Right *Flora Mander,* painted by Frederick Chester in 1881

A country home on an ancient site

In 1887 Theodore bought the early 17th-century Manor House built by the Wightwick family. Its situation offered an ideal site for a new house, a sheltered southerly slope with distant rural views of Shropshire, a stream and pools and potential for a garden.

Like other affluent Victorians, Theodore and Flora were moving their growing family out of an industrial town to a healthier location. Their son Lionel was born in 1888 while the new house was under way; he was followed by Alan in 1891. Wightwick was rural but only three miles from the factory, chapel and Town Hall, and it was near other Mander family homes.

The Manders wanted a comfortable home that reflected their aspirations and tastes. Theodore was not immensely rich, and had no intention of giving up business to become a country gentleman. Wightwick was planned as a family home in the country, not a country house at the heart of a large estate.

The business of building

Theodore chose a picturesque design by the architect Edward Ould, from Chester. It wasn't particularly large, with modest reception rooms facing south for sun and views, four bedrooms, nurseries and a service wing. Ould renovated the Old Manor House as servants' accommodation, and converted its farm buildings into stables. Theodore spent £9,492 on his new house – a large sum for those days, reflecting the high quality of materials and craftsmanship.

Between 1892 and 1893 Ould designed and built a new east wing, replacing the existing billiard room. With three large reception rooms

Left Ould's garden front design, drawn by Edmund Hodgkinson in 1889. The single-storey billiard room on the right faced east

Above From the south Wightwick's two building phases are evident, with the more richly patterned east wing on the right

Early electricity

Wightwick had electric light throughout by 1893. The original light fittings are still used and some early 100 volt light bulbs survive in working order but can't be used within the present system. To modern eyes the lighting level is very low, but it would have seemed bright compared to gaslight or oil lamps. It's hard for us to appreciate the novelty of electricity for the Victorian householder.

Early electrical systems could be troublesome and unreliable. Engineer Mr Dunn looked after Wightwick's heating system and the generating plant in the stables – the Mander boys called him 'Greasy Dunn'. A neighbour complained repeatedly about smoke from the generator chimney, so Flora had the 'Electric Engine' stopped while she was abroad. Connecting Wightwick to the local mains supply in 1904 solved the problem.

and five visitors' bedrooms, it doubled Wightwick's size. It may have been partly intended for entertaining business clients; the Manders didn't belong to the world of country house parties. Records don't survive, but Theodore must have spent at least as much on the east wing as he did on the earlier building.

Picturesque and practical

Theodore was a practical scientist. His house combined period details and traditional craftsmanship with modern technology. It was constructed using steel beams and concrete, and had central heating. It had a modern kitchen and bathrooms, even a Turkish bath.

Making a home

In 1884 Theodore Mander attended Oscar Wilde's lecture on 'The House Beautiful' in Wolverhampton. He made careful notes of what he heard, including three 'Rules in Art'. Wightwick was an opportunity to put them into practice.

We don't know how Theodore and Flora set about decorating and furnishing Wightwick, who advised them, or where they acquired much of the contents. Although the Manders bought from Morris and Company, they didn't employ the firm to decorate Wightwick. Their new home had comfortable interiors influenced by the Aesthetic Movement, with stained glass by Charles Kempe, Morris wallpapers and fabrics, eastern rugs, antique furniture and Chinese blue and white porcelain. Wightwick is a rare survivor of many Victorian houses decorated this way.

Living at Wightwick
Having started building in 1887, the Manders moved in before Christmas 1888. Theodore travelled into Wolverhampton every day to Manders and his public duties. In 1891 he became an alderman and on 9 November 1899 he was elected Mayor. Flora was active in local charities: an example of her fundraising work was the bazaar held at Wightwick in 1894 in aid of a home for orphans.

Religion was central to family life. Lionel rather bitterly remembered his father as 'an excessively good man of puritanical yeoman stock', who led morning prayers for family and servants every day. On Sundays they went to chapel, had a scripture lesson after lunch, sang hymns with Flora at the piano after tea before Theodore went out to preach, and ended with prayers at 10pm.

But the Manders also enjoyed themselves. Lionel wrote that Theodore was 'a fine shot, an enthusiastic fisherman and a keen rider to hounds'. There was croquet, tennis and cricket in summer and skating in the winter. The children and their cousins from The Mount performed *Snow White and the Seven Dwarfs* at Christmas in 1898. Geoffrey and Marjorie both became keen photographers. The Manders entertained family, friends and business associates. Flora held 'At Homes' for her women friends with refreshments and entertainment. They also welcomed guests as part of their public service. When the local Higher Grade School was opened the Manders gave a luncheon to celebrate the event.

Above Lionel, Marjorie, Flora, Geoffrey, Alan and Theodore Mander outside the Morning Room in the late 1890s

Rules in Art

Oscar Wilde, the famous author, poet and playwright, was a great advocate of Aestheticism, of 'art for art's sake'. The Aesthetic Movement influenced painters, architects and designers from the 1860s to the 1880s. The 'Rules' Theodore noted actually came from the ideas of the great art theorist John Ruskin and the designer William Morris, emphasising the importance of beauty and craftsmanship, and looking to the past for inspiration. Wilde seems to have paraphrased Morris's famous maxim: 'Have nothing in your houses that you do not know to be useful or believe to be beautiful'. Theodore had a Ruskin quotation carved in the Drawing Room panelling at Wightwick.

Right The *Snow White and the Seven Dwarfs* programme shows the Malthouse stairs

Triumph and loss

On 27 April 1900 Theodore and Flora Mander, Mayor and Mayoress, were presented to Queen Victoria on the royal train at Wolverhampton station. The Duke and Duchess of York, later King George V and Queen Mary came to Wolverhampton on 23 July, and made a brief private visit to Wightwick.

Seven weeks later Theodore was dead. On 28 August he fell dangerously ill whilst fishing in North Wales. He returned to Wightwick on 6 September. A second operation on a liver abscess at Wightwick on 14 September couldn't save him. He was only 47. Newspapers paid tribute to his kindness and generosity, his skill as a speaker 'on art, education and social subjects', and described him as 'an intense lover of art and horticulture'.

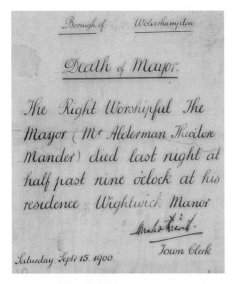

Four days after his death, Wolverhampton came to a standstill for his civic funeral as the procession made its slow, sad way from Wightwick Manor to Queen Street Congregational Church in Wolverhampton, and then past Wightwick to the burial in Pattingham churchyard.

A brief widowhood

It was a shattering blow. Normal life at Wightwick abruptly ended and the family scattered: Flora travelled abroad for six months with nine-year-old Alan, leaving Wightwick in the care of housekeeper Miss Smith; Marjorie went to school in Berlin; Lionel was away at Harrow School; and Geoffrey went up to Trinity College, Cambridge. On 20 January 1901 Geoffrey wrote to his mother about visiting Wightwick from The Mount where he was staying with his cousins, 'the rooms look very dismal all covered up'. Flora didn't really settle at Wightwick again until 1903. But her health was poor, and in 1905 she died in London – like Theodore, aged 47. Geoffrey was left responsible for his brothers; Alan was only 14.

Above The Duchess of York, in black, is in the centre with Flora to her left. The Duke of York is fifth and Theodore third from right

Left The official announcement of Theodore's death on 14 September 1900

Opposite, left Princess Prativa photographed by Rita Martin

Opposite, right Joan Wyndham sits at the feet of Miles Mander in a scene from the film *Loyalties* (1933)

Princesses in the family

After Flora died Marjorie went out to her uncle Martin Mander's sheep farm in New Zealand. There she met and married Gervas Nevile in 1910, and they later returned to England. Neither Lionel nor Alan went into the family business. Alan spent two unhappy years at sea on a tea clipper, the *Port Jackson*. In 1912 Lionel married an Indian princess, Princess Prativa Devi, daughter of the Maharajah of Cooch Behar. It ended with a scandalous divorce in 1922. Alan married Prativa's sister Princess Sudhira in 1914; their marriage lasted over 50 years.

From Wightwick to Hollywood

In the film *Wuthering Heights* (1939), starring Laurence Olivier and Merle Oberon, Mr Lockwood is played by Miles Mander – Lionel's professional name as a well-known actor, director, producer and writer. He was passionate about flying, motor and horse racing but ran up huge debts. After serving in the First World War, Miles made a successful career in British, European and Australian films. In 1935 he made his Hollywood debut in *The Three Musketeers*. He was a character actor best known for playing villains and English gentlemen. He appeared in, directed or wrote the screenplays for over a hundred films.

Geoffrey and Florence Mander

On 6 July 1907 a garden party for employees at Wightwick celebrated Geoffrey joining Mander Brothers and his marriage to Rosalind Florence Caverhill. There was a band, sports and 'Dancing after Tea'.

Like Flora, Florence was Canadian; she married Geoffrey in Montreal in 1906. Their daughter Mavis was born in 1908, followed by Mervyn in 1910 and Elizabeth in 1916. Photographs of them as babies and toddlers show Wightwick as a family home once more.

Like his father Theodore, Geoffrey was hard-working, thoughtful and energetic, and deeply committed to the family firm and to public service. After Harrow School he studied organic chemistry at Trinity College, Cambridge. Although modest by nature, he was less reserved and not so obviously serious as Theodore.

Above Geoffrey Mander in Royal Flying Corps uniform, 1918

Left The garden party at Wightwick in 1907

Photographs and his portrait reflect a determined but kindly and humorous character. He enjoyed shooting, hunting and fishing and played cricket, tennis and squash.

Radical politics

From early on Geoffrey was a committed, radical Liberal. Theodore's Conservative cousin Charles disapproved of him: 'He is very self opinionated, has no judgment or tact & is much too big for his boots, & has been ever since his father died'. Geoffrey remembered that when he supported the Labour candidate against Sir Alfred Hickman in the 1906 election it 'caused great indignation in Conservative circles in the neighbourhood and I found myself cut in the hunting field by some of them'. As a town councillor he caused a stir by proposing a minimum weekly wage of 24 shillings (£1.20) for council employees. At Wightwick Geoffrey and Florence hosted political functions for the Liberal Party, and ran classes for local people teaching useful skills such as gardening and dairying.

Wightwick for sale

At the outbreak of the First World War, Geoffrey tried to enlist but was rejected on health grounds. In 1917 he joined the Royal Flying Corps as a technical officer. He kept notes of flights, including one over Wightwick in 1917, 'circled round house about 100ft up'. He served in Egypt after the war. In 1919 Geoffrey returned to the business and to politics, but he and Florence were drifting apart. In 1920 he put Wightwick up for sale; it was advertised in *Country Life* magazine as 'one of the most unique half-timbered houses in England combining medieval atmosphere and modern convenience'. Most of the land and cottages were sold, but not the house. Florence moved to London, and they were divorced in 1930.

Below left Florence was always known by her second name

Speed!

As a young man Geoffrey was one of the first in Wolverhampton to own a motor car. In 1906 he was prosecuted for driving 'to the danger of the public' at a speed of around 12 miles per hour. The case was dismissed.

Practical politics and good business

At Mander Brothers Geoffrey put his radical convictions into practice. A profit-sharing scheme and pensions were introduced. In 1932 Manders became the first company in Britain to introduce the 40-hour working week.

Geoffrey believed his family's benevolent Christian attitude to their employees was the forerunner of modern welfare principles. Manders provided welfare, sports and social clubs, and Geoffrey hosted social events for the workforce at Wightwick. Employees' goodwill drove Manders' success, and the firm is still remembered with affection in Wolverhampton.

WITH BEST WISHES FOR
1931
FROM
Mr. GEOFFREY MANDER, M.P. & Mrs. MANDER
WIGHTWICK MANOR
WOLVERHAMPTON

MANDER AND THE DOLE CUT
THE TRUTH!

At 7-30 p.m. on Monday, September 28th, 1931, a division took place in the House of Commons on the 10% cut in the dole.

The cut was carried by 296 votes to 243.

MANDER VOTED AGAINST THE CUT.

This can be confirmed by anyone who visits the Free Library and looks up Hansard, the official report of Parliamentary proceedings. All the names are given.

UNEMPLOYED! STAND BY MANDER
NOW AS HE STOOD BY YOU THEN

Mander voted for the second reading of the Economy Bill as there were some cuts, such as the Army and Navy, he felt could not be avoided, but when in committee each point was taken separately.

MANDER VOTED AGAINST THE CUT.

Published by G. BENNISON, Lich Gates, Wolverhampton.
Printed by JAMES GIBBS, Wheeler's Fold, Wolverhampton.

Parliament

Determined to become a Liberal MP, Geoffrey first stood for election in 1920. After several unsuccessful campaigns he won the East Wolverhampton seat in 1929. He quickly built a reputation for his skilful use of 'parliamentary questions'. Journalist Percy Cater remembered 'the pinkly pugnacious Mr Mander waving above the battle of question-time like the banner of some cause or another'.

One cause was industrial relations, drawing on his experience. Another was foreign affairs. Geoffrey was a passionate advocate for the League of Nations. Like Churchill, he was one of the few who spoke out about the dangers of not taking a firm stand against aggression. After Geoffrey supported sanctions against Italy for its invasion of Abyssinia (Ethiopia), Mussolini attacked him in a newspaper, calling for a boycott of the Milan branch of 'Fratelli Mander'. Geoffrey was one of the first to highlight the danger Hitler posed. He fiercely criticised Neville Chamberlain's appeasement policy in his 1941 book, *We Were Not All Wrong*. He was proud that his name was on a Nazi list of dissidents who were to be rounded up after invading England.

Rosalie Mander

Liberal politics brought Geoffrey and Rosalie Glynn Grylls together. Twenty-three years younger, lively and formidably intelligent, she was secretary to a Liberal MP, and selected as Liberal candidate for Reading in 1930. Although Rosalie had grown up in Berkshire she was fiercely proud of her Cornish ancestry. Her lifelong friend Lady Longford recalled her at Oxford University as 'the exceptionally pretty young girl whose arrival was always heralded by the tap of elegant shoes'.

Geoffrey and Rosalie married in 1930. Some of the Mander family disapproved, dismissing her as 'the secretary'. Their son John was born in 1932. They spent much of their time in London, but at Wightwick political guests included the Asquiths and Vera Brittain. Rosalie began her successful writing career with a biography of Mary Shelley, published in 1938.

Coming to Wightwick

Rosalie recalled: 'When I married and first came to Wightwick in the 1930s, I regarded the place as old-fashioned and uncomfortable – which it was and is – but as I was much more interested in our small house in Westminster I made no attempt to "do Wightwick over". This was lucky, as it meant that when the National Trust accepted it later very little that was original had been changed.'

Left Rosalie Mander with her son John in the Hall at Wightwick

Opposite Geoffrey and Rosalie Mander's wedding on 30 November 1930

Politics and preservation

On 10 December 1937 newspapers announced that Geoffrey Mander had given Wightwick, its contents and a financial endowment to the National Trust.

The Manders' radical friend Sir Charles Trevelyan, who planned to give Wallington to the Trust, suggested offering Wightwick. Geoffrey was already a supporter of the Trust. He described Wightwick as 'one of the most beautiful modern houses in England', and the National Trust accepted it for its artistic importance. The gift reflected Geoffrey's political principles and Rosalie later wrote, 'He never regretted it, for he liked to think that the public should enjoy what had been his private property'.

Above The *Birmingham Post*'s coverage of the gift to the National Trust

Right Lady Mander with Ricky on the terrace. She loved cats, and always had one at Wightwick

Living with the National Trust

During the Second World War Geoffrey was Parliamentary Private Secretary to the Minister for Air and the Women's Auxiliary Air Force officers (WAAFs) occupied part of Wightwick. It survived, but the Manders' London house was bombed. In January 1945 Geoffrey was knighted for services to Parliament, becoming Sir Geoffrey Mander. But when Labour won a massive victory in the General Election in July he lost his seat – a bitter blow. He joined the Labour Party in 1948, and served as a county councillor.

Geoffrey and Rosalie continued to occupy and manage Wightwick. In his diary James Lees-Milne of the National Trust wrote of his visit on 23 April 1946, 'He is a very decent, good, thoughtful man. Left-wing' and 'Lady Mander talkative and pretty'. Their daughter Anthea, born in 1945, had unhappy memories of her childhood. The Wightwick routine always revolved around open days, although visitors could be a welcome diversion.

After Geoffrey died in 1962, Rosalie usually spent half the week in London and half at Wightwick. She was always there for Saturday and Bank Holiday open afternoons, giving lively guided tours. Tea for the volunteers was in her kitchen or on the terrace, with Lady Mander ('we volunteers never called her Rosalie') keeping several conversations going at once. The National Trust grew, and relationships were not always easy. Rosalie was delighted when an article about the Trust described her simply as 'fierce'. But she was kind and generous and particularly encouraged young volunteers.

Rosalie wrote many biographies and articles on 19th-century writers and artists, and frequently lectured in Britain and America. Her son John, also a writer, died in 1978. After Rosalie's death in 1988 her friend Mary Lutyens wrote, 'Seemingly so outgoing and sparkling, she was an intensely private person with depths of feeling she seldom gave one glimpses of'.

Rosalie was the last to live permanently at Wightwick. The family had kept away, but Anthea began taking a very active interest. A 'flat for all the family' was converted from the family bedrooms. Anthea wrote that it 'is everything a home should be, and Wightwick never was for me.' She died suddenly in 2004. Elizabeth, the last of Geoffrey's children, died in 2005. Mander family members still stay in the flat.

Above left **Rosalie** turning her hand to war work

Above **Lady Mander** giving a guided tour of Wightwick in the 1960s

A Growing Collection

Visitors from around the world come to Wightwick to see the collection of William Morris designs and Pre-Raphaelite art. Theodore and Flora Mander began the collection; Geoffrey and Rosalie developed it in partnership with the National Trust.

William Morris

William Morris (1834–1896) – 'Topsy' to his friends – was one of the greatest Victorian designers, with a genius for patterns, although he was more famous in his lifetime as a writer. In 1861 he founded what would become Morris and Company in partnership with his friends the Pre-Raphaelite artists Dante Gabriel Rossetti, Ford Madox Brown and Edward Burne-Jones and the architect Philip Webb. It grew out of working together to decorate Morris's home, Red House, at Bexleyheath (National Trust). The firm produced high-quality wallpapers, fabrics and carpets, embroideries, tapestries, tiles, stained glass and metalwork, furniture – and entire interiors.

Morris's designs were rooted in his deep understanding of materials and how to make things. They combine strong patterns inspired by historic designs with natural forms – flowers, plants, birds and animals. Morris preferred hand craftsmanship, but also designed for machine production. His daughter May later led the embroidery section of the firm. In the 1890s his Kelmscott Press produced exceptionally fine limited edition books. Morris and Co. closed in 1940. Sanderson's have continued to produce a range of Morris designs, now through their Morris and Co. subsidiary.

Left A corner of the Great Parlour with a Morris 'Sunbury' armchair covered in 'Strawberry Thief' cotton designed by William Morris, and Chinese blue and white porcelain

WILLIAM·MORRIS·

Morris's dilemma

Morris wanted his products to be available to all, but in reality only extremely wealthy clients could afford Morris and Co.'s more expensive work such as tapestries. Other customers like the Manders bought their cheaper wallpapers and fabrics. Morris himself complained of 'ministering to the swinish luxury of the rich', and in the 1880s became a very active socialist.

Above Portrait of *William Morris* painted by Cosmo Rowe in the 1890s

Left 'Acanthus' wallpaper designed in 1874 shows the strong pattern structure of William Morris's designs

Right Morris designed 'Honeysuckle' in 1876. It is one of his most complex patterns, symmetrical and on a large scale

Morris and Wightwick

Like many middle-class customers, Theodore and Flora Mander bought wallpapers, fabrics and furniture for their new home from Morris and Co. But they didn't commission the firm to decorate Wightwick, and Morris never visited. Morris and Company had a London shop and provided catalogues of their designs. You can see original 'Larkspur' wallpaper in the Library, hung in 1888. The Manders' decoration in 1893 was more expensive. 'Acanthus' wallpaper is one of Morris's most ambitious designs, requiring 30 different blocks and separate printings in 15 colours. The Manders used Morris fabrics on the walls, though apparently not for the curtains. The Drawing Room was hung with 'Dove and Rose' silk and wool. The Great Parlour hangings are 'Diagonal Trail' wool designed in 1893 by John Dearle; possibly this is the earliest example of this fabric being used in a house.

The Honeysuckle Room has less expensive 'Honeysuckle' printed linen. Morris used traditional vegetable dyes for fabrics; they have faded, so some of the original strong colours are now muted. The Manders also bought machine-woven carpets and rugs, although only fragments survive. Some chairs came from the Morris and Co. ranges inspired by 18th-century designs, for example, the 'Sunbury' wing chairs and a rush-seated mahogany 'Hampton Court' chair.

Collecting Morris

The National Trust accepted Wightwick partly for its original Morris decoration. Rosalie Mander remembered that 'The house at once took on new life with its sense of security and we set about acquiring things to add to original treasures'.

Geoffrey and Rosalie sought advice from Morris and Co. and the Manders and the Trust bought Morris wallpapers and fabrics. They redecorated some rooms using Morris wallpaper for the first time, notably 'Pimpernel' in the Billiard Room. Since Morris and Co. closed, the Manders and the Trust have acquired many more Morris furnishings through purchases and gifts. Geoffrey could drive a hard bargain: he paid £75 for the 'Pomona' tapestry design and 13 drawings for stained glass, including the *Minstrel Figure*, instead of the £100 asking price.

Left Philip Webb's drawing of a hare for *The Forest* tapestry

Below, left Design drawing for the *Pomona* tapestry. The figure was designed by Burne-Jones and the rest by Morris in 1884

Below A 'Rossetti' chair of ebonised beech from the Morris and Company Sussex range

Opposite Morris designed this *Minstrel Figure with Cymbals* about 1874. Geoffrey bought it in 1938

The collection

Wightwick's Morris character is much stronger today than it was in 1937 and it reflects most aspects of William Morris's work. You can see Morris and Co. designs used as he intended, with Morris paper or fabric on the walls of most rooms together with Morris curtains, furniture covers and cushions.

Textiles

Woven patterns include 'Bird and Vine', 'Bird' and 'Peacock and Dragon' in wool and 'Flower Garden' in wool and silk. 'Honeysuckle' and 'Strawberry Thief' are two of many printed designs. Embroidery includes a 'Rose and Olive' cushion designed by Morris. Curtains and a pair of sleeves by May Morris were bought from Kelmscott Manor. The Morris hand-knotted carpets, acquired by Geoffrey in 1961, are amongst Wightwick's finest works of art – much grander than Theodore's machine-made Morris carpets.

Tapestry is represented by original design drawings. 'Pomona' is by Morris and Burne-Jones. Philip Webb's drawings of a lion, raven, hare and fox were used in the 'Forest' tapestry made in 1887. In Theodore's time their owner Laurence Hodson lived at Compton Hall near Wightwick. The Trust

bought the drawings in 2014, supported by the National Art Collections Fund. The links to Morris and Co. and to Wolverhampton would have appealed very strongly to Geoffrey and Rosalie.

Stained glass

Morris and Co. made some of the finest Victorian stained glass. There are small panels of Milton designed by Madox Brown, and of Horace, Homer and Chaucer by Burne-Jones. Two Minstrels are by Morris. The drawings for stained glass are by Rossetti, Burne-Jones and Madox Brown; they include Madox Brown's *Christ and the Woman Touching the Hem of His Garment* and *Christ in Majesty* by Rossetti and Burne-Jones.

Books

Theodore owned several Kelmscott Press books. More Kelmscott volumes and original designs for letters and other details have been added. Geoffrey was interested in Morris's political ideas so collected related books and pamphlets.

Kelmscott Chaucer

The Kelmscott edition of the *Works of Geoffrey Chaucer* was Morris's greatest achievement in book production, and perhaps the finest book created in the 19th century. Wightwick's copy was given to the National Trust in 2007.

An Arts and Crafts house?

Theodore and Flora Mander also acquired work by Morris's associates and contemporaries and furnishings from many different periods and countries. Some of the original strong colours have faded or darkened with age, but the mix of colour and pattern still reflects their late Victorian tastes.

They went to Charles Kempe for stained glass. His windows are inspired by late medieval English and German glass, with rich greens and yellows and a lot of painted detail. Kempe's influence is particularly strong in the Great Parlour where his decorative colour scheme and plasterwork friezes intensify the 15th- and 16th-century feel. Geoffrey and Rosalie added more Kempe work.

Arts and Crafts

Decorative tiles in fireplaces are an important feature. Some rooms in the 1887 wing have tiles designed by William De Morgan, hand-painted with his distinctive flowers and creatures in rich colours and glazes. He was a friend of Morris and the firm sold De Morgan's work. Geoffrey, Rosalie and the Trust collected many more De Morgan tiles, vases and bowls.

W.A.S. Benson designed some of the light fittings. Like De Morgan, Benson was associated with the Arts and Crafts Movement. He designed furniture and metalwork made by his own company. He was a friend of Morris and in 1905 became chairman of Morris and Co.

Below, left Four De Morgan tiles. Top right *Bedford Park Anemone*; Top left Unnamed design; Bottom left *Single Rose*; Bottom right *Carnation*

Below The Great Parlour inglenook with Kempe decoration, Dutch tiles and Victorian sofas covered in Caucasian Sile carpets shows Theodore and Flora's tastes

Antique and modern

Theodore and Flora acquired most of the antique and antique-style English and European furniture, ranging in period from the early 17th to the 19th centuries, mingled with comfortable new armchairs and sofas. They collected the large quantity of Chinese and Japanese porcelain, particularly blue and white, very much in the Aesthetic Movement taste, and some English and European ceramics. Antique tapestries were hung in the Hall, and the fabric hangings in the Indian Bird and Oak Rooms are quite different to Morris designs. The Manders used fine eastern rugs and carpets not only on most floors but for curtains and upholstery. We have replaced some worn-out rugs to continue the effect.

Above Seventeenth-century oak furniture, a Victorian Bechstein piano and a curtain made from an Azerbaijani kelim in the Great Parlour

Right A comfortable Victorian armchair covered with eastern carpet in the Library. Burne-Jones designed the stained glass

Aestheticism and Arts and Crafts

Ruskin's and Morris's ideas inspired the Arts and Crafts Movement in Europe and America. It wasn't a distinct style but an approach to design, working and living based on understanding the qualities of materials and the joy of craftsmanship. Rather than imitating designs of the past, Arts and Crafts architects such as Philip Webb, Ernest Gimson and Charles Voysey took inspiration from their construction and craftsmanship.

Ould's deep interest in traditional materials and craftsmanship connects with Arts and Crafts, but he was chiefly interested in their picturesque and artistic potential. Theodore and Flora's tastes and home strongly reflected the influence of the Aesthetic Movement. While Wightwick is not itself an Arts and Crafts house, collecting since 1937 has enhanced the Morris and Arts and Crafts aspects of its interiors.

Wightwick and the Pre-Raphaelites

James Lees-Milne observed in his diary for 23 April 1946, 'The Manders' enthusiasm for the Pre-Raphaelites is infectious'. Geoffrey and Rosalie were pioneering collectors of the Pre-Raphaelites in the 1930s when Victorian art was very unfashionable. The collection they began is their greatest contribution to Wightwick and took it in a new direction.

The Mander family were never patrons of the Pre-Raphaelites, and didn't collect their work during the artists' lifetimes. The paintings, drawings and prints owned by Theodore and Flora and Geoffrey and Florence reflected conventional middle-class taste. Their family portraits and English and European scenes are mostly by artists little known today, and the Pre-Raphaelite collection displaced many of them. John Ruskin's fine drawing *Lake and Mountain* (below), possibly owned by Theodore, stands out as an exception.

Artistic rebellion

In 1848 seven very young men, led by Dante Gabriel Rossetti, John Everett Millais and William Holman Hunt, formed the secret Pre-Raphaelite Brotherhood. Ford Madox Brown was a close associate. They rebelled against the art establishment and sought inspiration from what they regarded as the 'purer' style of art before Renaissance masters such as Raphael.

Early Pre-Raphaelite art has subjects from the Bible, literature, the Middle Ages and contemporary life painted in brilliant colours or drawn with sharp outlines. Intensely realistic detail conveys symbolic meaning. Paintings such as Millais' *Ophelia* and Holman Hunt's *The Light of the World* are among the most famous of Victorian pictures. Their work initially provoked fierce criticism, but Ruskin's support helped them to gain success.

Pre-Raphaelitism quickly influenced other artists, but the Brotherhood fell apart in 1853. A second, very different but influential phase emerged from Rossetti's concentration on intense watercolours of medieval themes, focusing on imagination and colour rather than detail and meaning. In 1857 Rossetti, Morris, Burne-Jones and others decorated the Oxford Union debating hall with murals of stories from the legend of King Arthur. In the 1860s the original members of the movement developed in widely diverging directions. Their work influenced a younger generation in the 1870s and 1880s, notably Lucy Madox Brown, Marie Spartali Stillman and Evelyn Pickering (Mrs William De Morgan).

A Pre-Raphaelite passion

It was probably the direct links between the Morris firm and the Pre-Raphaelites that sparked Geoffrey and Rosalie's interest. Their first acquisition was a portrait of Jane Morris by Rossetti, completed by Madox Brown. They bought it for £14 in 1937, before the National Trust had formally accepted Wightwick. Collecting the Pre-Raphaelites quickly became a shared enthusiasm and then a partnership with the National Trust. The Manders bought from private owners, dealers and auctions. It wasn't just pictures: in 1939 they bought Pre-Raphaelite painted furniture with panels based on Rossetti pictures.

Above Jane Morris's face finely painted by Rossetti contrasts with the rest. After a stroke in 1893 Brown had to paint with his left hand

Opposite The Oak Room cabinet's paintings by Henry Treffry Dunn after Rossetti

Collecting the Pre-Raphaelites

Rosalie Mander said 'We were lucky in those years to get to know several descendants of the Pre-Raphaelites. We received many generous gifts, besides pictures on permanent loan, from those who were glad to find them appreciated and displayed for enjoyment. If only we had bought more then!'

In the late 1940s major paintings arrived: G.F. Watts's portrait of Jane Nassau Senior from her family and Burne-Jones's *Love Among the Ruins* from Lord Bearsted's bequest at Upton House.

The Rossetti connection

On 20 May 1948 James Lees-Milne noted in his diary, 'To tea with Lady Mander. A Pre-Raphaelite tea-party'. Guests included 'Mrs Angeli, William Rossetti's daughter, and Mrs Joseph (Holman Hunt's daughter). It was fun.' Mrs Angeli loaned many pictures to Wightwick. She described to Rosalie how they had been stacked on the pavement before a bomb destroyed her house during the war. They include many portraits of her Rossetti and Madox Brown relations; the Trust now owns them.

The collection grew steadily. Pioneering Pre-Raphaelite dealer Jeremy Maas recalled how in 1961 he was outbid for a group of drawings by Rossetti's wife, Elizabeth Siddal, 'by an elderly and distinguished-looking gentleman at about £120, thus creating a world record for her work'. The drawings were to be Geoffrey's last purchase, but Rosalie and the Trust continued collecting. Rosalie's last acquisition for Wightwick was a small Rossetti sketch of Walter Deverell.

Personal and quirky

The Manders' enthusiasms, the contacts they developed and opportunities that arose drove their collecting. Geoffrey and Rosalie had no plan to make a definitive collection of Pre-Raphaelite art. Their approach seems to have been more biographical, historical and literary than visual. Many of the pictures are about people, as individuals, used as models, or representing figures in a story. The Manders were interested in stories and associations; as well as pictures there are objects and furniture associated with the

Left Evelyn De Morgan painted *The Mourners* about 1917, prompted by the First World War. A label on the back reads 'The unhappy people, in their misery, are haunted by a vision of past happiness'

Pre-Raphaelites, including items which once belonged to Dante Gabriel Rossetti. The links with the artists and their families make this a collection of exceptional interest.

An active collection

Since Rosalie's death we have broadened the collection with pictures by artists not previously included, notably Spencer Stanhope. Coverage of female artists has expanded, including fine works by Spencer Stanhope's niece, Evelyn De Morgan.

Above *Lovers Listening to Music* of about 1855 is one of the Elizabeth Siddal drawings Geoffrey bought in 1961

Left *The Rescue*, painted about 1880 by John Roddam Spencer Stanhope. The intense colours and angular drapery are characteristic of his later work

Pre-Raphaelite Sisters

Jeremy Maas got to know Geoffrey and Rosalie. 'Thus it was that I met the first of the redoubtable band of ladies who were to contribute so much to Pre-Raphaelite studies in the 1960s and '70s.' Rosalie was one of the 'PreRaphaeladies' or 'the Pre-Raphaelite Sisterhood' (as journalist Ernestine Carter called them). Rosalie published *Portrait of Rossetti* as well as many articles on the Pre-Raphaelites.

Pre-Raphaelite family portraits

1 Holman Hunt's portrait of his daughter Gladys (Mrs Joseph) is characteristic of his intense drawing style; her niece Diana described Gladys as the rather alarming 'Big Aunt' of her childhood in her book *My Grandmothers and I*.

2 Madox Brown's *William Michael Rossetti by Lamplight* (1856) was a present to William's mother. The intimacy and directness, accurately rendered light and detail of this painting and Millais' of Euphemia (4) are characteristic of Pre-Raphaelite portraiture.

3 Drawings by Dante Gabriel Rossetti include this portrait of his sister, the poet Christina Rossetti.

4 *Euphemia Ruskin with Foxgloves* painted by Millais in Scotland in 1853 is a tender study of the woman who was to become his wife.

Collection highlights

Major pictures

2 John Roddam Spencer Stanhope's *The Gentle Music of a Bygone Day* (1873) combines strong colour and his love of the Renaissance art of Florence.

3 *The Tomb Scene from Romeo and Juliet* (1870) is Lucy Madox Brown's finest exhibited work, showing her characteristic strong composition and intensity of feeling.

4 G. F. Watts's superb 1858 portrait of Jane Nassau Senior has typically brilliant Pre-Raphaelite colour and intensely realistic detail, full of symbolic meaning.

5 Burne-Jones's *Love Among the Ruins*, painted in 1893–4 but based on an earlier version, is one of his finest late works, representing the ephemeral nature of youth and love. Its poetic feeling, subtle colouring and decorative qualities show his mature style and the strong influence of Italian Renaissance art in his work.

Pre-Raphaelite drawings

1 & 6 Elizabeth Siddal's watercolours *The Eve of St. Agnes* (c.1857) and *The Haunted Wood* (1856) have the intensity and imaginative feeling of Pre-Raphaelitism's second phase.

7 Millais' drawing *Queen Matilda Washing the Feet of Pilgrims* (1848) is in the distinctive early Pre-Raphaelite manner of spiky outlines and deliberately awkward compositions.

Fine drawings

1 Burne-Jones' *Girl in a Dress with Puffed Sleeves* is one of five mid-1860s studies of young women in red chalk on textured paper. They show his mastery as a draftsman and his growing interest in Italian Renaissance art.

2 Burne-Jones's delicate *Study of a Woman's Head* (1873) demonstrates equal skill in pencil. These signed works were for display, unlike the numerous drawings showing the artists' working practices, such as Burne-Jones's drapery studies for *King Cophetua and the Beggarmaid*.

3&4 A group of Rossetti's later drawings concentrate on images of beautiful women – he called them 'stunners' – in which beauty, colour and mood matter most. The collection includes representations of *Alexa Wilding* (4) and *Maria Zambaco* (3), who had a tempestuous relationship with Burne-Jones.

Exploring the House

An inscription with Theodore and Flora Mander's initials above the front door shows their pride in creating their new home. Other inscriptions carved on the east wing include 'The welcome ever smiles And farewell goes out sighing'.

Wightwick grew much bigger than they initially planned. Theodore built it in two phases that are almost two separate buildings with different characters, and form a rambling, very varied house on a comfortable scale. The main timbers are real structural framing.

Entrance

Here you see the house's original size and L-shaped plan. Edward Ould put his own stamp on the picturesque Old English style, developed by architect Norman Shaw and popular in the 1870s and 1880s. Wightwick combines sandstone with unmistakably Victorian red Ruabon brick and tile-hanging; the timber-framing derived from the Cheshire and Lancashire buildings Ould knew so well. Fine carving is by Edward Griffith, of Chester.

Wightwick is deliberately irregular and 'quaint', mixing Tudor, Elizabethan and Jacobean details, as if it has grown up haphazardly around a medieval tower. It has an old house's charm, while meeting the Manders' modern needs. The Elizabethan gatehouse at Little Moreton Hall in Cheshire inspired the two-storey porch inviting you in, although '1887' is prominently carved over the door. The cloakroom to its right was added in 1893. The servants' wing on the left is deliberately more simply detailed. Its Tudor-arched door is where luggage could be unloaded and taken up the back stairs.

South front and east wing

The two parts of Wightwick are immediately obvious from the terraces. The Old English west wing with red brick has its end splayed at an angle and a big upstairs window to the Day Nursery. Ould designed doors, sheltered seats and a balcony linking the house with its garden. His 1893 east wing set back on the right is on a grander scale and in a different spirit. Wholly timber-framed with much richer and more intricate patterns, it deliberately creates the look of a 15th- and 16th-century house.

Ould published a book on timber-framed houses in 1904, and you can see how they inspired him. The east wing's main section with windows set high and a bay window suggesting a great hall derives from Ockwells Manor in Berkshire, which dates from c.1450. Other details are drawn from houses such as Little Moreton Hall. The fine oak work is by Rattee and Kett of Cambridge, and James Brown of London supplied convincingly 'Tudor' patterned chimneys.

You could almost believe that the Manders had carefully restored an old house. But if it was a genuine medieval great hall, the big bay window would be at one end of the main range, not in the middle. The house's richly carved decoration includes windows with dragons and mermaids. Like Little Moreton Hall it has carved inscriptions but here they are literary quotations, from Shakespeare and the 17th-century poet Robert Herrick – a very Victorian touch.

Rooms to enjoy

Edward Ould skilfully created rooms combining comfort and artistic effect. He used period details, high-quality materials and craftsmanship to integrate the two parts of the house.

Welcome 1887

The Porch and Hall were always the main entrance for visitors. Exposed beams, oak panelling and antique furniture create an early 17th-century feel. Wallpaper friezes imitating embossed leather, originally crimson and gilt, once provided a splash of colour.

You immediately encounter the family in portraits: Geoffrey, Theodore and Flora Mander. With its Old English inglenook fireplace lined with

De Morgan plain tiles, the Hall sets the tone of their comfortable, welcoming home. It could be used as another sitting room. Like all the west wing rooms it is low and irregularly shaped, with a bay window and steps adding interest. It is deliberately dark, but Charles Kempe's stained glass windows provide glowing colour.

The steps up to the arch were the bottom of the main staircase until Ould removed it in 1893 to create a central hall hung with 17th-century Flemish tapestries. Here also are Pre-Raphaelite portraits of *Euphemia Ruskin with Foxgloves*

Above The Library. When space ran out the central shelves behind the wing chair were added across the door to the garden to take yet more books

Left The Hall's Kempe stained glass windows are dated 1888. The 'Bird' wool curtains and 'Hampton Court' chair are from Morris and Co.

1 Porch
2 Hall
3 Central Hall
4 Library

Anthea remembered that 'My parents more or less lived in the library'. Rosalie continued to use it after Geoffrey's death, with piles of books and papers on every surface and most of the chairs, so it was rarely open to visitors.

The books are well used and reflect the family's interests. Theodore's include books on religion, natural history, sciences and local history. Bound volumes of Parliamentary Debates are from Geoffrey's time as an MP. Geoffrey, Rosalie and the National Trust built up the large collection of books on Morris and the Pre-Raphaelites, including *The Collected Works of William Morris*, edited by May Morris. We still collect relevant books.

Transforming Wightwick
The late Monty Smith, who managed Wightwick from 1977 to 2000, had previously worked in Manders' interior design studio. With Rosalie Mander's support Monty opened the servants' wing for the first time. She was rather less enthusiastic about new inner casement curtains in all the rooms to replace the original ones she and Geoffrey had taken down in the 1930s to let in more light.

After Rosalie died Monty led a restoration programme that opened more of the house to visitors and rearranged many rooms. The family archive was gathered together from around the house, and is still yielding new information about the Manders and Wightwick.

and *William Michael Rossetti by Lamplight*. Ould built the new oak-panelled main staircase with its plasterwork frieze and ceiling, continuing the Jacobean theme. Rosalie Mander's portrait hangs on the stairs to the family bedrooms.

Library
Originally the dining room, in 1893 bookcases were fitted over the original Morris 'Larkspur' wallpaper but the serving hatch remains from its previous use. The Manders used the Library for study and as a sitting room. Geoffrey and Rosalie's daughter

Drawing Room 1887

1 Drawing Room
2 Morning Room

Victorian drawing rooms were emphatically the female domain. Here Flora Mander presided over 'At Homes' for her women friends, received afternoon calls and welcomed gatherings after dinner. Hidden behind the panelling and fireplace is a staircase to the boudoir, Flora's private sitting-room upstairs.

Its brightness deliberately contrasts with the dark Hall, with big windows facing south and west for afternoon and evening sun and the views. The L-shape, the bay windows and window seats were perfect for conversation in small groups.

Colour and comfort

The Italian Renaissance fireplace of about 1550 is lined with hand-painted De Morgan tiles. A quotation from *Modern Painters* by John Ruskin carved in the walnut panelling emphasises his influence on Wightwick's creation. The ceiling is delicately ornamented Jacobean-style plasterwork. Morris 'Dove and Rose' hand-loom woven silk and wool wall hangings, added *c.*1893, have faded from their original indigo blue.

Below The Drawing Room

In Flora's time the Drawing Room was comfortable but not ostentatious, and less crowded than many late Victorian drawing rooms. It has good marquetry furniture, mainly English or Dutch, and Chinese porcelain. The Hopkinson marquetry piano of about 1880 (a National Trust addition) is much grander than the upright piano that preceded it. After Geoffrey died the room was used less often, and in Rosalie's later years only occasionally, although she always put out her Christmas cards on the piano.

Collecting

Some of Geoffrey and Rosalie's earliest acquisitions are here. They bought the early Kempe stained glass from Old Place in Sussex, Kempe's own home. The Four Seasons illustrate the accompanying verse from *The Earthly Paradise* by William Morris. Pictures include John Ruskin's drawing *Lake and Mountain* and a drawing of his wife Effie by G.F. Watts.

Morning Room

Flora probably used this as a sitting room, as was usual for morning rooms. It has east and south windows for morning sun. Geoffrey and Florence used it with the same 17th- and 18th-century furniture as now, perhaps as a breakfast room. It became Geoffrey and Rosalie's dining room. In later years Rosalie used it only occasionally for guests.

De Morgan Rose tiles line the fireplace. Geoffrey moved the built-in cupboard, made from 17th-century Flemish window shutters, from the Library when the Morning Room was redecorated in 1910. The Morris 'Leicester' wallpaper designed by J.H. Dearle was hung in 1944.

Left William Morris's 1879 'Dove and Rose' design was one of several inspired by 16th- and 17th-century Italian fabrics

Above The Morning Room. Three of Rossetti's drawings of 'stunners' hang above the mid-18th-century dresser

Great Parlour 1893

Walking into the Great Parlour for the first time, its size and scale rising through two storeys are completely unexpected. Your initial impression is of a 15th-century great hall converted to a late Victorian sitting room. In medieval fashion there are no doors, just arches from the 'screens passage'.

Theodore and Flora Mander's approach to building Wightwick is summed up in the medieval French inscription above the fireplace that translates literally as 'faith to God, hospitality to friends'.

Heart of the house
Ould demolished the billiard room to make way for the Great Parlour. Halls were very popular as living rooms in Victorian country houses. The Manders used it for relaxing and entertaining, as an informal sitting room, for music, and for parties.

Colour, 'history' and comfort
Now mellowed with age, the Great Parlour was intended to be full of strong, glowing colour. To intensify the medieval effect Charles Kempe coloured the roof and fireplace and his stained glass including Saints George, Andrew and Patrick fills the windows. Kempe's coloured plasterwork frieze is inspired by plasterwork at Hardwick Hall in Derbyshire (owned by the National Trust), suggesting that the Parlour was perhaps enhanced in Elizabethan times. The frieze illustrates the ancient Greek myth of Orpheus and Eurydice; Geoffrey added appropriate quotations from the poets Milton and Addison.

But you're not meant to be deceived. The frieze includes a kangaroo and the true date '1893' is prominently carved above the fireplace. Period features were adapted to make the room convenient and comfortable. Radiators are concealed behind the Jacobean-style panelling and the great bay window is in the centre rather than at one end as it would be in a real medieval hall. The gallery is a bedroom landing, and what appears to be the open roof is actually a ceiling.

The Morris 'Diagonal Trail' wall hangings are original to the house. W.A.S. Benson designed the Flemish-inspired chandeliers and George Jack, the wall lights. Wall cabinets and shelves were designed to hold Chinese blue and white porcelain, very much in the Aesthetic taste, relieving the darkness of the wood. We had to re-create the effect after most of the porcelain was sadly stolen in 1991. The floor was always covered with eastern rugs, as it is today.

After the Second World War the Great Parlour gradually fell out of use. Monty Smith reinstated the original informal grouping of 17th-century furniture and comfortable sofas and chairs in 1992. It makes the room feel liveable despite its grandeur.

Love Among the Ruins
Burne-Jones was devastated when his original painting was badly damaged in a Paris photographer's studio in 1893. His hand-written note on the back says, 'The present picture I began at once, and have made it as like as possible to the other'. He thought the original was destroyed, but in fact it survived.

The Great Parlour is Wightwick's most impressive interior, both a living room and part of the circulation route between the drawing and dining rooms.

Billiard Room 1893

1 Lavatory
2 Turkish Bath
3 Billiard Room

Most Victorian country houses had a billiard room for recreation and relaxation, particularly for the male members of the household.

Theodore Mander's original billiard room was single-storey with a high roof and a large inglenook fireplace. A little remote from the rest of the house, it formed a self-contained gentlemen's suite with a lavatory (room with washbasins) and W.C. next to it. The Turkish Bath lay behind it. In 1893 a new lavatory and W.C. were built adjacent to the back hall, Theodore's business room and the Visitors' Staircase. Tip-up porcelain washbasins are set in a marble slab.

A new room

We don't know if Flora played, although mixed billiards was not unusual. By 1893 a segregated men's suite was beginning to seem outdated and the new Billiard Room leads directly from the Great Parlour and the Dining Room. Like all the 1893 reception rooms it is bigger and more richly decorated than its predecessor. The fine 16th-century style plasterwork ceiling and frieze showing signs of the Zodiac are believed to be by Leonard Shuffrey, a designer and manufacturer of plasterwork frequently employed by Ould. The inglenook has openwork posts cut from solid oak and Dutch tiles based on the Morris 'Daisy' design.

Turkish Bath 1887

Turkish baths were quite widespread in Victorian Britain, but they were uncommon in private houses, and few of these have survived. This one was probably intended for Theodore and male guests. It has glazed brick walls and concrete ceilings. A Constantine 'Convoluted Stove' that provided hot dry air survives in the basement. The warm room/bathroom now contains a Victorian bath from the Old Manor House. The outer cooling/dressing room became part of the new ground floor corridor in 1893.

Above The Billiard Room from the inglenook. The scoreboard is for Old English Pool rather than billiards

Play

The Manders and their guests probably played billiards during the day, particularly in poor weather, and in the evenings after dinner. We still have score books in Geoffrey Mander's handwriting. Large windows on three sides and the original electric light fitting over the table provide maximum illumination for the game. The Thurstons billiard table probably came from the previous room. It has been restored for visitors to use.

Raised seating was usual, giving a good view of the game in progress. Charles Dixon's watercolour of ships *The Manitoba and the City of Rome* is a typical billiard room subject. Billiard rooms might also be used for smoking, which had become socially acceptable by the late 19th century. Theodore was photographed with a cigarette in his mouth when the Chinese Ambassador visited Wightwick.

Collecting

Geoffrey and Rosalie chose the Morris 'Pimpernel' wallpaper in 1937. The Morris and Co. painted glass flower panels in the window came from the Wardle family; Morris learned indigo dyeing at their works in Leek, Staffordshire. *The Finding of Moses* – unfinished – is by William De Morgan. *The Mourners* is one of six pictures Evelyn De Morgan painted in reaction to the First World War.

Dining Room 1893

The dining room was one of the most important rooms in a Victorian house. Here the Manders ate family meals and entertained guests, with Theodore at the head of his table. He was committed to temperance but served wine to his guests.

Theodore and Flora's circle mainly consisted of their family and friends of similar social position, but they also entertained for business and public duties. Dinners for such guests would have been the most formal meals, with menus in French. In most Victorian country houses luncheon was less formal with simpler table settings.

Planned to impress

The new room is bigger, higher and altogether grander than its predecessor (now the Library). Dining rooms were considered to be masculine rooms, so it is more sombre than the Drawing Room. Suitably masculine Dutch tiles of ship designs line the plain Tudor-arched fireplace. Some of the unpolished walnut panelling may be from the previous billiard room; it doesn't all match. The fine Elizabethan-style plasterwork ceiling and frieze are probably by Leonard Shuffrey.

Above The Dining Room's built-in sideboard is conveniently placed next to the Serving Room hatch. There was originally another table in the window recess

Left Dutch tiles in the Dining Room fireplace

1 Serving Room
2 Back Hall and Corridor
3 Dining Room

Back Hall and Corridor 1893

The corridor to the servants' wing was built outside the Turkish Bath, incorporating its outer cooling/dressing room. It formed a rear entrance for tenants and employees visiting Theodore's business room (not open). The walls were originally painted. Geoffrey and Rosalie introduced the 'Trellis' and 'Daisy' wallpapers, two of William Morris's earliest designs.

Like many Victorian dining rooms this one faces east so gets the sun only at breakfast time – it looks brightest on a summer morning. The earlier dining room unusually faced south, but eating in full sun was generally thought unpleasant, so perhaps the Manders regretted it. There are chairs for 18, a typical number for a large Victorian dinner party.

A Benson light fitting hangs above the sideboard. Geoffrey acquired the fine Morris and Co. hand-knotted carpet. The pictures are mainly of the Rossetti and Madox Brown families, originally loaned by their descendant, Helen Rossetti Angeli. The Trust now owns them.

Serving meals

The Dining Room is as far as possible away from the Kitchen with doors and turns to prevent 'obnoxious kitchen odours'. The Kitchen prepared many dishes for the Dining Room, Nursery and the Servants' Hall, and the smells would have been very strong.

Food was expected to be invisible until served. Servants carried dishes from the Kitchen to the Serving Room; inner and outer hatches minimised visibility and noise, and the screen shielded the door from view. Speed and skill were needed to serve food hot. The butler, footman and maids served diners from the sideboards, known as *service à la russe*. With reducing numbers of domestic staff the Dining Room became increasingly impractical, and Geoffrey and Rosalie used the Morning Room instead.

Visitors' rooms 1893

1 Bathroom
2 Visitors' Staircase
3 Honeysuckle Room
4 Indian Bird Room
5 Acanthus Room

The comfortably furnished guest rooms, named after their original decoration, are entirely separate from the family bedrooms, providing mutual privacy. The best ones have good garden views.

In the 1930s Geoffrey Mander added quotations on the walls from favourite authors of the Pre-Raphaelites. The rooms were used less after Geoffrey's time, and very rarely in Rosalie's later years.

Visitors' Staircase

The decoration reflects lingering Aesthetic taste, with subdued green paintwork and a rare surviving rush matting dado. Morris 'Willow Boughs' wallpaper replaced the earlier 'Trellis' before 1937, but one section remains on the landing. The decorative 1893 radiator still works. Benson made the ceiling light.

Honeysuckle Room

This was a single bedroom. The Morris 'Honeysuckle' printed linen wall hangings are original. The fireplace tiles resemble De Morgan lustre designs but are by Maw and Co. May Morris designed the curtains of the late 18th-century bed. Its embroidered coverlet was 'Worked by Sarah Lilley Constant from 1910 to 1939'. The 'Sussex' chairs by Morris and Co. include the oval-seated 'Rossetti' design.

Bathroom

Family and visitors' wings each had one bathroom. The tiles, bath and heated towel rail are original but the washbasin was put in around 1937, replacing an earlier tip-up basin set in a marble top. Plumbed-in washbasins were not widespread before 1900; most people washed in their bedrooms.

Indian Bird Room

The usual provision for a Victorian couple was a bedroom and dressing room. This and the Acanthus Room next door could be that or be used as two single rooms. The rooms are ingeniously planned with the dividing wall staggered to create alcoves for the beds.

Left A Royal Worcester Aesthetic Movement moon flask and part of the Indian Bird Room's wall-hangings

Like most of the visitors' rooms they have Georgian-inspired fireplaces with Dutch tiles.

The loose pattern of the printed linen wall hangings is quite unlike any Morris design, but the Manders followed their own tastes. The bed is made from 17th-century carved timber and hung with Morris 'Wey' printed velveteen. The Royal Worcester red moon flasks are Japanese-inspired Aesthetic Movement pieces.

Geoffrey saw the quotation from Walter Scott's *The Talisman* in a bedroom at William Morris's home, Red House. Pictures include some of Burne-Jones's superb red chalk studies of young women and *Brother Conrad of Offida* by Marie Spartali Stillman.

Acanthus Room

The green Morris 'Acanthus' wallpaper replaced the 1893 original in browns. The remarkable bed made in Italy or England around 1860 incorporates Italian marquetry, mother of pearl, and ivory panels originally made c.1700. These show Adam and Eve and other scenes from the Bible. The pictures include pencil studies by Burne-Jones.

Above The Acanthus Room. The watercolour above the Morris 'Sussex' armchair is by Alfred Parsons. Theodore Mander commissioned him to redesign the garden

Oak Room
1893

1 Daisy Room
2 Gallery
3 Oak Room

The Oak Room suite was always for the Manders' most important guests. The main room continues the Great Parlour's medieval theme; with its oak-ribbed barrel roof it is reminiscent of a solar, a medieval lord's private chamber which adjoined the great hall.

Beams and Morris 'Diagonal Trail' wool curtains mark the positions of lost panelled partitions that originally divided the bedroom from a dressing room. The fireplace's carved quotation is from Coleridge's narrative poem, *The Rime of the Ancient Mariner*. The original wall hangings survive only in the room beyond the open screen.

Geoffrey's alterations

The Oak Room once housed the bed Charles II is said to have slept in when hiding from the Parliamentarians at Moseley Old Hall in 1651. Geoffrey bought it in 1913 and, around the same time, he removed the partitions and blocked up the open screen of turned balusters. The Manders'

Below The Oak Room bed was believed to have been used by Swinburne. Geoffrey paid £1 for it. The carved panels are reversible

Pre-Raphaelite painted furniture

The extraordinary cabinet, folding bed and mirrors have paintings by Rossetti's studio assistant Henry Treffry Dunn, based on Rossetti pictures. The carvings are by Thomas Keynes. The mirror frames were inspired by Rossetti's designs for the Oxford Union murals in 1857, the mirrors representing the windows of the Debating Chamber.

They came in 1939 from 2 The Pines, Putney, home of Rossetti's friends Theodore Watts-Dunton and the poet Algernon Charles Swinburne.

most important guests slept in this room, including former Prime Ministers Lloyd George and Clement Attlee. The Kempe stained glass portraying Charles I and his adviser Archbishop Laud came from Old Place in 1937. After Geoffrey helped the National Trust acquire Moseley Old Hall in 1962, the royal bed was returned there.

The room today

In 1994 we put back the beams (found in the stables) and reinstated the balusters to unblock the screen. The fine hand-knotted carpet is from Morris and Co. The large portrait drawing by Rossetti is Alexa Wilding, one of his favourite models. Rossetti owned the pair of Chinese blue and white vases and the Flemish water cistern that appears in one of his paintings, *La Bella Mano*.

Gallery

Rosalie found the settle in Cornwall. Gothic Revival architect G.F. Bodley and Charles Kempe designed it for Light Oaks, a house near Manchester. The paintings of the Four Seasons are similar to Kempe's stained glass windows in the Drawing Room.

Daisy Room 1893

This has been a single bedroom, Geoffrey's study, the housekeeper's sitting room, an office, and a store room. It was reinstated as a bedroom in 1991, and has been used occasionally. The original Morris 'Daisy' wallpaper was replaced in 1946. Pictures include drawings and watercolours by Millais, Holman Hunt and May Morris.

Above 'Daisy' was William Morris's first wallpaper to be produced, in 1864. The mirror is 18th century, made in India

Visitors, family and servants

The Pomegranate Passage behind the Great Parlour links the visitors' rooms, family rooms and servants' wing. It was primarily for the Manders and their guests, but servants used it to serve all the bedrooms. From the housemaids' closet leading off it they carried clean water to the bedroom washstands, and brought the waste water back.

Morris's 'Pomegranate' paper was hung before 1937. The wall hanging based on Burne-Jones's painting *The Mill* was embroidered by the Royal School of Needlework in about 1908. Rossetti appears as Chaucer in one of the Morris stained glass panels.

Family rooms 1887

The west wing was always the Manders' private space. The portraits are of Geoffrey's brothers Lionel and Alan, his first wife Florence and his five children. After Geoffrey died Rosalie used only a few rooms, and some were let. The bedrooms are now the Mander family's private apartment, so are not open.

Main staircase and corridors

In 1893 a new panelled Jacobean-style staircase replaced the original bathroom. Its newel posts are finely carved with wild flowers. The plasterwork ceilings modelled with birds and fruit are possibly by Shuffrey. Kempe stained glass fills the window of the earlier staircase landing, now a broad corridor.

Above **A corner of the Pomegranate Passage with the back stairs beyond. The electric bellboard for summoning servants is close to the housemaids' closet**

Opposite above **Mander children's toys and books in the Day Nursery**

Opposite below **A puppy chasing a cockerel above the Night Nursery fireplace**

1 Pomegranate Passage
2 Night Nursery
3 Day Nursery
4 Main stairs
5 Corridors

The Nurseries

The Mander children mainly lived here. The location of the Nurseries next to the family bedrooms is unusual, suggesting Theodore and Flora wanted to be close to their children; Victorian nurseries were usually more remote. Most of the fittings and furniture are from their time, but after Geoffrey and Florence's first child Mavis was born in 1908 both rooms were re-decorated. Toys and books from the 1880s to the 1950s are still here. The Nurseries were restored in 1989–91.

Day Nursery

The children played and ate their meals here. It's sunny and cheerful, with views of the garden from the seat in the huge window. Geoffrey and Rosalie probably added the cut-outs of cars, steam engines, animals and birds for their son John, who was born in 1932. John made the dolls-house for his sister Anthea. She remembered, 'The increasingly shabby day nursery was used as a "playroom" until I left Wightwick at the age of sixteen'. Later Rosalie used it, strewn with books and papers, to write her books – from downstairs you could sometimes hear her typewriter. Among the gramophone records is Geoffrey's election song 'Vote, Vote, Vote for Geoffrey Mander'.

Night Nursery

The children's nurse slept with them. The Minton 'Days of the Week' fireplace tiles are intended to amuse and instruct. Sporting artist and illustrator Cecil Aldin designed the printed frieze of puppies chasing chickens, ducks and ducklings.

Making Wightwick work

Servants were essential to running a Victorian house, but they were kept largely out of sight. At Wightwick they worked and lived in the servants' wing, the tower and the Old Manor House. The 1893 addition needed more servants so Ould enlarged the servants' wing, with new first-floor bedrooms and a bathroom on the second floor.

Around 1900 the senior servants – housekeeper, butler and cook – ran their own departments and managed five maids and a footman. The Manders, as you might expect, looked after their servants. Housekeeper Emma Smith ran Wightwick very capably while Flora was abroad after Theodore died. Her sympathetic letters to Flora give a picture of life at Wightwick with the house largely closed up and the number of servants reduced.

After the First World War the number of servants gradually declined. Rosalie remembered that 'When I came to Wightwick the gardener's wife was housekeeper; her resentment at my arrival was not improved by my failure to impress her'. The last housekeeper was Mrs Griffiths; her daughter Margaret was Wightwick's curator from 1948 to 1973.

Back stairs and corridors 1887
These gave access to family and servants' rooms and were in constant use. Servants used the stairs to carry luggage up from the side door. The electric bell board still works.

The cook's department
The cook and kitchen maid did the more skilful cooking in the Kitchen. It would have been busy and very hot. The Kitchen was made worse by facing west, so in summer it was flooded with sun just as dinner was being cooked. It was never modernised; Geoffrey and Rosalie adapted the butler's pantry as their kitchen instead. There are no sinks in the Kitchen; the scullery maid did the wet and dirty jobs, basic cooking and washing up in the Scullery, remodelled in 1893.

Above The Kitchen. The Eagle Range & Gas Co. of Birmingham made the cooking range. It still works

1 Game Larder
2 Laundry
3 Scullery
4 Servants' Hall
5 Kitchen
6 Larder
7 Back Stairs

boiler) and a pump which supplies the housemaids' closet upstairs with rainwater collected from the roof. The larder for storing pheasants, other game and uncooked meat was added later.

Servants' Hall

The servants ate their meals and spent their limited free time here. Typically it is as far away as possible from the family rooms with no view of the garden. It was extended in 1893, and was always simply furnished with chairs and tables. The large table and glazed, fitted cupboard are original, but the piano was not here in the days of servants.

Right Original shelves in the Scullery

Both Kitchen and Scullery have glazed brick walls for easy cleaning. A maid lit the up-to-date Eagle cooking ranges early every morning. Most of the original fittings and furniture and many of the utensils are still here, although the scullery dresser is a recent replica.

The larder, with slate shelves and shaded from the sun, keeps food cool whatever the weather. The room off the Scullery was designed for storing and preparing vegetables, but has been used as a laundry. It has a copper (an open top

An Underrated Garden?

On 9 July 1888 Theodore Mander noted 'First plate of strawberries gathered at Wightwick'.

Wightwick still feels like a country garden, with rural views to Shropshire. Designers Alfred Parsons and then Thomas Mawson worked on it in the spirit of the Arts and Crafts Movement. The structure of evergreen hedges and topiary, terraces, stonework, walks and vistas largely designed by Thomas Mawson creates interest all year round. In spring drifts of daffodils and a carpet of bluebells are followed by colourful banks of rhododendrons and azaleas. In summer herbaceous borders and roses bring colour to formal areas.

A family garden

Each generation of Manders enjoyed the garden with family and friends. They played tennis, croquet and bowls on the lawn, and boated, skated, fished and bathed in the pools. Babies were put out in the garden in their prams, and toddlers played on the terrace. The Manders hosted garden parties, sports and other events for charity, for employees and for the Liberal Party.

Gardening at Wightwick

We know little about the Wightwick family's garden. A 1762 map drawn for John Wightwick shows the Old Manor House with a small enclosed garden and another enclosed area of six rectangular plots. A large orchard contained four small pools. The upper pool

Above Boating on the lower pool in the 1930s. Geoffrey and John Mander are in the canoe. Elizabeth is on the left, and Rosalie on the right

remains, but by 1840 the other three had been combined to form the present lower pool.

The Manders were not expert gardeners, but Theodore and Geoffrey took an active interest and kept notes of progress. Theodore was interested in plants, and his travels abroad included plenty of 'botanising'. Architect Edward Ould and Theodore's head gardeners may have advised him on shaping the garden. The sloping site was levelled to build the house; Ould's design shows a formal lawn with a stone retaining wall. The garden evolved gradually. There were box balls, banks and flower beds along the south front, and a terrace and beds on the west.

A Redesign

In 1899 Theodore brought in the Parsons Partridge Partnership. Writing to Walter Partridge, Parsons was scathing about Wightwick's existing garden 'no coherence & no leading ideas, & the immediate surroundings of the house about as bad as it could be'. Theodore Mander seemed 'to think that I could just say straight off how to make

it perfect'. On 29 July Partridge wrote to Theodore that 'Our object is to make the grounds much more compact & less rambling & disjointed than at present'.

The focus was on design and planting rather than construction work. Partridge proposed two years' work done bit by bit so the grounds would be tidy by the summer as Theodore wanted.

Above Elizabeth, John and Rosalie Mander playing cricket on the upper terrace in the 1930s

Left Anthea Mander (on the left) with her niece Koko playing tennis in the 1950s

Alfred Parsons (1847–1920)
As a successful painter and illustrator, landscapes, gardens and flowers were Parsons' favourite subjects. His gardens reflected an Arts and Crafts approach, with great care in the choice of materials and yew hedging and topiary creating structure. Unostentatious planting of English hardy plants and old varieties of roses provided colour and composition. Parsons designed around 70 gardens, including Great Chalfield Manor in Wiltshire (National Trust).

An Edwardian garden

On 7 October 1900 Partridge wrote that Theodore Mander's death meant 'everything has to be cut down in the garden'.

But Flora was still buying plants, and Parsons and Partridge met at Wightwick in December 1900, so work was presumably continuing. On 18 July 1899 Parsons had 'pegged out the line of a proposed narrow paved terrace round the garden front of the house, which would have many uses as you will see when you go there, & leave a broader space for croquet lawn & flower garden. It will also be in keeping with the quaint character of the house.' The Formal Garden's hedges and topiary are probably largely due to Parsons, but we don't know exactly what was finally proposed or how much of it was carried out.

Flora Mander and Mawson

It was Flora who took the biggest single step in shaping the garden as we now see it, when she commissioned Thomas Mawson to redesign the garden in 1904. His design was transformational and is the basis of the garden today. Mawson probably came to the Mander family's attention because he laid out East Park in Wolverhampton in 1895–6 when Theodore was a town councillor. In 1901 a copy of Mawson's book *The Art and Craft of Garden Making*, published in 1900, was in the Great Parlour.

Above Yew hedges and herbaceous borders in the Formal Garden frame views of the house

Left Mawson designed the retaining walls, oak balustrades and steps. Narrow courses of red tiles add interest to the stonework

Long Walk and the Yew and Holly Walk. Formality, structure and sensitive use of traditional materials near the house and gradually softening into informality further away is characteristic of Mawson's Arts and Crafts approach.

Wightwick revisited

Geoffrey Mander went to Mawson for more improvements. Mawson prepared an elaborate design. In 1910 Geoffrey noted, 'built flagged terrace and wall in front of house. June. Also circular steps outside dining room'. But Mawson's proposed design for beds in the Formal Garden, water garden by the upper pool and new formal layout for the kitchen garden remained just a plan.

Thomas Hayton Mawson (1861–1933)

Thomas Mawson was the leading landscape designer of his day. He worked, not just in Britain, but in the United States, France, Germany and Holland – and for Queen Alexandra in Denmark, creating over two-hundred gardens. Mawson had quite a lot in common with his clients, the Manders, as a successful businessman, a Congregationalist and a committed Liberal.

Transformation

For many years we thought that little was done after Flora's untimely death in 1905, but recent research indicates that many of Mawson's proposals were carried out. He made dramatic changes, imposing strong architectural form and order, and created an entirely new area of garden to the south. The upper lawned terrace was raised and formalised with rose beds and a balustrade on a retaining wall. Mawson introduced steps leading down to the 'New Lawn' with yew topiary drums and formal hedging. To the west he laid out the

Change and revival

Geoffrey put his own stamp on the garden, planting many trees, shrubs and flowers from 1914 to 1917. Reflecting his interest in historic and literary associations and to mark the three-hundredth anniversary of Shakespeare's death in 1916, Geoffrey planted the flowers and herbs mentioned in *Hamlet,* Act IV, Scene 5.

But in 1920 Geoffrey put Wightwick up for sale. Most of the land surrounding the garden was sold and for a time little seems to have been done in the garden until Geoffrey planted many rhododendrons and laurels in 1927–8.

A garden of associations

With the gift of Wightwick to the National Trust, Geoffrey and Rosalie took a new interest in the garden. For them, associations mattered more than the actual plants. Rosalie remembered, 'We collected plants from the gardens of famous people for the beds below the terrace: from Kelmscott, from Kempe's garden at Lindfield, and also from Dickens' home at Gads Hill and Tennyson's at Farringford'. May Morris sent plants from Kelmscott Manor 'characteristic of the garden in my Father's day'.

The Manders brought politics into the garden. Labour leader Clement Attlee planted a hornbeam, chosen by Geoffrey because as a boy William Morris loved the hornbeams in Epping Forest. A cedar commemorates Conservative Prime Minister Stanley Baldwin; his mother Louisa Macdonald was married in Wolverhampton and her sister Georgiana married Edward Burne-Jones. Geoffrey placed Gothic Revival stonework from the Houses of Parliament in the garden, acquired when it was repaired in 1933.

Recognition and revival

After the Second World War parts of the garden were simplified to reduce costs, and housing development increasingly changed its formerly rural setting. For a while it was overshadowed by the house and its collection, but with growing public interest in late Victorian and Edwardian gardens, its significance started to be appreciated. In the late 1980s we began restoring and enhancing it, guided by Mawson's original plans discovered in the house and using designs from Mawson catalogues. Since 2007 a new kitchen garden has been created, inspired by Mawson's 1910 plan. The War Memorial Garden made in 2010 reinforces the links between Wightwick, Mander Brothers and its employees.

A near miss

As a contribution to 'Dig for Victory' during the Second World War the flower beds were turned over to vegetables – Burne-Jones's grandson Lance Thirkell helped with this. But Geoffrey's attempt to get the garden back under control almost ended in disaster on 31 March 1946. To get rid of dry grass on the south front, unmown for about five years, he set fire to it.

'It was very dry & spread rapidly finally burning up 8 box trees in front of the library and drawing room. A beam in the roof over our bedroom began smouldering. I telephoned for the N.F.S. [fire service]. With their help & a stirrup pump worked by Derrington [head gardener] & others it was put out.'

The box balls were not replanted until 1991.

Left Geoffrey and Rosalie planting a bed by the house in the 1950s

Below The south front. The box balls Theodore planted in front of the house were left to grow very large

Opposite Clement Attlee planting the hornbeam held by Geoffrey Mander 8 March 1953, as recorded in Geoffrey's notebook

The Formal Garden, orchard and Yew and Holly Walk from the tower roof

Formality around the house

Thomas Mawson insisted that 'to give a proper connection between the house and garden a formal arrangement near the house is essential'.

At Wightwick, terracing, walls, balustrades, clipped hedging and topiary, lawns and flower beds create different levels and form compartments. Straight lines and simple geometric shapes – cylinders, rectangles, circles – are softened by the planting.

House and forecourt

Edward Ould intended Wightwick to be covered with climbing plants, and today wisteria (Rosalie Mander's cat climbed it to an upstairs cat flap), yellow banksiae rose, Virginia creeper and a grape vine grow on the south front. Ould's proposed drive from the Bridgnorth Road through the garden was, however, never created; high yew hedges enclose the forecourt instead of the proposed iron railings and gates.

Long Walk and Formal Garden

Geoffrey placed stonework from Big Ben's clock tower at the entrance to Mawson's Yew Walk. Parsons probably first laid out the Formal Garden and may have suggested the topiary peacocks. The flowerbeds are modified from Mawson's 1904 plan, with roses and herbaceous borders as Mawson preferred. In 1991 Monty Smith designed the pergola and seat, with posts for climbers, from Mawson designs. Climbing roses yellow 'Alberic Barbier' and 'Goldfinch' and red 'Parkdirektor Riggers' are combined with clematis.

Terraces and lawns

The Manders played tennis on the east lawn until the 1960s. Mawson created the upper lawned terrace with rose beds and the oak, stone and tile balustrade. The Manders used his stone-flagged terrace for sitting out. The craftsmanship in traditional materials and construction reflects Arts and Crafts influence, while the detailing subtly echoes the house. The view down to the pool is at its very best when the rhododendrons are in flower.

The lower lawn was previously a field, so the purple-twigged lime and the copper beech, planted by the Duke and Duchess of York, were outside the garden until 1904. Mawson created a new lawn and a strong south axis with yew drums. The long Chelsea Border is named after plants Geoffrey bought at the Chelsea Flower Show. In 2001, the Magnolia Border was added on the other side.

Nuttery and bridge garden

Mawson's round steps link the tennis lawn, nuttery and bridge. Amongst the hazelnuts, ferns and ivy is more stonework from the Houses of Parliament. Theodore installed a bridge over Wightwick Bank leading to a new garden of tulips, roses, currants and gooseberries; Geoffrey turned it into a fruit garden in 1908. The current bridge was built in 1949, and has been extensively repaired. Like its predecessor it is inspired by the Mathematical Bridge at Queen's College, Cambridge.

The sundial
The sundial was originally the centre of a Circular Garden with four flower beds, since grassed over. The inscription is in Flora's commonplace book of favourite quotations.
  'Light and shade by turns
  But love always'

The informal garden

Above The orchard with Wightwick's picturesque skyline rising above

Mawson believed that, 'the further we proceed from the house the freer should be the treatment of the details of the garden scheme'.

Moving west the formality softens, merging into the orchard and longer grass, the pools and woodland. It's an approach characteristic of Mawson and other designers influenced by the Arts and Crafts Movement. There are attractive views of the house framed in gaps in the trees, from across the lower pool or from the orchard.

Yew and Holly Walk

Mawson laid this out with alternating Irish yews and 'Golden Queen' hollies as a semi-formal route into the informal garden. Geoffrey called it the Addison Walk after the writer Joseph Addison. The memorial to Mander Brothers employees who died in both World Wars came from the John Street premises in Wolverhampton. It was re-erected here in its own new garden in 2010. The Grigg House, rebuilt in 2009 after a fire, is thatched with heather from the Long Mynd in Shropshire.

Orchard and willow grove

In 1887 this was still a field. The orchard of traditional apple varieties is shown on Mawson's plans. It's at its best in spring, with great drifts of daffodils. Geoffrey planted 350 willows 'behind pool' in 1916. The willows' vivid scarlet stems are a flash of colour in winter and early spring, followed by blue camassias. Geoffrey laid out the Ice Age boulders, deposited in the area by a glacier, in 1957.

Kitchen Garden

The Kitchen Garden provided food for the Manders and their servants. It remained in production until the early 1980s, when it was grassed over. The Peach House built by specialists Richardson of Darlington in 1891 is the only survivor of the glasshouses. Monty Smith designed the new formal kitchen garden inspired by Mawson's unexecuted 1910 plan. It is planted with traditional varieties of fruit and vegetables.

Woodland

Theodore Mander probably planted the narrow woodland strip across to Tinacre Hill; he called it Tinacre Walk. You barely notice the surrounding houses, even in winter. The dell near the end may be the rock garden which Theodore created in 1899.

Right The Kitchen Garden in spring

The paddock and pools

The grass down to the lower pool was an orchard in 1762. The Manders used it as a paddock, and it was grazed by horses until the late 1990s. We pulled back the railings to bring it into the garden. Both Theodore and Geoffrey enlarged the lower pool, and Geoffrey stocked it with trout for fishing. Geoffrey planted rhododendrons around the pools. In late spring they create banks of vivid colour hanging over the water, with sweet scents from azaleas in pastel shades. Ground cover around the upper pool is comfrey and pulmonaria 'Mawson's Blue'. Japanese acers add autumn colour.

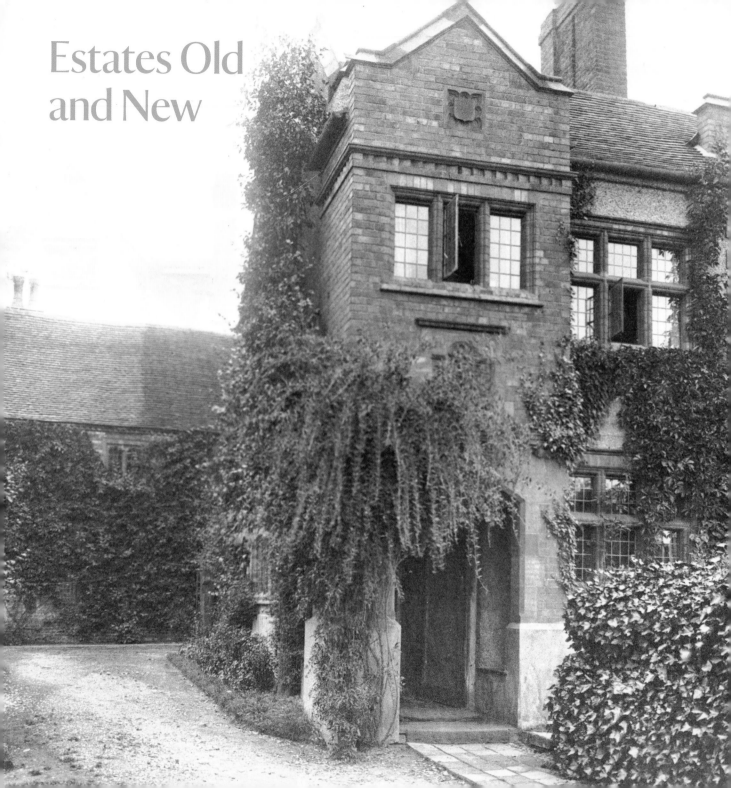

Estates Old
and New

The Wightwick family who held the small estate from the 1200s onwards later prospered as lawyers and clergymen. The Old Manor House's front door may come from the timber-framed house which they built in about 1500. It was probably Francis Wightwick and his son Alexander who rebuilt the house in brick c.1600–30.

Alexander's son Francis lived at Dunstall Hall near Wolverhampton, and Wightwick ceased to be the family's main home. In 1815 Wightwick was sold to the Hinckes family. Around this time everything to the left of the Old Manor's porch was demolished and a new external wall and a two-storey rear extension were built. Wightwick was let to farmers, the Moore family, until the 1880s.

Theodore Mander retained the 'Manor House' to accommodate servants and it gradually became known as Old Manor House. Ould rendered the walls, added Ruabon brick dressings and mullioned windows, and installed fireplaces. Above the porch is the Wightwick coat of arms. The old kitchen still has its large fireplace and ceiling hooks for hams.

The Malthouse

The Wightwicks built this around 1600, possibly as a barn. The Moores used it to malt barley for brewing. Ould blocked windows and doors, inserted Tudor-style Ruabon brick windows, and added the outside staircase. He removed the top floor to create a spacious recreation room open to the roof. The fireplace has an improving

inscription LABOR IPSE VOLUPTAS ('work is a pleasure in itself'). In the mid-1890s it housed Wightwick Manor School, attended by the Mander children and their cousins. In 1928 Geoffrey converted half of it into a squash rackets court that remained in use until 1982.

R.I. Ledoux of Montreal made the family sleigh c.1890 – a reminder that Flora was Canadian. The photographic dark room of about 1900, probably used by Geoffrey and Marjorie, is a rare survival.

Stable block

Theodore was a keen rider and the Victorian Manders travelled by carriage. Ould remodelled the old farm buildings as stables and coach house and created a drive. The yellow brick paving once had a glazed roof for washing carriages under cover. Geoffrey adapted the coach house as a 'motor house' for his prized cars. In 1913 he 'set back drive gates and widened drive for 16.20 Sunbeam bought July'. Years later his son John's pottery kiln was housed in the stables. Horses occupied some of the stables until the late 1990s.

Above Wightwick Manor School pupils with their teacher outside the Old Manor House. Marjorie Mander stands on the left. Alan (with curly hair) is in front of her, and Lionel sits on the rug on the right

Left The Old Manor House with the Malthouse behind it, photographed in the 1890s

Keeping Wightwick Alive

Although the Manders owned Wightwick Manor for just 50 years they continued to enrich it under the National Trust's much longer ownership. Now that none of the family lives here permanently, keeping Wightwick alive is a greater challenge.

We try to keep the feeling of a family home with the accretions of daily life that were never cleared away. Pictures, objects and furniture are still added and moved around as they have been for over a hundred years. Although Wightwick is now on the edge of a city, we maintain as much as possible of the original country garden feel through careful planting and protecting views.

Conservation

Wightwick has many fragile fabrics, wallpapers, pictures, furniture and objects that are very vulnerable to light and wear. Visitor numbers have tripled since the early 2000s. We carefully control light levels and you can really help us care for Wightwick by trying not to touch. Rooms and garden areas are closed from time to time for essential work. Your membership or entrance fee helps to fund our day-to-day care and specialist conservation.

Welcome

Wightwick is now open almost every day. Our volunteers are crucial to Wightwick's welcoming feel. In the spirit of the Manders it continues to develop and welcome visitors as it always has.

Left Volunteers admire the Kempe stained glass in the Drawing Room bay window

50 Walks in
SHROPSHIRE

First published 2003
Researched and written by Julie Royle

Produced by AA Publishing
© Automobile Association Developments Limited 2003
Illustrations © Automobile Association Developments Limited 2003

Published by AA Publishing (a trading name of Automobile
Association Developments Limited, whose registered office
is Millstream, Maidenhead, Windsor, SL4 5GD; registered
number 1878835)

ois Ordnance Survey® This product includes mapping data licensed from
Ordnance Survey® with the permission of the
Controller of Her Majesty's Stationery Office.
© Crown copyright 2002. All rights reserved. Licence number 399221

ISBN 0 7495 3632 2

A01418

A CIP catalogue record for this book is available
from the British Library.

The contents of this book are believed correct at the time of printing.
Nevertheless, the publishers cannot be held responsible for any errors
or omissions or for changes in the details given in this book or for
the consequences of any reliance on the information it provides. This
does not affect your statutory rights. We have tried to ensure
accuracy in this book, but things do change and we would be grateful
if readers would advise us of any inaccuracies they may encounter.

We have taken all reasonable steps to ensure that these walks are
safe and achievable by walkers with a realistic level of fitness.
However, all outdoor activities involve a degree of risk and the
publishers accept no responsibility for any injuries caused to
readers whilst following these walks. For more advice on walking
safely see page 128. The mileage range shown on the front cover is
for guidance only – some walks may exceed or be less than these
distances.

Visit the AA Publishing website at www.theAA.com

Paste-up and editorial by Outcrop Publishing Services Ltd, Cumbria
for AA Publishing

Colour reproduction by LC Repro
Printed in Italy by G Canale & C SPA, Torino, Italy

Legend

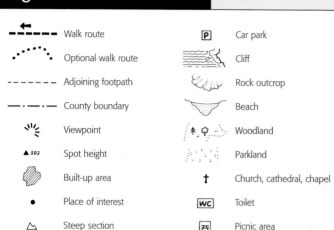

← – – – – –	Walk route	P	Car park
⋅⋅⋅⋅⋅⋅⋅	Optional walk route		Cliff
– – – – –	Adjoining footpath		Rock outcrop
–⋅–⋅–⋅–	County boundary		Beach
☀	Viewpoint		Woodland
▲ 392	Spot height		Parkland
	Built-up area	†	Church, cathedral, chapel
•	Place of interest	WC	Toilet
△	Steep section	🌲	Picnic area

Shropshire locator map

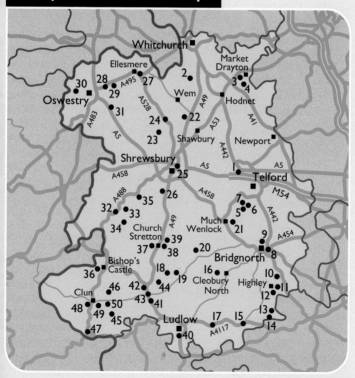

Contents

WALK		RATING	DISTANCE	PAGE
1	All Around The Wrekin	🚶🚶🚶	8½ miles (13.7km)	8
2	Branching Out from Prees	🚶🚶🚶	10 miles (16.1km)	11
3	Gingering it Up at Market Drayton	🚶🚶🚶	5¼ miles (8.4km)	14
4	Drayton and the Colehurst Loop	🚶🚶🚶	8¼ miles (13.3km)	17
5	A World First at Ironbridge	🚶🚶🚶	4¼ miles (6.8km)	18
6	Exploring Shropshire's China Town	🚶🚶🚶	5 miles (8km)	20
7	Revolution at Coalbrookdale	🚶🚶🚶	5 miles (8km)	23
8	Up Jacob's Ladder to Rindleford	🚶🚶🚶	6½ miles (10.4km)	26
9	Way to Go at Bridgnorth	🚶🚶🚶	4 miles (6.4km)	29
10	Trust in Dudmaston	🚶🚶🚶	5 miles (8km)	30
11	Regeneration at Alveley	🚶🚶🚶	5 miles (8km)	32
12	Highley Enterprising and Enjoyable	🚶🚶🚶	5½ miles (8.8km)	35
13	The King's Wood at Wyre	🚶🚶🚶	5 miles (8km)	38
14	Over the Border to Far Forest	🚶🚶🚶	7½ miles (12.1km)	41
15	In a Twist at Cleobury Mortimer	🚶🚶🚶	4¾ miles (7.7km)	42
16	At Liberty on Shropshire's Highest Hill	🚶🚶🚶	7 miles (11.3km)	44
17	Bedlam on Clee	🚶🚶🚶	8¼ miles (13.3km)	47
18	Close to the Edge at Diddlebury	🚶🚶🚶	6¼ miles (10.1km)	50
19	From the White House to Little London	🚶🚶🚶	8¼ miles (13.3km)	53
20	A Walk on the Wild Side at Wilderhope	🚶🚶🚶	3 miles (4.8km)	54
21	Paying Homage to St Milburga	🚶🚶🚶	6¼ miles (10.1km)	56
22	Drama at Clive and Grinshill	🚶🚶🚶	5¼ miles (8.4km)	59
23	Here be Dragons	🚶🚶🚶	5½ miles (8.8km)	62
24	A House Called Grumpy at The Witterage	🚶🚶🚶	8 miles (12.9km)	65
25	Shrewsbury: Islanded in Severn Stream	🚶🚶🚶	6 miles (9.7km)	66
26	Gone to Earth on Lovely Lyth Hill	🚶🚶🚶	8 miles (12.9km)	68
27	Meres, Mosses and Moraines at Ellesmere	🚶🚶🚶	7¼ miles (11.7km)	71
28	From Castle to Canal	🚶🚶🚶	6 miles (9.7km)	74
29	Round the Waterways at Frankton	🚶🚶🚶	8 miles (12.9km)	77

Contents

WALK		RATING	DISTANCE	PAGE
30	Place Your Bets at Oswestry	🚶 🚶 🚶	4 miles (6.4km)	78
31	The Full Monty at Queen's Head	🚶 🚶 🚶	6½ miles (10.4km)	80
32	Hope for the Dormouse	🚶 🚶 🚶	9½ miles (15.3km)	83
33	Back to Purple	🚶 🚶 🚶	4½ miles (7.2km)	86
34	Sitting in the Devil's Chair at Stiperstones	🚶 🚶 🚶	3½ miles (5.7km)	89
35	The Lion of Pontesbury	🚶 🚶 🚶	4 miles (6.4km)	90
36	Life and Death in Bishop's Castle	🚶 🚶 🚶	7 miles (11.3km)	92
37	Sheep Shape the Mynd	🚶 🚶 🚶	7½ miles (12.1km)	95
38	Shapely Seductive Strettons	🚶 🚶 🚶	6 miles (9.7km)	98
39	From Cwms to Caer Caradoc	🚶 🚶 🚶	2½ miles (4km)	101
40	Breadwalk to Bone Bed	🚶 🚶 🚶	5¼ miles (8.4km)	102
41	Over the Edge at Stokesay	🚶 🚶 🚶	6¼ miles (10.1km)	104
42	Steaming up Wart Hill	🚶 🚶 🚶	6 miles (9.7km)	107
43	Folly on Wenlock Edge	🚶 🚶 🚶	6½ miles (10.4km)	110
44	Land of Hope and Glory	🚶 🚶 🚶	8¼ miles (13.3km)	113
45	And So to Bedstone	🚶 🚶 🚶	5 miles (8km)	114
46	Follow the Buzzard to Bury Ditches	🚶 🚶 🚶	5½ miles (8.8km)	116
47	On Offa at Knighton	🚶 🚶 🚶	8 miles (12.9km)	119
48	Under the Sun at Clun	🚶 🚶 🚶	5½ miles (8.8km)	122
49	Over Black Hill to the Valley of Cwm	🚶 🚶 🚶	9½ miles (15.3km)	125
50	The Wood Colliers' Legacy at Clunton	🚶 🚶 🚶	3¾ miles (6km)	126

Rating: Each walk is rated for its relative difficulty compared to the other walks in this book. Walks marked 🚶 🚶 🚶 are likely to be shorter and easier with little total ascent. The hardest walks are marked 🚶 🚶 🚶 .

Walking in Safety: For advice and safety tips ➤ 128.

Introducing Shropshire

It lacks a coastline, and none of its hills quite achieves mountain status, but Shropshire has just about every other desirable feature a discerning walker could wish for. Perhaps nowhere else in England will you find a county so deeply rural and with so much variety. But don't take my word for it. Choose a clear day, then make your way to the top of The Wrekin, and look down on that 'land of lost content' so wistfully evoked by A E Housman, the author of *A Shropshire Lad*.

Take binoculars with you and trace the course of Britain's longest river as the Severn sweeps through the county, from the Breidden Hills in the west to Wyre Forest in the south east, effectively dividing Shropshire in two. To the north is a patchwork of dairy fields, hedgerows, copses and crops, broken at intervals by rugged sandstone ridges, such as Grinshill or Nesscliffe, and dissected by a complex canal network. Spilling over the border into neighbouring Cheshire and North Wales is the unique meres and mosses country, with serenely smooth lakes glinting silver in the early morning light, interspersed with russet-tinged expanses of alder-fringed peat bog, where only the cry of the curlew disturbs the silence.

South of the Severn lies the Shropshire Hills Area of Outstanding Natural Beauty. Where to start? There is almost too much. With Wenlock Edge perhaps, one of the most famous escarpments in the country, despite being not especially high or dramatic. It's only when you walk the Edge that you fully discover what a magical place it is – glorious woods and unexpectedly steep slopes plunging to innumerable secret valleys, meadows, streams and farmhouses, all tucked away, invisible from the outside world.

If the Edge superficially lacks drama, that could never be said of the Stretton Hills, rising magnificently above the little town of Church Stretton, especially Caer Caradoc, with its shockingly steep southern slopes and a prehistoric fort encircling its summit. Across the Stretton Gap lies the Long Mynd. Viewed from The Wrekin, the Mynd is a dark bulky smudge. Seen from Caer Caradoc, it's an undulating plateau cut by valleys so steep they're often almost vertical. But look at the Mynd from the south and it takes on a very different character, more like a range of round-topped hills. In reality, the Long Mynd is all of these things, and it offers endless walking possibilities, not to mention a view to equal, or even surpass, that from The Wrekin. To stand on its western tops, looking

---

PUBLIC TRANSPORT ⓘ

Over the years, bus services in Shropshire have improved dramatically everywhere except Clun Valley. Every walk in this book was accessed easily by public transport. The county council is keen to increase the use of public transport, as are other interested parties such as the National Trust. Several leisure bus services are aimed specifically at walkers, but ordinary, everyday services will get you there. Details are available from Traveline on 0870 608 2 608, while tourist information centres and libraries have free timetable booklets.

across the Onny Valley towards Wales and the setting sun, is to gaze on a scene so sublime you'll be itching to get out there. Near at hand beckons Stiperstones, its long crest jagged with rocky tors, and south of it Heath Mynd, Stapeley, Bromlow Callow and innumerable others rolling away to the border. Further south and west, Offa's Dyke snakes over the gloriously remote rounded tops of Clun Forest, which merge imperceptibly with the Kerry Hills of Radnorshire, where that loveliest of rivers, the Teme, has its source.

And let's not forget the Clee Hills. Brown Clee dominates the Severn Valley near Bridgnorth, providing a worthy backdrop for exquisite Corve Dale. It never looks better than in early morning mist, its intricate patchwork slowly emerging as the sun breaks through. And then there's Titterstone Clee, rearing high above Ludlow. Its slopes are scarred by quarrying and blighted by radar installations, yet its massive presence and charisma remain undimmed, and the view from its southern flank is claimed to be the finest in England.

Using this Book

Information panels
An information panel for each walk shows its relative difficulty (➤ 5), the distance and total amount of ascent. An indication of the gradients you will encounter is shown by the rating ▲ ▲ ▲ (no steep slopes) to ▲ ▲ ▲ (several very steep slopes).

Maps
There are 30 maps, covering 40 of the walks. Some walks have a suggested option in the same area. The information panel for these walks will tell you how much extra walking is involved. On short-cut suggestions the panel will tell you the total distance if you set out from the start of the main walk. Where an option returns to the same point on the main walk, just the distance of the loop is given. Where an option leaves the main walk at one point and returns to it at another, then the distance shown is for the whole walk. The minimum time suggested is for reasonably fit walkers and doesn't allow for stops. Each walk has a suggested map. Laminated aqua3 maps are longer lasting and water resistant.

Start Points
The start of each walk is given as a six-figure grid reference prefixed by two letters indicating which 100km square of the National Grid it refers to. You'll find more information on grid references on most Ordnance Survey maps.

Dogs
We have tried to give dog owners useful advice about how dog friendly each walk is. Please respect other countryside users. Keep your dog under control, especially around livestock, and obey local bylaws and other dog control notices.

Car Parking
Many of the car parks suggested are public, but occasionally you may find you have to park on the roadside or in a lay-by. Please be considerate when you leave your car, ensuring that access roads or gates are not blocked and that other vehicles can pass safely. Remember that pub car parks are private and should not be used unless you have the owner's permission.

All Around The Wrekin

A Shropshire classic with added value – The Wrekin and The Ercall.

•DISTANCE•	8½ miles (13.7km)
•MINIMUM TIME•	3hrs
•ASCENT / GRADIENT•	1,585ft (485m) ▲▲▲
•LEVEL OF DIFFICULTY•	🚶🚶 🚶🚶 🚶🚶
•PATHS•	Woodland footpaths, urban streets, quiet lanes, 2 stiles
•LANDSCAPE•	Hills and woods on the edge of Wellington
•SUGGESTED MAP•	aqua3 OS Explorer 242 Telford, Ironbridge & The Wrekin
•START / FINISH•	Grid reference: SJ 651113
•DOG FRIENDLINESS•	Dog heaven, except on firing days (► note below)
•PARKING•	Belmont or Swimming Pool East car parks, both on Tan Bank, off Victoria Road, Wellington
•PUBLIC TOILETS•	Victoria Street car park, between bus and train stations
•NOTE•	Rifle range on The Wrekin – warning notices posted, but take care on firing days

BACKGROUND TO THE WALK

Those who live in Shropshire know that The Wrekin is more than just a hill. For all true Salopians it is a sort of focal point and symbol of Shropshire, the embodiment of home, a sentiment implied in the traditional toast 'To all friends around The Wrekin'. Although it reaches only a modest 1,323ft (407m), its splendid isolation makes it seem higher. This illusion is strengthened by its shape: while basically a whaleback, it appears conical from certain angles, like a mini-mountain, giving the impression of an extinct volcano. It isn't, though it is volcanic in origin, an eroded remnant of a vast chunk of rock thrust to the surface around 700 million years ago, putting it among the oldest rocks in the world.

Fact or Fiction

If that origin seems a bit mundane, you might prefer the alternative provided by local folklore, which tells of the giant Gwendol Wrekin ap Shenkin ap Mynyddmawr (or the Devil in another version) who was on his way to Shrewsbury to dam the River Severn with a shovelful of soil. He met a cobbler who guessed what he was up to, showed him the sackful of shoes he was carrying and told him he had worn them all out trying to find Shrewsbury. Frustrated, Gwendol dumped his shovelful on the spot, sparing Shrewsbury from flooding and creating The Wrekin. (It didn't work, however – Shrewsbury floods nearly every winter.)

Ancient Rock

The return leg of the walk takes you through The Ercall Nature Reserve. The Ercall (pronounced arkle) is a small, steep, wooded hill important for its geology as well as its woodlands and wildlife. It has been much quarried and the sheer quarry faces are exciting to explore. Much of The Ercall is composed of Wrekin quartzite, a hard, white, crystalline rock around 535 million years old. It also has what geologists call an intrusion of granophyre, a fine-grained granite formed 560 million years ago, and a source of china clay. The great civil engineer Thomas Telford (1757–1834) used Ercall granophyre when he

resurfaced the Roman Watling Street to create his much admired Holyhead Road, on which
the modern A5 is based. Do stop to read the information boards in the nature reserve if you
would like to know more about the geology and ecology of The Ercall, which is managed by
Shropshire Wildlife Trust in partnership with Telford and Wrekin Council.

Walk 1

Walk 1 Directions

① Walk along **Tan Bank** away from
the town centre. Cross **Victoria
Road** and go forward a little way,
still on Tan Bank, before turning
left on a path just after the police

station. Walk to **New Church Road**
and turn right. At **Holyhead Road**,
turn left, then cross to **Limekiln
Lane**, noticing the Old Hall School
(built in 1480) on the corner. Soon
the slopes of The Wrekin appear, as
Limekiln Lane heads under the
M54 into open country.

② At the end of the lane, go straight on into **Limekiln Wood**; the path leads along the edge of the wood at first. When you reach a junction, go to the left, but a few paces further on fork right into the heart of the wood. Ignore any branching paths, sticking to the well-trodden main route. Arriving at a T-junction by some ruined buildings, turn right, descend to a junction and turn left, then left again when you come to a road.

> **WHAT TO LOOK FOR** ⓘ
> **Limekiln Wood** is full of intriguing humps and hollows, overgrown now by ferns and ivy but still hinting at its former role as a quarry. Coal and limestone were dug here and much of the limestone was burnt on site in kilns, two of which survive (they're not on the route of this walk). The resulting lime was used in agriculture and building.

③ Turn right on the access road to **Wrekin Farm**. When you reach **Wenlocks Wood**, leave the farm road, turning right on a field-edge footpath which heads towards The Wrekin. A stile soon gives access to its eastern slopes. Go forward a few paces, then turn left.

④ Branch right where a signpost indicates a permissive path. Follow this round the hill to a cross path;

> **WHERE TO EAT AND DRINK** ⓘ
> The **Dun Cow** on Duke Street and the **White Lion** on Crown Street in Wellington are traditional pubs. **Café del Manso** next to the bus station has outside tables, very pleasant on sunny days. But my vote goes to **Flapjacks**, a friendly tea room and restaurant on Bell Street at the end of Tan Bank. No dogs allowed, unfortunately, but children are welcome and there is a reasonable veggie selection.

> **WHILE YOU'RE THERE** ⓘ
> Why not visit one of the National Trust's more unusual properties? You'll pass close by it when you cross Holyhead Road towards the end of the walk. A Victorian suburban house called **Sunnycroft**, it is typical of many built for prosperous professionals and businessmen, and has survived largely unaltered, its original contents still in place. The garden has pigsties, stables, orchards and even a wellingtonia avenue.

turn right, joining the Shropshire Way for the climb over the summit ridge. As you approach the northern end, keep left when the path forks, then left again by a prominent beech tree, descending through woods. At the edge of the woods, leave the Shropshire Way and turn right to meet a lane.

⑤ Turn right to a T-junction, join a footpath opposite and pass between two reservoirs before meeting a lane, where you go left. As you draw almost level with **Buckatree Lodge**, turn right into **The Ercall Nature Reserve**. Go straight on along a bridleway, past some impressive former quarries and a pool. Before long you come to a junction: ignore a path doubling back towards the quarries and go forward a few paces to find that the main track swings left and climbs to the top of **The Ercall**.

⑥ As Wellington comes briefly into view through the trees, turn right on a ridge-top path. As you begin to descend, the path forks. Go to the right and shortly join a track which passes under the **M54**. Keep straight on along **Golf Links Lane** to **Holyhead Road**. Cross to a footpath opposite. When you reach a road (**Roseway**) turn right, then left on to **Tan Bank**.

Branching Out from Prees

An exploration of Whixall Moss, together with two branches of the Shroppie.

•DISTANCE•	10 miles (16.1km)
•MINIMUM TIME•	3hrs 30min
•ASCENT / GRADIENT•	98ft (30m)
•LEVEL OF DIFFICULTY•	
•PATHS•	Some road walking (take care on blind bends on Post Office Lane), about 20 stiles (some in disrepair)
•LANDSCAPE•	Dairy country, canals, Whixall Moss
•SUGGESTED MAP•	aqua3 OS Explorer 241 Shrewsbury
•START / FINISH•	Grid reference: SJ 537337
•DOG FRIENDLINESS•	On lead in nature reserves and where cattle present, some electric fences
•PARKING•	Where bridleway meets lane by Prees Station, take care not to block access
•PUBLIC TOILETS•	None on route

BACKGROUND TO THE WALK

North Shropshire is meres and mosses country. Meres are lakes or ponds, but mosses are perhaps less familiar. Very simply, they are raised peat bogs, which may not sound particularly interesting. Reserve judgement until you have explored Whixall Moss, part of Fenn's, Whixall and Bettisfield Mosses National Nature Reserve (NNR). Only the best or rarest places receive NNR designation, but Whixall is also a European Special Area of Conservation and a Wetland of International Importance. Since most of our mosses have been destroyed by forestry, agriculture and peat digging, it is also extremely rare. Commercial peat cutting ceased here in 1991 and since then work has been in hand to restore the moss, as far as this is possible.

Endangered Habitat

A moss is waterlogged, stagnant and acidic. Despite this, or because of it, 1,700 insect species can be found in this habitat. The trouble is, some are so specialised they can't easily survive elsewhere, which is one reason why mosses are so important. The raft spider, for instance, is very much at home here, as is the rare white-faced darter (a damselfly). Uncommon birds of prey such as the hobby patrol the skies and the increasingly scarce snipe finds a refuge here in winter. Characteristic plants include cotton sedge, bogmoss, cross-leaved heath, bog rosemary, cranberry and sundew – a carnivorous plant which feasts on insects. When mosses are drained for peat cutting such species are inevitably lost.

There are few rights of way through the reserve but, in 2001, a partnership between English Nature, the Countryside Council for Wales and British Waterways developed three circular trails, parts of which are included in this walk, along with the adjacent Llangollen Canal. Canal-side fens overflow with plants such as great hairy willowherb, water figwort and flag iris. In places carr has developed – a damp woodland, characterised by species such as alder and willow. Mallard ducks, mute swans and kingfishers haunt the canal, along with dragonflies and damselflies. If you're really lucky you might even see a water vole.

Walk 2 Directions

① Join the bridleway by the signal box. After a few paces you'll see a blocked stile, so use the gate near by instead. Go into a field and follow the right-hand edge to a stile. Cross to the other side of the hedge, but continue in the same direction. Keep straight on across four more fields to the **B5476**.

② Walk along the road opposite (**Post Office Lane**) and keep straight on at two junctions. Take extra care along here. Turn right by **Whixall Social Centre**, then left on to a driveway before **Church Farm**.

③ At **Farthing Cottage**, turn right on the Shropshire Way. Cross a field, passing a pond, then continue across the next field. Go slightly left across a third field to a pair of stiles and a footbridge. Don't cross these, but leave the Shropshire Way, turning left to a gate opening into a large field. Turn left, keeping about 100yds (91m) from its left-hand edge. On reaching a row of three large oaks, go diagonally right towards a gate and then cross another field to a lane.

④ Turn right, then left at a junction and straight on at the next. Join the first path on the right after **Whixall School**, taking particular care while stepping off the dodgy stile. Cross three fields to the Llangollen Canal and cross **Roundthorn Bridge**,

where an information board tells you about the NNR. Take a leaflet from the box here – it acts as a permit to enter the reserve. Turn right, then left, following the orange-coded **Mosses Trail**.

⑤ At Point 8 on the trail, turn left to meet the canal at **Morris' Bridge**. Turn right on the tow path to a canal junction, then cross **Roving Bridge** to join the Prees Branch. The tow path changes sides at **Dobson's Bridge**. Beyond **Whixall Marina** the canal is disused and has become a Shropshire Wildlife Trust nature reserve.

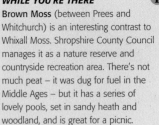

⑥ Meet a lane at **Waterloo Bridge**. Turn left, then immediately right, signposted 'Abbeygreen and Edstaston'. Keep straight on past the Abbeygreen turning, but turn left when you come to a T-junction. The lane is joined by the Shropshire Way and heads into **Edstaston**.

⑦ Leave the Shropshire Way and turn left on a footpath which crosses fields to the **B5476**. Turn left, then cross to a lane. Follow it past **Edstaston Hall** and a couple of farms until you can turn left on a bridleway which heads for the railway, then follows it to **Prees Station**. If you're catching a train, remember to signal the driver, as you would for a bus, because Prees is a request stop.

Walk 3

Gingering it Up at Market Drayton

Enjoy a veritable feast of gingerbread men and Cheshire cheese on the Staffordshire border.

•DISTANCE•	5¼ miles (8.4km)
•MINIMUM TIME•	2hrs
•ASCENT / GRADIENT•	165ft (50m)
•LEVEL OF DIFFICULTY•	
•PATHS•	Streets, tow path, sandy track and quiet lanes; field paths and 6 stiles on Walk 4
•LANDSCAPE•	Market town, canal and mixed farmland
•SUGGESTED MAP•	aqua3 OS Explorer 243 Market Drayton
•START / FINISH•	Grid reference: SJ 674344
•DOG FRIENDLINESS•	On lead between Point ④ and Walkmill Bridge and in dairy fields on Walk 4
•PARKING•	Car park on Towers Lawn, next to bus station
•PUBLIC TOILETS•	At bus station

BACKGROUND TO THE WALK

In 1245, at the behest of Abbot Simon of Combermere Abbey, Henry III granted Market Drayton a charter for a Wednesday market and two annual fairs. Marketing has been its main role ever since, serving a large area of rural Shropshire, Staffordshire and Cheshire. Abbot Simon wasn't just thinking of the local peasants and farmers – his monks had their own produce to sell. They cultivated vines and kept honeybees, as well as participating in dairy farming, which flourished in the fertile countryside. Food has always been the main focus for Market Drayton's traders and, even today, the town is full of small, independent shops selling a wide range of locally made produce. Every Wednesday Cheshire Street is still submerged by a flood of colourful stalls heaped high with food, along with goods from the Staffordshire Potteries. So you can buy your cake and the plate to eat it from too.

Sweet-toothed Town

To compete in the modern world, Drayton now markets itself and the theme is still food, as it tries to entice tourists to the 'home of gingerbread'. First made here in 1817, for many years there were four gingerbread dynasties in town, each with its own secret recipe. People then enjoyed gingerbread in 'junks as big as my foot', but nowadays you can buy it fashioned into hearts, teddy bears, sheep or footballers.

Traditionally, Draytonians dunked their gingerbread in port and one of the most popular recipes already contained rum. Billington's gingerbread is still made locally to a secret recipe, but Drayton also boasts plenty of other specialities, such as damson jam, damson cheese and damson gin, which possibly goes down well with a bit of rum-soaked, port-dunked gingerbread. Go into one of the bakers in town and you can choose from other local treats like butter buns, lardy cakes and oven bottoms, while pikelets and oatcakes from the Potteries are popular too. Since the 16th century, Drayton has been famous for dairy

Walk **3**

goods. Yogurt is made in a factory on the edge of town, but farm-made yogurts are also on sale in the shops, along with excellent cheeses. It is said that the only unpasteurised Cheshire cheese still made in England comes from Market Drayton.

Clive's Contribution

Robert Clive was born near Market Drayton in 1725 and went to school there. He terrorised the town as a boy, even running a protection racket. His despairing family packed him off to India where he achieved great wealth and prestige in the process of establishing British supremacy there. Despite his fame (or notoriety), it's his culinary contribution they celebrate in Drayton. At the Clive and Coffyne (a coffyne is a pie case) they serve an award-winning Clive of India Pie which is said to be based on a recipe given by Clive in 1768 to the bakers of Pézenas in France. He has also, rightly or wrongly, been linked to the gingerbread tradition because of his involvement in the spice trade.

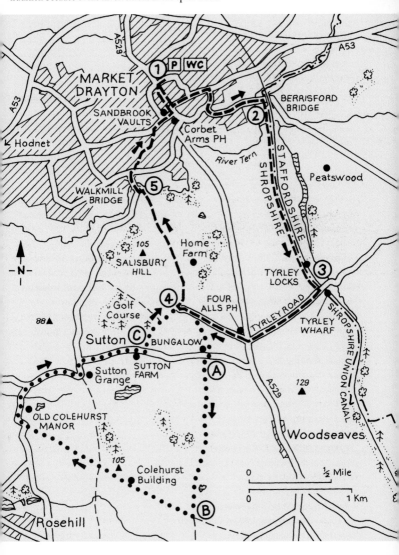

Walk 3 Directions

① Walk past the bus station, cross at the zebra crossing, then turn left down **Queen Street** to the Buttercross and left on **Stafford Street**. Go straight on at the first junction, right at the next on to **Great Hales Street** and then left on **Berrisford Road** (use the easily missed footway on the left until forced to join the road).

WHERE TO EAT AND DRINK
The **Four Alls** is a popular place with lots of outside seating, ideal for families with dogs. Market Drayton has many friendly, attractive pubs – if you appreciate period buildings you'll want to try them all. You'll pass several of the best on this walk. Special mention must go to the **Corbet Arms**; the landlord in 1885 was my ancestor, Richard Wycherley.

② You'll soon come to **Berrisford Bridge**, also known as 40 Steps Aqueduct, which carries the Shropshire Union Canal over the road. Go up the steps and turn right on the tow path. This part of the Shroppie system was originally the Birmingham and Liverpool Junction Canal, which went from Autherley to Nantwich. The engineer was Thomas Telford and the boldness of his design is apparent along this stretch, with its massive cuttings and embankments. The deep cutting on the approach to **Tyrley Locks** has its own microclimate, and positively drips with ferns, mosses and liverworts. The tow path marks the county boundary – this stretch of the canal is in Staffordshire.

③ At bridge 60 by **Tyrley Wharf** go up to the lane (**Tyrley Road**) and turn left. This leads to the main

road (**A529**) and a pub called the **Four Alls**. Cross with care to **Sandy Lane**. After 600yds (549m) a footpath leaves the lane on the left – this is where you branch off for Walk 4. If you're doing Walk 3 only, continue along the lane.

WHILE YOU'RE THERE
Hodnet Hall Gardens at nearby Hodnet, about 5 miles (8km) south west of Market Drayton, is worth a visit, with over 60 acres (24.3ha) of landscaped gardens around an Elizabethan-style house built in the 1870s. Enjoy the woodland walks and lovely water gardens with their chain of ornamental ponds.

④ **Sandy Lane** comes to a T-junction with a track. Turn right here; it's still Sandy Lane, but this part is a private road and dogs must be kept on leads. It heads north towards Drayton, overlooked by Salisbury Hill, where a Yorkist army under the Earl of Salisbury camped in 1459 before heavily defeating a Lancastrian force twice the size.

⑤ When you meet a road, turn right to cross the River Tern at **Walkmill Bridge** (a packhorse bridge). Cross **Walkmill Road** and go up **Kilnbank Road** opposite. This leads to **Shropshire Street**; turn right. After passing **Sandbrook Vaults**, turn left past the Buttercross to **Cheshire Street**, which leads back to **Towers Lawn**.

WHAT TO LOOK FOR
With a flight of five locks and a group of gorgeous buildings, **Tyrley Wharf** is a place to linger. It's hard to imagine this was once a real working wharf – rough, tough, noisy, smelly and mucky. It served the Peatswood Estate and was also a change-over point for the tow horses, which were expected to do about 25 miles (40km) a day.

Drayton and the Colehurst Loop

A longer, more rural walk through dairy pasture, providing a glimpse of a medieval manor house.

See map and information panel for Walk 3

•DISTANCE•	8¼ miles (13.3km)
•MINIMUM TIME•	3hrs 30min
•ASCENT / GRADIENT•	213ft (65m) ▲▲▲
•LEVEL OF DIFFICULTY•	👫 👫 👫

Walk 4 Directions (Walk 3 option)

This additional loop to Walk 3 at Market Drayton will give you a greater feel for the real character of the area, with its mix of lush meadows full of dairy cattle contrasting with huge, prairie-like arable fields.

Leave Walk 3 between Points ③ and ④, about 600yds (549m) after the **Four Alls** pub, where a footpath leads off the lane on the left. It begins as a short green lane which quickly brings you to a gate and stile. Go into a dairy pasture and walk across it towards a bungalow at the far side. As you approach the bungalow you should change to the other side of the hedge, but continue in the same direction, past the bungalow towards a lane (Point Ⓐ).

Turn right, then first left on a short green lane, which may be overgrown with nettles. Cross a stile into a pasture and go straight on along its edge, then across a stile to the next pasture.

The right of way goes straight across, passing through a cluster of small pools. You may find you can't get through due to the denseness of the vegetation round the pools. If so, pass to the right of them, then continue across the field to the far side. Make sure you're heading in the right direction by checking that there's a hedge over to your left, a group of trees in the far left corner and then a lower hedge at the far side of the field. Head for this and you should soon see a gate and stile which confirm you're on the right track. Cross the stile and continue straight on across an arable field to intercept a farm track (Point Ⓑ) at the far side.

Turn right and walk to a lane. Turn right again, passing a large and very impressive timber-framed house, **Old Colehurst Manor**. Turn right when you get to the next two junctions, signposted to Sutton and then to Woodseaves.

After passing **Sutton Farm**, go left on a bridleway (Point Ⓒ) just before a modern house. Walk along the field edge to the right of a hedge, then join a track and turn right to rejoin Walk 3 at Point ④.

Walk 5

A World First at Ironbridge

The world's first iron bridge, cast in 1779, still graces the Severn Gorge below Benthall Edge.

•DISTANCE•	4¼ miles (6.8km)
•MINIMUM TIME•	1hr 30min
•ASCENT / GRADIENT•	426ft (130m) ▲ ▲ ▲
•LEVEL OF DIFFICULTY•	👫 👫 👫
•PATHS•	Mostly excellent, muddy in places, lots of steps (down only), 1 short stretch is narrow and eroded, 5 stiles
•LANDSCAPE•	Wooded hills and mixed farmland above Severn Gorge
•SUGGESTED MAP•	aqua3 OS Explorer 242 Telford, Ironbridge & The Wrekin
•START / FINISH•	Grid reference: SJ 672033
•DOG FRIENDLINESS•	Will love woods, but keep under control in fields
•PARKING•	Bridge Car Park at south end of Iron Bridge
•PUBLIC TOILETS•	In The Square at Ironbridge

Walk 5 Directions

The little town of Ironbridge is built of mellow brick, its attractive buildings clinging in tiers to the north side of the gorge, overlooking the River Severn. Though it is part of a UNESCO-designated World Heritage Site and a major tourist centre, it has not lost its charm, retaining a maze of steep, narrow streets, which mingle with patches of woodland, open to the public and managed by the Severn Gorge Countryside Trust.

The iron bridge itself was built by Abraham Darby III, grandson of the man who started it all by smelting iron ore with coke (► Walk 7), and it's a supremely graceful structure. Do take the time to explore the bridge – walk across it, gaze down from its parapet, walk underneath it, admire it from the steep streets to the north. But do all that later, otherwise you might not be able to tear yourself away from

Ironbridge to get on with the walk. Without crossing into Ironbridge, and with your back to the bridge, turn right into **Benthall Edge Wood**, taking a track that passes under a disused railway bridge. When the track comes to an end, cross over a stile on the left and turn left, going uphill to arrive at a major path junction.

Turn right here and stay on the main path, ignoring branches from it. The path runs through damp, jungly woodland, climbing steadily. When it emerges into the open at one point, care is required as it's narrow and eroded. So don't get too carried away with the view of The

---

WHERE TO EAT AND DRINK ⓘ

You'll be spoilt for choice in Ironbridge. Possibilities include the **Tontine Hotel** opposite the bridge and the **Station Hotel** by the car park, both with outside tables. **Ironbridge Tea Room** welcomes dogs and also does takeaways. **Peacocks Pantry** is a very welcoming tea room, with a children's play area.

Wrekin (or the power station) that you forget to watch where you're putting your feet. The path improves as you return to the wood and soon after this it merges with a track coming from below and then with another from the left. Keep on in much the same direction, forking left uphill a few paces further on, along a tree-lined path above a forest road. When you get to the edge of the woods, cross a stile and continue along the edge of meadows on the **Shropshire Way**, soon bearing a little left to pass a house, joining a track to a lane. Turn left and then, after 400yds (366m), join a path at a gate on the left where a sign requests you to keep your dog on a lead.

WHILE YOU'RE THERE

A good starting point for understanding Ironbridge is the **Museum of the Gorge**, in a Gothic warehouse built in the 1830s by the Coalbrookdale Company. The displays concentrate on the history of the gorge and include a huge scale model showing it as it was in 1796.

The path runs by the right-hand hedge along the edges of three fields, then straight across a fourth to a gate at the far side. Keep going by field edges to meet a track by **Benthall Hall Farm**. Turn right, then left on to a lane by **St Bartholomew's Church**, an interesting building and worth a visit – just check out that sun dial! Adjacent Benthall Hall, which was built of stone in the 16th century

presents a stunning face to the world. It's quite something inside as well, and as it's owned by the National Trust you can have a look round. There are plaster ceilings and lots of carved oak. Mr and Mrs Benthall still live there so it's a real home, with a warmer feel than many National Trust properties.

Continue down the lane a few paces to find a footpath which crosses a field in front of the hall. Go through a gate at the far side, after which the path continues along a field edge, meeting a track at the far side. Turn right and at a junction carry straight on along a lane. Approaching another junction, turn left into **Workhouse Wood** (owned by the Woodland Trust).

The path soon forks – carry straight on here. At the next junction turn right, then left at a T-junction, and straight on at two subsequent junctions. As you approach the far side of the wood, turn right on a path that runs along its edge at first. Before long, as you return to **Benthall Edge Wood**, you'll come to the first of several flights of wooden steps, interspersed with boardwalks, all of which makes the steep descent easier, if rather over-civilised. At a boardwalk junction turn right, down more steps, then left. Keep going down until you come to a waymarked junction; turn right here on a path that leads out of the wood to a lane. Cross over, then descend to the iron bridge.

WHAT TO LOOK FOR

Benthall Edge Wood is a real jungly tangle of trees, shrubs and ferns. You'd never guess this was once the scene of frenetic industry, but look more closely and you'll spot the clues. The hummocky nature of the ground and the presence of deep pits point to the fact that Benthall Edge Wood was mined and quarried for coal and limestone from the 13th century onwards. In the 19th century it was almost cleared of trees, so it's heartening to look at the natural regeneration that has occurred since industry ceased.

Exploring Shropshire's China Town

Woodland, the River Severn and fascinating industrial remains make for a superb walk in Ironbridge Gorge.

•DISTANCE•	5 miles (8km)
•MINIMUM TIME•	2hrs
•ASCENT / GRADIENT•	295ft (90m)
•LEVEL OF DIFFICULTY•	
•PATHS•	Mostly excellent, though path through Lee Dingle is quite rough and may be muddy, 1 stile
•LANDSCAPE•	Woodland and riverbank
•SUGGESTED MAP•	aqua3 OS Explorer 242 Telford, Ironbridge & The Wrekin
•START / FINISH•	Grid reference: SJ 677033
•DOG FRIENDLINESS•	No sheep or cattle so can run fairly freely
•PARKING•	Next to Bedlam Furnaces on Waterloo Street, between Ironbridge and Jackfield Bridge
•PUBLIC TOILETS•	At Ironbridge end of Waterloo Street

BACKGROUND TO THE WALK

Coalport china is famous the world over, and rightly so, for it's exquisite stuff. The story of how it came to be made here is interesting too. Coalport, which is much smaller today than it was at its peak, was planned as a canal-river interchange and a complete new town by ironmaster William Reynolds. Between 1788 and 1796 he built warehouses, workshops, factories and cottages on formerly undeveloped land by the river. Crucially, he also constructed the Shropshire Canal to link the East Shropshire Coalfield with the River Severn. The terminus was at Coalport Wharf, between the Brewery Inn and Coalport Bridge.

Monument to Industry
The canal greatly aided the new town's development, especially after the completion of the Hay Inclined Plane in 1793. This is one of the country's major industrial monuments, the best preserved and most spectacular of its kind. It was the means by which boats were transferred from the top to the bottom of the gorge. Equivalent to 27 locks, but worked by only four men, it could pass six boats in an hour, a feat which would have taken three hours using a lock system. The boats were carried up and down the almost 1 in 4 gradient on wheeled cradles. The incline is now part of Blists Hill Museum, but you can see part of it on this walk. After the canal was superseded by a railway it silted up, became overgrown and was infilled during the 1920s. It was partially restored in 1976 and again in the 1990s.

In 1795 the Coalport China Company was founded by John Rose in the large building which is now a youth hostel and café. Across the former canal is a later china works, now Coalport China Museum, showing factory life and manufacturing techniques. Even if you don't go inside the museum, the whole site, with mellow brick buildings and enormous kilns, is wonderfully evocative. China manufacture ceased here in 1926 when the company moved to the Potteries. Coalport China is now part of the Wedgwood group.

① To the left of the furnaces (as you stand facing them) a path climbs into parkland, then zig-zags up through a succession of wisteria-covered pergolas and flights of steps. Turn right at the top, then left on **Newbridge Road** to a junction.

② Pass to the left of the **Golden Ball Inn**, then turn right at the junction with Jockey Bank, past **Victoria Cottage**. Go left at another junction and through a gate into a wood called **The Crostan**. A stepped path climbs to a junction

where two paths are indicated. Take the right-hand one, climbing by the woodland edge to another waymarked junction.

③ Turn right on a bridleway, which runs across two meadows into woodland. Continue through the wood, with **Lloyd's Coppice** clinging to the steep slope on your right. Fork left at two junctions; at the second one the bridleway leaves the trees to continue between woodland and houses.

④ A stile on the right gives access to **Lee Dingle**, where a path descends towards the road. Cross

Walk 6

Legges Way, turn left under two bridges, then soon right on a footpath by the entrance to **Blists Hill Museum**.

⑤ Ignore a path branching left and carry straight on past a line of wooden posts. Turn right on a footpath by the last post, skirting the Blists Hill site and soon entering woodland. Ignore paths branching left and keep close to the museum site. Soon you'll see the canal through the trees. When the path enters grassland, it forks; keep left, with trees between the path and the canal. At the next junction turn right, glimpsing the top of the great **Hay Incline**.

> **WHILE YOU'RE THERE**
> Blists Hill Museum re-creates the sights, sounds and smells of a late Victorian town. The staff wear period costume and you can exchange your money at the bank for Victorian coinage to spend in the shops or pub. Watch someone mucking out a pigsty, operating a steam engine or pouring iron in a foundry, or learn about the scary side of Victorian medicine in the chemist's shop.

⑥ Following signs for Coalport, descend to a junction by a bridge. Turn left on the **Silkin Way**, then immediately right and right again past the **Shakespeare Inn** and **Tunnel Tea Rooms**. Cross a road bridge, then turn left across the **Shropshire Canal** and left again on the tow path. Re-cross the canal at the next footbridge and walk past the **China Museum**, Coalport Youth Hostel and Slip Room Café. Join Coalport **High Street** and continue in the same direction, rejoining the **Silkin Way** opposite the **Brewery Inn**. Follow the track to **Coalport Bridge**, then cross over the river.

> **WHERE TO EAT AND DRINK**
> There are numerous possibilities mentioned in the route description. All look appealing, most allow dogs and several offer children's menus and vegetarian choices. The **Boat Inn** is particularly interesting, with its mural of a Severn trow (flat-bottomed, square-sailed trading vessel), and past flood levels marked on the door. It has a garden and riverside tables, as do the **Brewery Inn** and the **Woodbridge Inn**. The museums and craft centre all have cafés.

⑦ Turn right on the Severn Way, which passes through **Preen's Eddy** picnic area, then climbs away from the river to continue along a former railway trackbed. Turn right at signs for Silkin Way via Jackfield Bridge and you'll come to the **Boat Inn**. Head towards Ironbridge past lovely cottages and **Maws Craft Centre**.

⑧ As you approach a black-and-white-painted former pub, a path takes you on to its access track, bending left into woodland. Turn right towards Ironbridge, soon joining **Church Road**. Pass **Jackfield Tile Museum** and the Calcutts House, then carry straight on at **Jackfield Sidings**, passing the **Black Swan**. When a bridge crosses the path you can access the river. Cross **Jackfield Bridge**, then turn left past the **Robin Hood Inn** and the **Bird in Hand** to return to **Bedlam Furnaces**.

> **WHAT TO LOOK FOR**
> Bedlam Furnaces were built in 1757 by the Madeley Wood Furnace Company and taken over by William Reynolds in 1794. They were used to smelt iron ore and are blast furnaces similar to those developed by Abraham Darby I. If a blast furnace was allowed to cool its lining would crack, so smelting was continuous, with employees working 12-hour shifts.

Revolution at Coalbrookdale

An absorbing walk in the wooded hills and valleys where the Industrial Revolution began.

•DISTANCE•	5 miles (8km)
•MINIMUM TIME•	2hrs
•ASCENT / GRADIENT•	770ft (235m) ▲▲▲
•LEVEL OF DIFFICULTY•	🚶🚶🚶
•PATHS•	Woodland paths, lots of steps (mostly descending), may be fallen trees at Strethill, 2 stiles
•LANDSCAPE•	Wooded hills of Severn Gorge
•SUGGESTED MAP•	aqua3 OS Explorer 242 Telford, Ironbridge & The Wrekin
•START / FINISH•	Grid reference: SJ 664037
•DOG FRIENDLINESS•	Excellent, but keep under strict control at Strethill (sheep)
•PARKING•	Dale End Riverside Park, just west of Museum of the Gorge
•PUBLIC TOILETS•	In Museum of the Gorge car park

BACKGROUND TO THE WALK

People have been smelting iron for many centuries, but production was originally small scale because smelting was dependent on timber which first had to be made into charcoal – a slow and laborious process. All that changed at Coalbrookdale in 1709 when Abraham Darby I perfected a method of smelting iron with coke instead of charcoal. It may sound a small thing, but it sparked a revolution that changed the world. At long last iron could be made cheaply in large quantities and it came to be increasingly used in many areas of engineering.

World Leader

By 1785 the Coalbrookdale district had become the foremost industrial area in the world. It was particularly celebrated for its innovations: the first iron bridge, the first iron boat, the first iron rails and the first steam locomotive. Tourists came from far and wide to see the sights, and artists came to paint it all – furnaces lighting up the night sky was a favourite subject. Decline eventually set in due to competition from the Black Country and South Wales and the area fell into decay. Since the 1960s, the surviving industrial relics have been transformed into a fascinating collection of museums and the gorge has been designated a UNESCO World Heritage Site. Perhaps even more remarkable than the industrial heritage is the way nature has reclaimed sites of industrial despoilation and made them beautiful again. These regenerated woods and meadows are managed by the Severn Gorge Countryside Trust and are accessible to the public.

Taking Care of the Workers

The ironmasters were paternalistic types who built decent houses for their workers and took an interest in their moral well-being. When you walk through Dale Coppice and Lincoln Hill Woods you will be using the Sabbath Walks, designed by Richard Reynolds to provide healthy Sunday recreation for his workers. The idea was that this would keep them from drinking, gambling and sexual promiscuity. A rotunda was erected at one viewpoint, but has since been demolished, though you can still enjoy the view. It's mostly woodland now, but you will see the remains of a great quarry that bit deep into Lincoln Hill. It extends so far underground that tours of its limestone caverns were popular with 19th-century day-trippers. Bands played in the illuminated caverns and thousands came on excursion trains from the Black Country and Birmingham.

Walk 7 Directions

① Follow the **River Severn** upstream, using the Severn Way, and pass under two bridges. After the second one, bear away from the river towards **Buildwas Road**. At the road, turn left for a few paces, then cross to a footpath that ascends through woodland. Keep close to the edge until a waymarker directs you obliquely right.

② Cross a stile and continue in the same direction over pastureland. Pass under a pylon, then join a farm track and turn left through a gate. Follow the hawthorn hedge on your right to a junction, turn left on a bridleway and follow it along field edges, then across the middle of a meadow to a lane. Turn left.

③ Leave the lane when it bridges a road, turning right on a farm access track (Shropshire Way). Go through a gate on the right, just before **Leasows Farm**, then downfield to enter **Lydebrook Dingle**. A path descends through the wood, beyond which you continue along a path called **Rope Walk**.

④ Descend some steps on the left into **Loamhole Dingle**. Cross **Loamhole Brook** at a footbridge and climb steps on the other side to a T-junction. Turn right on what is mostly boardwalk and, when you reach **Upper Furnace Pool**, cross it on a footbridge to meet the road.

⑤ Your onward route is to the left, but a short detour right leads to the **Darby Houses**, Tea Kettle Row and the Quaker Burial Ground. Resuming the walk, go down to **Darby Road** and turn right beside the viaduct and the **Museum of Iron**. Turn left under the viaduct at a junction with **Coach Road**. Follow the road past the museum and Coalbrookdale Works to a junction.

> **WHILE YOU'RE THERE** ℹ
> The **Museum of Iron** brings the Darbys'
> achievements to life. It includes the
> Darby Furnace where it all began and it
> has much to say about the lives of those
> who lived and worked in the area during
> this period of momentous change.
> Equally fascinating are the ironmasters'
> homes near by (known as the **Darby
> Houses**) and the charming terrace of
> workers' houses at Tea Kettle Row.

⑥ Cross to **Church Road**, turn left after the Wesleyan chapel on the corner and enter **Dale Coppice**. Follow signs for Church Road at the first two junctions, but at the third ignore the Church Road sign and keep straight on. Leave the wood to enter grassland and go forward a few paces to meet a track. Turn left, then shortly fork right, staying on

> **WHERE TO EAT AND DRINK** ℹ
> There is lots of choice, such as the
> **Swan**, a very attractive place which is
> open all day. Well-behaved dogs and
> children are welcome in the bar area, but
> no dogs where food is served. There's a
> special children's menu. Almost next
> door (the other side of Lincoln Hill
> limekilns), the **Malthouse** is equally
> attractive and also welcomes children,
> and dogs in the bar or outside.

the track. Go left at another junction, then right at the next two. Dale Coppice is on your right, a cemetery on your left.

⑦ A gate accesses **Dale Coppice**. Turn right, then soon left, going downhill to a junction marked by a bench. Turn right, then left when a sign indicates Church Road, and left again beside the road.

⑧ Turn right into **Lincoln Hill Wood** and follow signs for the Rotunda, soon arriving at a viewpoint where the Rotunda formerly stood. Descend a very steep flight of steps to a junction. Turn right, then left down more steps and left again, signposted to Lincoln Hill Road. Cross the road to a footpath opposite, that descends to the **Wharfage**. Turn right past Lincoln Hill lime kilns and the **Swan** to **Dale End Riverside Park**.

> **WHAT TO LOOK FOR** ℹ
> Upper Furnace Pool in Loamhole Dingle
> is the pool that powered the bellows that
> blew the furnace where Abraham Darby
> first smelted iron with coke. The area of
> open water has been reduced by a
> profuse growth of **marsh horsetail**.
> This primeval-looking species is the
> evolutionary successor to the giant tree-
> like horsetails that were a major element
> in the swamp vegetation that 300 million
> years ago formed the coal measures.

Walk 8

Up Jacob's Ladder to Rindleford

A spectacular combination of sheer cliffs and secluded valleys at Bridgnorth.

•DISTANCE•	6½ miles (10.4km)
•MINIMUM TIME•	2hrs 30min
•ASCENT / GRADIENT•	540ft (165m) ▲▲▲
•LEVEL OF DIFFICULTY•	🏃🏃 🏃🏃 🏃🏃
•PATHS•	Steep and eroded in parts (beware landslips), 2 stiles
•LANDSCAPE•	Wooded cliffs, bracken-filled valleys and mixed farmland
•SUGGESTED MAP•	aqua3 OS Explorer 218 Wyre Forest & Kidderminster
•START / FINISH•	Grid reference: SO 720934
•DOG FRIENDLINESS•	Generally excellent, but keep on leads in The Batch
•PARKING•	Severn Park, off A442 on east bank of Severn at Bridgnorth
•PUBLIC TOILETS•	Severn Park, also Listley Street in Bridgnorth

BACKGROUND TO THE WALK

The most dramatic of Shropshire towns, Bridgnorth clings to the top of a sandstone cliff. Or at least High Town does – for Bridgnorth is two towns in one, with Low Town occupying the riverside. The two are linked by a modern road, seven ancient stairways, a cartway and a funicular railway. This has a gradient of 2 in 3 and has been operating since 1892. Until recently it was Britain's only inland cliff railway and it remains the only electrically powered one, with colliery-type winding gear.

A Touch of Europe
It's often said that Bridgnorth, with its clifftop setting, resembles a continental town and if you do this walk you'll get an inkling of what is meant. It's only when you climb to the viewpoints on High Rock and Pendlestone Rock that you really get to see Bridgnorth in context. The modern town sprawls in the background, but the old town is distinct from it in a way reminiscent of many European countries. The Spanish, for instance, usually preserve an old town and build a modern one next to it, while here in Britain we knock it down and build on top. This is not the case in Bridgnorth. It does look almost continental from High Rock, perched on its cliff and watched over by its twin church towers. The red sandstone one to the north belongs to St Leonard's, the original parish church. During the Civil War it was used as an ammunition store by Royalist troops. When the Roundheads scored a direct hit, the ensuing fire proved disastrous. It was skilfully rebuilt, but is now redundant. The classical-style church to the south is built of white sandstone and dedicated to St Mary Magdalene. It was constructed between 1792 and 1794 to the design of Thomas Telford, replacing the Norman chapel attached to Bridgnorth Castle, and is now the parish church.

A Troglodyte's Dream
Bridgnorth's cliffs are formed from sandstone, a soft, easily eroded, easily hewn rock. The sandstone country of south Shropshire, north Worcestershire and south Staffordshire is riddled with caves, natural and man-made, many of which were inhabited until the 1960s.

This is not so grim as it sounds – caves are warm in winter and cool in summer. When equipped with electricity and piped water, they can be far more salubrious than some types of conventional housing. There are still plenty of former cave-homes in Bridgnorth, including some on Cartway which were last inhabited in 1856. Others beside the river have brick-built extensions, while Lavington's Hole looks like a cave, but is actually the entrance to a tunnel dug under Castle Hill by the Parliamentary forces during the Civil War.

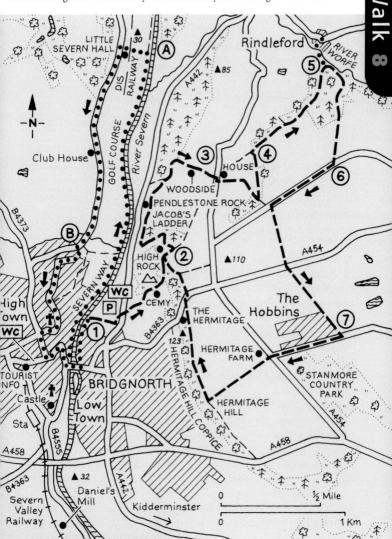

Walk 8 Directions

① Cross the **A442**, turn left, then right, signposted 'cemetery'. At the cemetery take the adjacent footpath, climbing steeply. The gradient eases and you turn right on a fenced path into woodland, then climb again, to the cliff top. At the wood's edge, turn left to reach a waymarked junction at the top of **High Rock**.

Walk 8

② Fork left, descending at first before the path (known as **Jacob's Ladder**) levels out to contour in an undulating fashion round High Rock and then **Pendlestone Rock**. At a junction, keep to the higher path which soon swings right. Leaving the trees behind, it passes **Woodside farm**, then merges with the farm access track.

③ Meeting a lane, turn right for a few paces, then left on a footpath. Pass a house, go through a gate into a field and proceed along the edge until a waymarker directs you diagonally to the far corner. Go through a gate and turn left through a narrow field. Cross a stile at the far side and keep straight on through a valley.

④ Meet a track at the far side, opposite a sandstone building, then turn right along a steep-sided valley. Reaching a junction, go straight on along a grassy path through bracken, leaving the main path, which bends right. Eventually you come to a junction with a sandy track beside the **River Worfe**.

⑤ Your onward route is to the right, but first it's worth a short detour to the left to explore the lovely hamlet of **Rindleford**. Resuming the walk, return to the junction and follow the River Worfe

on the sandy track which soon swings right, then climbs gently out of the valley.

⑥ Turn right when you reach a lane, heading towards Bridgnorth, until a signpost on the left indicates a footpath along a field edge. This leads to the **A454** and continues on the other side, past a housing estate called **The Hobbins**.

⑦ Turn right on another road, past **Stanmore Country Park**, to the A454. Cross to a footpath opposite, by **Hermitage Farm**. It runs to the top of Hermitage Hill, where you turn right through **Hermitage Hill Coppice**. As you approach the B4363, descend to a lower path to visit **The Hermitage**, then walk to the road and cross to a footpath opposite. Follow this along the cliff top to rejoin the path which descends past the cemetery to the **A442** and **Severn Park**.

Way to Go at Bridgnorth

A short stretch of the Severn Way and a chance to explore beautiful Bridgnorth.
See map and information panel for Walk 8

•DISTANCE•	4 miles (6.4km)
•MINIMUM TIME•	1hr 30min
•ASCENT / GRADIENT•	Negligible
•LEVEL OF DIFFICULTY•	

Walk 9 Directions (Walk 8 option)

This short walk is interesting in that it gives you a different perspective on Walk 8, allowing you to view High Rock and Pendlestone Rock from the valley. It also includes a short stretch of the Severn Way, a long distance trail that follows the river from source to sea. Best of all, this walk provides an incentive to explore the unique and charming town of Bridgnorth.

Walk downstream from **Severn Park** by the river, cross the bridge, then walk upstream on the **Severn Way**. After passing the last house, the path continues along the edge of playing fields and then along the edge of a golf course.

Cross a stile at the far end of the golf course (Point Ⓐ) and turn left along a field edge, then cross an embankment. This marks the course of the dismantled Severn Valley Railway – though it survives as a steam line between Kidderminster and Bridgnorth, the northern part of the line, from Bridgnorth to Shrewsbury, has been lost. Go straight on along a stony track that passes to the right of

Little Severn Hall to meet a lane. Turn left and follow the lane towards **Bridgnorth**.

At the edge of town, after passing the turn for Bramble Ridge (Point Ⓑ), take a footpath on the left which climbs through trees then levels out and soon arrives at a junction. Go to the right, shortly emerging on a stony track bordered by bungalows. It soon bends left and heads towards Bridgnorth, acquiring a tarmac surface along the way. When it bends right, keep straight on past Mold Court to **St Leonard's Close**. Turn right, then right again to **High Street**.

If you enjoy interesting old towns, make a point of exploring every inch of Bridgnorth. Get a free town map from the tourist information centre on Listley Street to ensure you don't miss anything. It really is a very special little place. However, if you want a direct route back to your starting point, turn left down **High Street**, then left on a steep lane called **Cartway** which descends to the river (notice the caves in the sandstone here, which were still being used as dwellings until the middle of the 19th century). Cross the bridge and walk upstream to return to **Severn Park**.

Trust in Dudmaston

Riverside, woods, a traditional estate and great views feature on this easy walk from Hampton Loade.

•DISTANCE•	5 miles (8km)
•MINIMUM TIME•	2hrs
•ASCENT / GRADIENT•	328ft (100m) ▲ ▲ ▲
•LEVEL OF DIFFICULTY•	🚶🚶 🚶 🚶
•PATHS•	Easy to follow and easy to use, 4 stiles
•LANDSCAPE•	Woods, parkland and farmland in and above Severn Valley
•SUGGESTED MAP•	aqua3 OS Explorer 218 Wyre Forest & Kidderminster
•START / FINISH•	Grid reference: SO 747865
•DOG FRIENDLINESS•	On lead near livestock, can run free on green lanes and woods – consult any National Trust notices posted
•PARKING•	National Trust car park by River Severn at Hampton Loade
•PUBLIC TOILETS•	None on route

Walk 10 Directions

Hampton Loade is a tiny place famous for its cable ferry. Apart from a seasonal ferry at Worcester, this is the last working ferry on the River Severn. At the time of writing its future is in doubt, but everybody hopes Bridgnorth District Council will enable it to be saved. Perhaps a way can be found to keep it going, much to the benefit of the walkers, anglers and railway enthusiasts who are its main users – railway enthusiasts because on the other

side of the river is Hampton Station, on the Severn Valley Railway. It's well worth crossing to visit the station, which is full of character (in fact, the best way to arrive at Hampton Loade is by train and ferry). Great wicker baskets of damsons used to be loaded on to the trains here and transported to Manchester to be made into dyes for the cotton trade. Those days may be long gone, but something of their atmosphere lingers still.

The object of this walk, however, is Dudmaston, so begin by walking upriver. Cross a footbridge as you approach a waterworks, then fork right, heading away from the river to enter woodland. The path climbs to a junction, where you branch left to walk the length of **Long Covert**. After about ¾ mile (1.2km) the path is joined by another from the right. It then arrives at a clearing, where you turn right on another path which follows the rim of a dingle to a junction by a bench. Turn left, descending towards a brook.

> ### WHILE YOU'RE THERE ⓘ
> A short detour from the walk will take you into **Quatt**, a model estate village designed by London architect John Birch in 1870. The timber-framed bus shelter is a more recent addition, but reaches the same high standard. The 18th-century Dower House is a handsome building and the brick church opposite, rebuilt in 1763, contains many fine tombs of the Wolryche family who lived at Dudmaston.

Ignore an ornamental footbridge and continue on the same side a little further until you can cross the brook at stepping stones. Climb out of the dingle into the pasture/parkland which surrounds **Dudmaston Hall**, following a track which takes you through a gate, to the right of farm buildings, then straight on to a waymarker post. Now turn left to join Dudmaston's access road.

WHERE TO EAT AND DRINK ⓘ

You might enjoy the **Stables**, the National Trusts's tea rooms at Dudmaston, though opening hours are limited. The friendly **River and Rail** pub at Hampton Loade is open every day, with food from noon onwards. A huge variety of drinks, snacks and meals is available and dogs are welcome in the large garden/paddock.

To continue with the walk, turn right to the **A442**. If, however, you intend to visit Dudmaston Hall, this is as good a time as any (check opening hours in advance as they're fairly limited). Dudmaston is one of the National Trust's nicest properties. The estate has been in the same family for 850 years and the 17th-century hall retains the atmosphere of a family home, because that is what it is – it's occupied by Sir George and Lady Labouchere, who gave it to the National Trust in 1978. It contains an outstanding collection of contemporary art and a wealth of

exquisite botanical art from earlier centuries. The extensive gardens and grounds are gorgeous and offer a variety of walks.

On arriving at the **A442**, cross over to a lane opposite and walk along it for about 600yds (549m). If you prefer, you can use a footpath on the left that runs beside the lane for much of that distance. Leave the lane on the right on a field-edge bridleway. Descend into a valley, then climb out of it again and continue to a footpath junction in a field corner. Turn left, still on the bridleway, and follow the field edge to a lane.

The bridleway continues opposite, by a field edge. In the corner, turn left for a few paces, then through a gap and along the edge of the next field, with woodland (**Witheridge's Rough**) on your right. At the end of the wood, close to the corner, join a track and turn right, enjoying excellent views now of Wenlock Edge, The Wrekin and the Clee Hills. Leave the track when it turns right to a farm and go straight on instead, through sheep pasture. At the far side, turn left on another track, with woodland on your left and a hedge on your right. After the hedge comes to an end, a sudden view is revealed of the Clee Hills. Leave the track at this point, and walk down to the A442. Cross over and go down the lane opposite to **Hampton Loade**.

WHAT TO LOOK FOR ⓘ

Dudmaston is one place where you can see the survival of almost all the traditional attributes of a south Shropshire estate: the hall, landscaped gardens and parkland, woodland, farmland and a village of estate cottages (Quatt). The National Trust works with the community and gives priority to local people when letting cottages. It also promotes local facilities and places certain restrictions on its tenant farmers so that they have to take environmental concerns into account, retaining sheep pasture, for instance, instead of converting every field to crops.

Regeneration at Alveley

Woods, meadows and green lanes – a great day out in the Severn Valley.

•DISTANCE•	5 miles (8km)
•MINIMUM TIME•	2hrs 30min
•ASCENT / GRADIENT•	425ft (130m) ▲ ▲ ▲
•LEVEL OF DIFFICULTY•	🚶 🚶 🚶
•PATHS•	Riverside paths, green lanes, can be uneven and slippery in places and shallow streams in winter, 12 stiles
•LANDSCAPE•	Meadows, woods and gentle slopes
•SUGGESTED MAP•	aqua3 OS Explorer 218 Wyre Forest & Kidderminster
•START / FINISH•	Grid reference: SO 753840
•DOG FRIENDLINESS•	On lead near Hampton Loade (tame ducks), visitor centre and cattle by river
•PARKING•	Visitor centre at Severn Valley Country Park, Alveley
•PUBLIC TOILETS•	At visitor centre

BACKGROUND TO THE WALK

The Severn Valley Country Park straddles the river, linking the former coal-mining communities of Alveley and Highley. Alveley Colliery Bridge, a footbridge known locally as Miners' Bridge, provides the physical linkage, enabling walkers to cross from one side to another. Both Alveley and Highley have a long history of mineral extraction. Quarrying was important in the beginning, especially at Alveley, but coal mining began in the Middle Ages at Highley. It was 1935 before a shaft was sunk at Alveley, but not very long after that the mine became uneconomic. It closed in 1969, leaving high unemployment and a ruined landscape. Natural regeneration began at once, with pioneer species such as silver birch recolonising the fertile soils. Meanwhile, an industrial estate was built to provide jobs for some of the miners, while others found work in Bridgnorth or Kidderminster.

Back to Nature

Once the industrial estate was established, a landscape reclamation scheme was launched in 1988, to give a helping hand to the natural process. The transformation of the post-industrial landscape has been so successful that it's hard to believe that the woods, meadows, ponds and wetlands of the country park have replaced a scene of spoil heaps and dereliction. The site has cultural significance too, and every year a Miners' Memories Day is held at the visitor centre. Ex-miners meet up to share their memories and perhaps to marvel at the changes. Well dressing and tree dressing have recently been introduced to the park in an attempt to re-establish traditional rural customs which can foster a sense of involvement with both landscape and community.

Almost a Rainforest

There are waymarked trails within the country park, but it also acts as a gateway to other footpaths in the Severn Valley. Tow paths run along both banks of the river, but Alveley is also at the heart of a superb network of green lanes, many of them deeply sunken after generations of use. Some use stream beds, which occupy dingles carved out by tributaries of the Severn. Though they're often dry underfoot in summer, all are tree-hung, fern-filled refuges for wildlife. The Severn is no Amazon, yet there are places where you could almost believe yourself to be on the fringe of some great rainforest as you follow centuries-old footpaths threading their mossy way through high-banked dingles extravagantly clothed in layers of fern. Holly, ash and wild cherry meet overhead, casting a soft green shade in which delicate wild flowers such as wood sorrel and wood anemone flourish in spring.

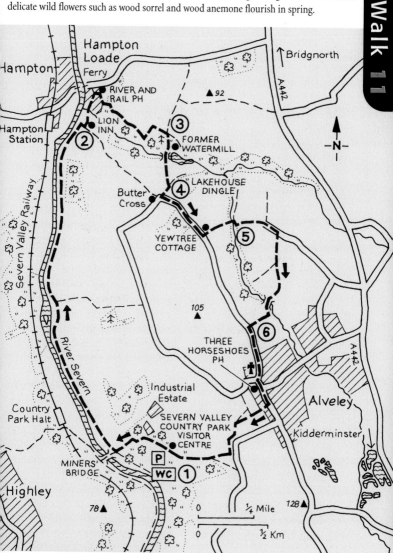

Walk 11 Directions

① Walk down to the river from the country park visitor centre, using whichever route you prefer, though you'll find the **History Trail** (red arrows) takes you directly to **Miners' Bridge**. Don't cross the bridge, but descend steps to the riverbank and walk upstream for nearly 2 miles (3.2km).

② Follow a short track to the car park of the **Lion Inn**. Turn left past Old Forge Cottage to **Hampton Loade**, then turn right past a house called The Haywain (just before the **River and Rail** pub). A waymarked path leads up through the garden into a wood, then along the edge of a field bordering the wood. Go along two sides of the field to reach the top left corner, cross a stile, turn right and cross another stile in the next corner. Proceed to a track and turn right.

WHAT TO LOOK FOR ⓘ

When you reach Point ④ in this walk you will have arrived at an ancient crossroads that is marked by the enigmatic **Butter Cross**. Its sandstone shaft is topped by a round head with a Maltese cross carved on both faces. Nobody knows what it signifies or even how old it is. One suggestion is that it marked the site of a medieval market.

---

③ After a few paces, look for a waymarker indicating a path on the right. It descends through woodland to **Lakehouse Dingle**. Pass a former watermill, cross a footbridge and keep going along a pebbly track. When you meet a concrete track, turn right to a junction with a lane.

④ Turn left, staying on the lane until you've passed **Yewtree Cottage** and its neighbour. Take a left turn after the second cottage. There is no signpost or waymarker, but it's a well-defined field-edge bridleway.

WHILE YOU'RE THERE ⓘ

The **Severn Valley Railway** operates a full steam-hauled service from May to the end of September and a reduced service the rest of the year. The stations are beautifully kept – the nearest to Alveley are Highley and Hampton Loade, one reached by the Miners' Bridge, the other by the only surviving cable ferry operating on the Severn. Country Park Halt is even closer and was opened recently to allow easy access to the country park by train (► Walk 12).

At the bottom of the field look for a gap in the hedge, where the way descends through trees to a dingle.

⑤ Turn right, climb up to meet a lane and turn right again. After 100yds (91m), join a track on the right. When it bends right, keep straight on instead, along a tree-lined green lane. Before long it becomes narrower and deeply rutted as it descends to a brook. Cross at the stepping stones, or at a nearby footbridge. The track then swings left beside the brook for a while before turning sharp right.

⑥ Turn left when you meet a lane and walk into **Alveley**. Go through the village centre, passing some delightful cottages, the church, pub, shop and bus stop, then turning right on a footpath next to the premises of IGM. The path descends to a junction where you turn left until you reach a field through which well-trodden paths descend to the country park.

WHERE TO EAT AND DRINK ⓘ

There is a drinks machine at the **visitor centre** and other refreshments are sometimes available. The well-stocked **shop** in Alveley village is next to the **Three Horseshoes**, which claims to be Shropshire's oldest pub (1406). The friendly **Lion** at Hampton Loade serves home-cooked food, while the equally friendly **River and Rail** opened only in 2001. It offers drinks (including tea and coffee), snacks and meals all day, from noon till late, with good veggie choices. Dogs are welcome in the large garden/paddock.

Highley Enterprising and Enjoyable

Trace the history of Highley's miners on a Severn Valley sculpture trail.

•DISTANCE•	5½ miles (8.8km)
•MINIMUM TIME•	2hrs 30min
•ASCENT / GRADIENT•	490ft (150m) ▲▲ ▲
•LEVEL OF DIFFICULTY•	🚶 🚶 🚶
•PATHS•	Woodland, pasture and riverside tow path, 16 stiles
•LANDSCAPE•	Two wooded valleys and ridge between
•SUGGESTED MAP•	aqua3 OS Explorer 218 Wyre Forest & Kidderminster
•START / FINISH•	Grid reference: SO 745830
•DOG FRIENDLINESS•	On leads along east side of Borle Brook, in pastureland near Whitehouse Farm and in Highley churchyard
•PARKING•	Severn Valley Country Park, Station Road, Highley
•PUBLIC TOILETS•	At car park

BACKGROUND TO THE WALK

The first thing to say about this walk is yes, it is a weird shape! That's purely because of the appalling state of some of the other local footpaths, but don't let that put you off. The paths on this route are fine and it's an excellent walk in beautiful countryside.

Victorian Town

You don't expect to find mining towns in Shropshire, but Highley is one, albeit in miniature. An ex-mining town, to be precise, but if that conjures up a depressing image, Highley confounds expectation again. Its terraces of well-built, well-preserved and obviously well-loved Victorian houses are trim, attractive and harmonious, their period features mostly intact and their gable walls and window sills all painted bright red in an idiosyncratic touch which may sound disastrous, but actually works perfectly. The Victorian (or possibly Victorian-style) street signs are charming too.

Mines and Quarries

Quarrying was important here long before mining – some of the stone for Worcester Cathedral came from Highley. Although coal mining began in the Middle Ages, large-scale operations commenced only in 1878, peaking in the 1930s. Highley Mining Company also opened collieries at Kinlet and Billingsley. Most of the coal dug at Highley went down a tramway to Highley Station on the Severn Valley Railway (SVR). The tramway is now a footpath, which you'll follow on this walk. Tramways and railways were built to link the other mines to the SVR as well. Billingsley Colliery Railway ran along the west bank of Borle Brook, joining the SVR at Brooksmouth. A tramway ran along the east bank and both are now footpaths, also used in this walk.

If you've done Walk 11, you'll know that the mines closed in 1969 and the former industrial areas on both sides of the river have been transformed into a country park. Highley has also gone in for some public artwork, including a sculpture trail, known as the

Seam Pavement Trail, by West Midlands artist Saranjit Birdi. This is a series of seven bronze plaques depicting Highley's past. The imaginative designs incorporate miners' nicknames gleaned from archive information and consultation with locals. The names, including such gems as Dick the Devil, Flaming Heck and Joyful Clappers, were passed down through the generations, forming what Saranjit calls a seam through time. The plaques are terrific, with possibly the most striking being *Trail Boss*, *Name Poem* and *Plough and Lady*. The latter depicts Lady Godiva (of Coventry fame), who owned Highley Manor in the 11th century. Saranjit Birdi is also responsible for the sculpture *A Song of Steam Trains* at Highley Station.

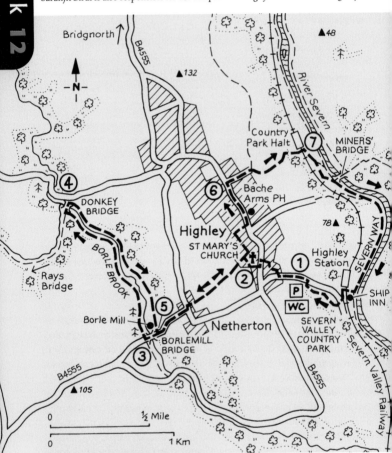

Walk 12 Directions

① Turn left up **Station Road**. When you're almost at the top, turn right at a sign for the Seam Pavement Trail. Follow a footpath (**Smoke Alley**) to the main road. Turn left, then cross to a footpath to **St Mary's Church**.

② Go through the churchyard of St Mary's, leaving it by the side of timber-framed **Church House**. Make your way down a stony track, then pass to the left of **Springfield**, on a public footpath which runs along field edges to reach a lane. Walk down another lane almost opposite, which is signposted 'Borle Mill and Kinlet'.

Walk 12

③ Cross **Borlemill Bridge** and turn right on a public footpath. It's hidden among conifers, but it's opposite an easily seen path on the other side. After passing a house, continue along field edges and then through the woodland which borders **Borle Brook**.

④ The path arrives at **Donkey Bridge** (an 18th-century packhorse bridge), which you will need to cross. Before you do so, however, it's worth going a few paces to the left to see an old railway bridge. (If you're keen to trace the Billingsley Colliery Railway as far as you can, you should turn left on a bridleway which goes to Rays Bridge, but you'll have to return the same way, owing to the impassability of other footpaths). Having crossed Donkey Bridge, turn right to walk back along the other side of **Borle Brook**. Don't

walk by the brook itself, instead take a higher path, through woods and meadows.

⑤ Turn left when you come to the lane and retrace your steps to **Highley**. Pass to the left of the church and left again on **Church Street**. Follow it to **High Street** (again watching for the pavement trail plaques) and turn left.

⑥ Turn right on **Vicarage Lane**, which will take you past four 400-year-old pollarded beeches, known locally as the Seven Sisters (some say there were once seven trees, others say it's Severn Sisters), to a junction where you fork right over a cattle grid. The track descends to four gates. Go through the one on the right.

⑦ Cross the railway by **Country Park Halt** and turn right, passing through woodland. At a junction with a surfaced track, turn left to **Miners' Bridge**, then join the Severn Way, signposted to Highley Station. When you reach the **Ship Inn**, built for bargemen and opened in 1770, another signpost directs you to Highley Station. Cross the line, then turn left until you come to a path climbing through woods. This is the former tramway and it goes directly up taking you back to the car park.

The King's Wood at Wyre

A gorgeous leafy walk around Kingswood and Buttonoak in Wyre Forest.

•DISTANCE•	5 miles (8km)
•MINIMUM TIME•	2hrs 30min
•ASCENT / GRADIENT•	575ft (175m) ▲ ▲ ▲
•LEVEL OF DIFFICULTY•	🚶 🚶 🚶
•PATHS•	Woodland and field paths, 2 stiles (plus 4 on Walk 14)
•LANDSCAPE•	Mostly broadleaved woodland, with some conifers
•SUGGESTED MAP•	aqua3 OS Explorer 218 Wyre Forest & Kidderminster
•START / FINISH•	Grid reference: SO 743784
•DOG FRIENDLINESS•	On lead in Longdon Orchard and on path to Kingswood
•PARKING•	Forestry Commission car park at Earnwood Copse, on south side of B4194, west of Buttonoak
•PUBLIC TOILETS•	None on route

BACKGROUND TO THE WALK

Wyre Forest is shared between Shropshire and Worcestershire, with Dowles Brook forming the county boundary. It was once a royal hunting forest, but the place name Kingswood is the only obvious reminder of that today. In the days of the Norman kings, the forest stretched from Worcester to Bridgnorth. It's considerably smaller today, and partially afforested with alien conifers, but it remains one of the largest and finest semi-natural woodlands in the country.

The Mighty Oak

Despite the conifers, there is still lots of broadleaved woodland, including species such as beech, silver birch, rowan, holly and hazel. But English oak is overwhelmingly dominant. There are two types of English oak – common (also known as pedunculate) and sessile (sometimes called durmast). Common oak usually dominates in the Midlands, but not in Wyre Forest, where the sessile oak is king. The underlying coal measures mean that much of the forest soil is acidic, the preferred habitat of the sessile oak.

English oak supports more wildlife than any other British tree, including an impressive 284 insect species. For centuries local people were also dependent on oak, which provided timber for houses, ships, pit props, fencing and a multitude of other uses. Small timber was used by broom makers and basket weavers, and also served as firewood. Oak twigs were bound together in bundles and used to make tracks suitable for horse-drawn carts, while oak bark, rich in tannin, was used for curing leather in the local tanneries. The forest is dotted with hamlets, such as Buttonoak, which grew out of woodland clearings known as assarts, where squatters settled illegally to make a living as basket weavers, broom makers or charcoal burners. The latter were known locally as wood colliers.

Walk here in autumn and you will see squirrels and jays everywhere, busily burying acorns for the winter. Some will be retrieved in due course, but those forgotten will germinate in spring to launch a new generation of oak trees. Unless, that is, the saplings are eaten by deer. Fallow deer are very common in Wyre and I have never walked in the forest without seeing several. Go quietly, with your dog on a lead, and you should see some too.

0 ½ Mile
0 1 Km

B4194

① Bewdley

▲150

P

EARNWOOD COPSE

Button Oak PH

ELAN VALLEY PIPELINE

② Buttonoak

▲140

-N-

⑦

MANOR HOLDING

Kingswood

LONGDON ORCHARD

Wyre Forest

③ KINGSWOOD FARM

⑥

BRAND WOOD

WIMPERHILL WOOD

▲85

SHROPSHIRE

WORCESTERSHIRE

④ ⑤

DOWLES BROOK

Dismantled Railway

THE NEWALLS

Ⓐ FOREST DELL

New Parks

CYCLEWAY

Far Forest

▲135

GREENWOOD

Ⓑ

PLOUGH LANE

Oxbind Coppice

Plough Inn

A4117

Kidderminster

Fingerpost

Visitor Centre

Ⓒ

A456

A456

Callow Hill

Walk 13

Walk 13 Directions

① Walk through a gate on to a forest road and immediately turn right on a footpath (no signpost or waymarker) into **Earnwood Copse**. Keep straight on at all junctions, eventually joining a sunken path not far from the edge of the forest. If you shortly pass under an overhanging yew tree you will know that you're on the right path (not that you're likely to go wrong, but forestry operations can sometimes bring about slight changes to the path network).

> **WHERE TO EAT AND DRINK** ⓘ
> The **Button Oak** is on the main road at Buttonoak. It's a friendly place, well used to welcoming walkers, including children. Dogs are welcome too, but not in the bar when food is being served. There's a pleasant beer garden outside.

② The path descends to meet what looks like a firebreak but is actually the route of the Elan Valley pipeline, bringing Welsh water to Birmingham. Turn right here and cross a footbridge on the edge of the forest, to the right of the pipeline. Walk up a bank into arable fields and then follow a waymarked field-edge footpath uphill. When you reach the top, go through a hedge gap and turn left towards the hamlet of **Kingswood**.

③ Soon after passing a sensitively restored timber-framed cottage (**Manor Holding**), you come to a T-junction at the edge of the forest. Go a few paces to the left towards **Kingswood Farm** and then you'll see a track that swings right to enter the forest. Keep straight on at all junctions, walking through **Brand Wood**.

④ You'll soon reach **Dowles Brook**. Don't cross (unless you're doing Walk 14); turn left on a bridleway that runs beside it. Follow the bridleway for 1¼ miles (2km), with **Wimperhill Wood** on your left.

⑤ Turn left on another bridleway, which first passes through a marshy area, then climbs through scrub and young woodland. It's waymarked and easily followed. After crossing a forest road, go straight on, but turn right at the next waymarked junction before swinging left to resume your original heading. After crossing a stream, the bridleway turns right as it climbs above the rim of a steep valley.

⑥ Turn sharp left (still on the bridleway) through a gap between two fenced areas, where birch and other natives are regenerating fast following clear felling of the conifers that grew here. You're approaching **Longdon Orchard** now, a conservation area where your dog must be under strict control. At the next junction go left, into conifers, then soon turn right.

⑦ Turn right when you meet the Elan Valley pipeline again, then very soon left, still on the bridleway. Follow it up to the edge of the forest near **Buttonoak**, then turn left to return to **Earnwood Copse**.

> **WHILE YOU'RE THERE** ⓘ
> **Bewdley** is in Worcestershire and it's well worth a visit. Once a busy Severn port, it now caters for tourists instead of boat builders and bow-hauliers (the men who pulled the boats upstream before somebody invented towing horses). Bewdley's waterfront is said to be the finest in the Midlands, and anybody who appreciates 17th- and 18th-century architecture will love this little town.

Over the Border to Far Forest

See the other side of Wyre Forest by slipping over into Worcestershire.
See map and information panel for Walk 13

•DISTANCE•	7½ miles (12.1km)
•MINIMUM TIME•	3hrs
•ASCENT / GRADIENT•	853ft (260m) ▲ ▲ ▲
•LEVEL OF DIFFICULTY•	🚶 🚶 🚶

Walk 14 Directions (Walk 13 option)

Leave Walk 13 at Point ④, crossing **Dowles Brook**. A few paces up the bank is a junction. Turn right, cross a tributary stream and turn left up a leafy green tunnel by the woodland edge. The path soon meets a surfaced track; continue in the same direction, passing between the abutments of a dismantled rail bridge. At a junction, turn left past **The Newalls** (Point Ⓐ) on another tree-lined hollow way that leads back into the forest. After descending to cross a brook it climbs to a lane by **Forest Dell**. Turn right, and soon right again.

Reaching a junction at the end of **Sugars Lane** (Point Ⓑ), go through a hedge gap opposite and along the left-hand field edge, over a stile in the corner and along an enclosed

---

WHAT TO LOOK FOR ⓘ

Linger at Dowles Brook and you might see **birds** such as dippers, kingfishers or grey wagtails, all of which occur along the brook. **Crayfish** and young **trout** may be seen in the brook itself, with a little bit of luck.

---

path to **Plough Lane** at Far Forest. Turn left and walk to a junction, then turn right on a track running past a house called **Greenwood**. The track forks at **Brantwood**. Take the right-hand option, along the edge of the forest, with private woodland beyond the fence on your right.

Descend to a brook, cross at a footbridge, climb a stile and go uphill, following yellow-painted posts. At a T-junction marked with yellow arrows, turn right, then go straight on at the next, following a tree-lined track out of the forest towards **Callow Hill**. At another T-junction (Point Ⓒ), turn left on a bridleway, which soon returns to the forest. In a few paces fork left, then left again where blue arrows indicate. At the next fork you can take either branch as they soon merge. Keep following the blue arrows (actually white arrows on a blue background) to meet a cycleway. Turn left and follow it towards **Dowles Brook**. Look for waymarkers and a sign sending you left to a bridge (but ignore the next waymarker unless you want to ford the brook). Cross back into Shropshire and turn left to Point ⑤ on the main route, where you head up into **Wimperhill Wood**.

Walk 15

In a Twist at Cleobury Mortimer

Hills, valleys and a crooked spire in the land of the Marcher lords.

•DISTANCE•	4¾ miles (7.7km)
•MINIMUM TIME•	2hrs
•ASCENT / GRADIENT•	558ft (170m) ▲ ▲ ▲
•LEVEL OF DIFFICULTY•	🏃🏃 🏃🏃 🏃🏃
•PATHS•	Mostly field paths across pasture, about 10 stiles
•LANDSCAPE•	Pastoral country with secluded valleys and panoramic views
•SUGGESTED MAP•	aqua3 OS Explorer 203 Ludlow or 218 Wyre Forest & Kidderminster
•START / FINISH•	Grid reference: SO 672757
•DOG FRIENDLINESS•	On leads almost all way
•PARKING•	Childe Road car park, Cleobury Mortimer
•PUBLIC TOILETS•	Eagle Lane

Walk 15 Directions

It's hard to say whether Cleobury Mortimer is a town or a village. Once the stronghold of Norman baron Ralph Mortimer, who built a castle here and soon established control over much of the border country, it's certainly a delightful place. The Mortimers went on to rule the Marches for centuries, but their centre of power soon moved to Wigmore, then to Ludlow, and Ralph's castle at Cleobury was eventually destroyed by Henry II in 1155.

As you leave it behind, do stop occasionally to glance back at the view of Cleobury, set against the backdrop of the Clee Hills and dominated by the spire of St Mary's Church, which has a marked twist in it. This is due to the warping of the timbers and has admitted Cleobury to the membership of an exclusive club – the slightly bizarre-

sounding European Twisted Spires Association. The only other British member is Chesterfield.

Walk through the alleyway under the **Talbot Hotel** to the main street. Go down **Eagle Lane** opposite and, when the lane bends right, cross a stile into a field. Follow the hedge up to the top corner and go diagonally to the top right corner of the next field. Cut across the corner of another, then go diagonally across the next to meet the far hedge, in line with a solitary oak. Follow the right-hand hedge down to **Rowley Brook** and turn right to cross a bridge into cattle pasture.

> **WHAT TO LOOK FOR** ⓘ
> **Reaside Farmhouse** is an outstanding early 17th-century sandstone building, with gables, a marvellous porch and star-shaped brick chimney stacks. The late 16th and early 17th centuries were periods of great prosperity when yeoman farmers all over the country built themselves fine houses like this.

Go diagonally right, climbing to the top of a rise. Cross a stile in the hedge, squeeze past another and go straight on by the left-hand hedge, along the edge of sheep pasture. As you go through a gate, a superb panorama of fields, woods and hedges presents itself, with all of Worcestershire spread out in front of you, rising to the Malvern Hills. As you go forward, Herefordshire comes into view on your right, with the Black Mountains marking the Welsh border.

Go down the next field, passing through a gate, then left on a track towards **Reaside Farm**. Pass between the farmhouse and its outbuildings, through a gate into a field, forward past an oak tree (complete with treehouse), then left down a slope. Cross two fields to a footbridge and cross the **River Rea**. Go to the far right corner of the next field and through a gate to join a track. Follow it for a few paces to an open gateway, then leave it, passing through a gap on the left instead. Go forward along a short grassy track parallel with a farm track then, at the end, go left along a leafy tunnel to meet a lane.

Turn left along the narrow, high-banked lane for nearly ½ mile (800m), until you can turn right on a stony track, which leads past **The Rookery**, then down to the River Rea. Cross the Rea on a footbridge to the right of a weir. This peaceful spot by the weir was once the site of

a charcoal furnace, built in the 16th century for smelting iron ore. Go forward to cross a stone bridge and follow a track that soon curves to the left and climbs to pass **Mawley Hall**. When you come to a junction with another track, turn right past paddocks, then left at a footpath sign. The path descends to go round three sides of a walled garden, before reaching a junction where you branch right towards the river.

WHERE TO EAT AND DRINK
The **Talbot Hotel** welcomes children and dogs in the bar or the beer garden, and there are several other pleasant pubs in Cleobury. **Sarah's Tearoom** is very friendly and welcomes children and walkers, but not dogs. There are also some great shops such as **Ashley's Cake Shop**, **Brown's Corner Bakery** and the **Top Nosh Deli**.

Having crossed the Rea again, keep straight on across sheep pasture, until a waymarker directs you diagonally downhill, back to the river. Follow it to a lane. You can take this back to Cleobury or, better still, look for a grassy bridleway on the left, climbing to the left of a stone house, then on through grassland and along a leafy tunnel. Once houses take over at Mortimer Hill, start looking for a path on the right that cuts through to **Lion Lane**. Turn left, following the lane to **Church Street**. Turn left again and cross to the **Talbot** passageway back to **Childe Road**.

WHILE YOU'RE THERE
Neen Sollars, a village on a ridge between the River Rea and Mill Brook, lies south of Cleobury. There are lovely walks, substantial traces of the dismantled Bewdley-to-Tenbury railway (including a viaduct) and a 14th-century church with an exceptional monument to explorer Humphrey Conyngesby, who was born in 1567. Described as 'a perfect scoller… and a greate traveyler', he disappeared without trace in 1610. The monument was erected in 1624, by which time his family had obviously given up hope of his return.

At Liberty on Shropshire's Highest Hill

Taste an exhilarating sense of freedom on Brown Clee's upland commons.

•DISTANCE•	7 miles (11.3km)
•MINIMUM TIME•	3hrs 30min
•ASCENT / GRADIENT•	1,460ft (445m) ▲ ▲ ▲
•LEVEL OF DIFFICULTY•	🕺 🕺 🕺
•PATHS•	Generally good, but can be very boggy in places, 5 stiles
•LANDSCAPE•	Hill, moorland, pasture and plantation
•SUGGESTED MAP•	aqua3 OS Explorer 217 The Long Mynd & Wenlock Edge
•START / FINISH•	Grid reference: SO 607871
•DOG FRIENDLINESS•	Excellent, but under strict control near sheep
•PARKING•	Cleobury North picnic site, on unclassified road west of Cleobury North
•PUBLIC TOILETS•	None on route

BACKGROUND TO THE WALK

Choose a clear day for this walk, because the stunning view from Abdon Burf, the higher of Brown Clee's twin summits, extends from the Cotswolds to Cadair Idris. At 1,770ft (540m), Brown Clee is Shropshire's highest hill, overtopping its sibling, Titterstone Clee, by 23ft (7m), and Stiperstones by just 13ft (4m). Brown Clee may be high, but it's not wild, though it appears so in places. It is a perfect illustration of just how intensive rural land use can be. There's hardly anything this hill hasn't been used for at one time or another in its long history.

Settlement and Land Use

Nobody knows when people first started making use of the Clee Hills, but three forts were built on Brown Clee in the Iron Age. Those on Abdon Burf and Clee Burf have been destroyed by quarrying. A third, Nordy Bank, still stands guard on Clee Liberty. Iron-Age people must also have hunted on the hills, and the tradition continued for centuries, with the Clees part of a royal forest for a time.

Brown Clee Hill must have been used for stock grazing since the hill forts were built, or even before that. More recently, in the Middle Ages, all of the hillside above the encircling roads was common land, divided between several parishes, while an outer ring of parishes also had grazing rights. Stock from the outer parishes was driven to and from Brown Clee on tracks known as outracks or strakerways, most of which are now footpaths or bridleways. Many are deeply sunken through long use, and commoners' sheep and ponies still graze Clee Liberty.

Medieval Mining

Mineral extraction also has a long history in the Clee Hills. Brown Clee is riddled with shafts and is said to be the highest ex-coalfield in Britain. Ironstone was dug from the coal measures from the Middle Ages onwards and fed a number of forges around the hill. More recently, a type of volcanic rock called dolerite (also locally known as dhustone) was exploited, mostly for road building, and the ruins of a stone-crushing plant still disfigure Abdon Burf. Wagons then transported the stone down a steep incline to the railway at Ditton Priors. Quarrying ceased in 1936 and the incline is now a footpath (though not a right of way), used in this walk to gain access to the hill. You can still see parts of the actual tramway in places.

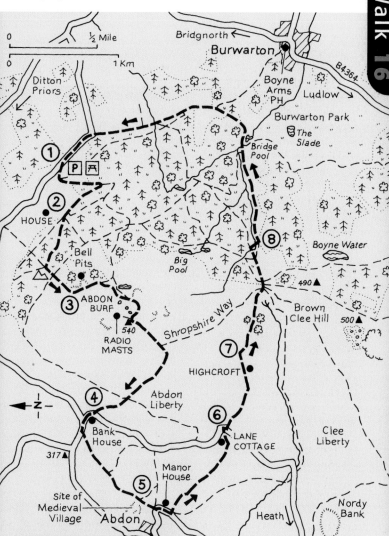

Walk 16 Directions

① Cross a stile and walk uphill. Intercepting another path by a bench, turn left; shortly you have

plantation on your left, woodland on your right. When the track forks, go right to meet another track, then right again. Soon you're walking by the edge of woodland, with a field on your right.

② There are two houses below and, as you draw level with the second one, you will see a small clearing on your left. On the edge of it a faint path begins to rise diagonally through plantation. It soon becomes clearer and quickly leads to a steep straight track (the former tramway). Join this, shortly crossing a cattle grid on to pastureland.

③ The track turns sharp left, leaving the tramway incline. It's an easy walk to **Abdon Burf**, with its ugly wireless station and awesome views. Stand next to the trig pillar, with the radio masts on your right, and look south west to see a path descending the hill. Follow it down to a line of posts. Go through the line and keep descending by a fence. The path swings right, becoming a hollow way.

> ### WHAT TO LOOK FOR ⓘ
> Just after the cattle grid crossed in Point ②, there is a profusion of mounds, with corresponding depressions. These are the remains of **bell pits**, an early form of mining which involved digging a short shaft and working the seam from the foot of it as far as was safe, leaving a pit with a bell-shaped profile.

④ Turn right when you meet a lane, then left at a junction and soon left again, at a stile. Go along the left-hand edges of a series of meadows, and maintain the same direction as the path merges with the remains of an old green lane.

⑤ As you approach **Abdon**, a stile gives access to a garden. Go straight through, with signs directing you past the house and down a hollow way to a lane. Turn left past farm buildings and continue to a collection of barns. There's a stony track opposite – walk a few paces along it to a bridleway on the left. Follow it uphill to **Lane Cottage**.

⑥ Bear right to a lane and cross to a stile opposite. Go up a steep pasture towards a fence/hedge on the skyline. Cross it at a stile and continue to the top left corner of the next field, then turn left on a track. When you reach **Highcroft**, the track continues as a hollow way.

> ### WHERE TO EAT AND DRINK ⓘ
> The **Boyne Arms** at Burwarton is full of character. Its name derives from the family that owns much of Brown Clee Hill. Many walkers stop here for a drink and home cooking, so you can expect a friendly welcome.

⑦ Go through a gate into pasture and follow the right-hand fence to the top corner. Pass through a gate and continue to a line of beeches on the summit ridge. Go forward through the beeches, then straight on along a track, which descends through woodland, plantation and bracken to a junction. Turn right.

⑧ The track crosses a stream. This is where you leave it to head downhill, following the stream. When you meet a track, turn left. After 600yds (549m) you'll come to a junction. Branch right here if you want the pub or bus stop at **Burwarton**. If not, keep left to return to the picnic site.

> ### WHILE YOU'RE THERE ⓘ
> Visit the hamlet of **Heath**, west of Brown Clee. The renowned Heath Chapel stands alone in a field and is the purest example of Norman church architecture in Shropshire. The chapel is surrounded by the earthworks of a deserted medieval village, with the remains of streets, enclosed fields, house platforms and fish ponds.

Bedlam on Clee

A terrific walk on one of Shropshire's highest and most charismatic hills.

•DISTANCE•	8¼ miles (13.3km)
•MINIMUM TIME•	3hrs 30min
•ASCENT / GRADIENT•	1,330ft (405m) ▲▲▲
•LEVEL OF DIFFICULTY•	👫 👫 👫
•PATHS•	Good but rough, uneven and/or boggy in places, 2 stiles
•LANDSCAPE•	Moors and upland pasture with industrial remains
•SUGGESTED MAP•	aqua3 OS Explorer 203 Ludlow
•START / FINISH•	Grid reference: SO 595753
•DOG FRIENDLINESS•	Good, but keep under close control near sheep and cattle
•PARKING•	Car park/picnic site/viewpoint opposite turning for Kremlin Inn on A4117 on eastern edge of Cleehill village
•PUBLIC TOILETS•	Cleehill village

BACKGROUND TO THE WALK

L ocals say the view from Clee Hill is the finest in England and it's hard to disagree. After all, where else can you see from the Brecon Beacons to the Peak District, from Snowdonia to the Cotswolds? It's stunning. But before getting too carried away with the view, we need to sort out some names, which can be confusing in these parts. For instance, it's Cleehill village, but Clee Hill. However, strictly speaking, Clee Hill is just the area that is currently being quarried, north east of the village. The top is Titterstone Clee Hill. Naturally, not everybody calls it that – to many who live in sight of it, in Shropshire and neighbouring counties, it's just Clee Hill or The Clee.

What's in a Name?

And then there's Bedlam. The original Bedlam was the Hospital of St Mary of Bethlehem, a lunatic asylum (as they used to be called) in London. What few people know is that Bedlam is also a Victorian quarrying settlement on Clee Hill. If you can get hold of an old map, you'll see it called by that name, and if you go to Bitterley you'll see a road sign indicating Bedlam. Look at the excellent map displayed at Cleehill picnic site – Bedlam is marked on it too. Unfold your modern, state-of-the-art OS map, however, and you'll look in vain for it. It may be apocryphal, but the story goes that Bedlam's residents don't like its name because of its associations, and would prefer to rename it Titterstone Village. The Ordnance Survey plays safe by not naming it at all. Still, it's reassuring to note that somebody in Bedlam has a sense of humour, as you will see when you pass Hullabaloo House.

There are other intriguing names on and around Clee Hill: Sodom, for example, but perhaps it's best not to inquire too closely into that. Random, Crumpsbrook, Hopton Wafers, Cramer Gutter, Rugpits, Titrail, Lubberland, Angelbank, Applecake Hill, Cadbury, Pastycraft, Hackenchop, Hilluppencott, Hemm and Hoopits all have their own charm. Many names relate to wildlife, such as Kitesnest, Hawkwood, Magpie Hill, Brown Owls, Lapwing, Foxwood and even Wormsacre. Others relate to the industrial heritage of the area. The bridleway you join at Cleeton St Mary, for instance, is marked on old maps as Limers' Lane, though it's often referred to as the Random bridleway nowadays because it passes Random.

Walk 17 Directions

① Walk up the track opposite the picnic area, towards the unusually named **Kremlin Inn**. Before you reach it, go through a rusty bridle gate on the left and along a track. After the first 220yds (201m), the right of way runs to the left of it, but can be very difficult – most walkers use the track.

② Meet the radar station access road by **Hedgehog House** and turn right. Walk to the end of **Rouse Boughton Terrace** and go through a gate on the left to meet a track. Don't follow it; turn right along the edge of a pasture instead. Continue along the edge of the next field and through a gate in the corner to meet the **Shropshire Way**, which goes to the right. Ignore it and go straight on, cutting the corner of the field,

Walk 17

aiming to meet and then follow the left-hand boundary after about 300yds (274m).

③ Continue in the same direction through the next field to the left corner, then follow a track down to cross **Benson's Brook** at a bridge. Climb out of the valley on a track which passes the abutments of a former tramway bridge (part of Bitterley Incline, but called Titterstone Incline on OS maps), before arriving at **Bedlam**.

④ Turn left into the hamlet, then immediately fork right past The Old Shop House and Hullabaloo House towards **Titterstone Clee Hill**. A gate gives access and a path takes you to the right. After passing a house, it cuts a broad swath through the bracken.

⑤ Leave this path when you come to **Bitterley Incline** again. Climb on to the embankment, joining the Shropshire Way. Continue uphill now towards the ruined quarry buildings ahead. Pass to the right of the main quarry, then go left to the top.

⑥ Just to the north of the trig pillar is a cairn, the **Giant's Chair**. Look north towards Brown Clee Hill to see Callowgate, a red-roofed farm at the northern edge of the moorland. Aim for this, picking the best way down the slope and then across the brackeny moorland.

⑦ When you reach **Callowgate**, leave the Shropshire Way and turn right by the moorland edge. Joining a lane at **Cleetongate**, turn right and walk to the village of **Cleeton St Mary**. Turn right past the church, right again past almshouses, then left on to the **Random bridleway**, which runs along the moorland edge. Keep just to the right of a fence, except where you need to cut a corner – it's obvious when you come to it.

WHAT TO LOOK FOR
This is a great place to see **raptors** such as the buzzard or the kestrel – watch the latter for a while and you'll understand why it is also called the windhover. You're also increasingly likely to see a **raven** or two. This impressive member of the crow family suffered a sharp decline in numbers, but is now making something of a comeback in the wilder parts of western England, including Clee Hill.

⑧ When the fence makes a very sharp left turn, keep straight on to meet the radar station access road. Turn left to **Rouse Boughton Terrace** then retrace your steps to the start.

WHILE YOU'RE THERE
Visit **Hope Bagot**, a lovely village tucked away on the southern slopes of Clee Hill and approached along deeply sunken lanes. There are some fine Georgian houses, particularly Hope Court and the Old Vicarage, and a 16th-century timber-framed cottage. The small church is Norman, with a possible Saxon arch over the entrance to the vestry. An ivy-draped holy well in the churchyard is sheltered by a great yew tree, believed to be over 1,600 years old.

Close to the Edge at Diddlebury

Former drovers' roads link the crest of Wenlock Edge to the meadows of beautiful Corve Dale.

•DISTANCE•	6¼ miles (10.1km)
•MINIMUM TIME•	3hrs
•ASCENT / GRADIENT•	689ft (210m) ▲▲▲
•LEVEL OF DIFFICULTY•	🚶🚶 🚶🚶 🚶
•PATHS•	Mostly good but ford on Dunstan's Lane can be deep after rain, 10 stiles (8 more on Walk 19)
•LANDSCAPE•	Wooded ridge of Wenlock Edge, patchwork of Corve Dale
•SUGGESTED MAP•	aqua3 OS Explorer 217 The Long Mynd & Wenlock Edge
•START / FINISH•	Grid reference: SO 479875
•DOG FRIENDLINESS•	On lead near livestock; notices warn sheep chasers will be shot
•PARKING•	Car park/picnic site on east side of unclassified road between Middlehope and Westhope
•PUBLIC TOILETS•	None on route

BACKGROUND TO THE WALK

Wenlock Edge needs a book to itself, so all you will get here is the merest glimpse, but it should whet your appetite for more. This great tree-clad escarpment is one of Shropshire's most famous landscape features, partly because it plays a role in A E Housman's collection of poems entitled *A Shropshire Lad* and is also the subject of a choral poem by the composer Vaughan Williams. It is best seen from the west, appearing as an unbroken escarpment running from the Severn Gorge to Craven Arms. From the east it is more elusive, rising almost imperceptibly. Within a basic ridge structure, it seems to form a series of waves or steps, and consists for part of its length of two parallel edges, divided by Hope Dale.

Ancient Woodland

Wenlock Edge was formed of Silurian limestone about 420 million years ago. Developing as a barrier reef in a tropical sea on the edge of a continental shelf, it was built up from the accumulation of sediments and the skeletons of marine creatures such as corals, brachiopods and crinoids. Earth movements and erosion then sculpted it into the escarpment we see today.

Most of it is wooded, and much of this is ancient woodland, growing on steep slopes where there has been continuous tree cover since the end of the last ice age. The dominant species is ash, which has a special affinity with limestone, but many other types are present. Beneath the trees are lime-loving shrubs such as spurge laurel, spindle and dogwood. The ground flora is rich and varied, especially along the rides and in newly coppiced areas where flowers respond to the increased light by growing more profusely and attracting many butterflies.

Exploitation

In the past, the Edge was always seen as a valuable resource to be exploited. Timber provided building materials, tools and charcoal for iron smelting. Limestone was used for building, for making lime, for iron smelting and, more recently, as an aggregate. This latter use still continues and there are unsightly quarries between Presthope and Much Wenlock, where you can walk the ridge and look down on the unedifying spectacle of monstrous machines digging up Shropshire so that heavy lorries can carry it away. There's nothing like that on this walk, where the quarries you pass are small ones, long since abandoned and now transformed by nature into mossy, fern-filled caverns of green.

Walk 18 Directions

① Turn left out of the car park along the lane. When you come to a junction, turn left again, signposted 'Middlehope'. Keep straight on at the next, signposted 'Upper Westhope', where the road becomes a track and soon bends left towards a house. Go through a gate on the right instead and along a grassy bridleway that soon enters woodland. Keep straight on at two cross paths.

② The bridleway emerges into pasture; keep straight on along the left-hand edge to the corner. Go through a gate and turn right on a field-edge path, which soon becomes a wide track.

③ Having passed a cottage, and with a group of barns ahead, look for blue arrows that direct you sharp right. Keep left above **Corfton Bache**, a deep valley, until more blue arrows send you zig-zagging down into the valley. Follow it to the road at **Corfton** and cross to a lane opposite.

④ As the lane degenerates into a track, look on the left for a footpath starting at an iron kissing gate. Go diagonally left across cattle pasture to a prominent stile at the far side. Cross a farm track and walk to the far right corner of an arable field.

> ### WHERE TO EAT AND DRINK ⓘ
> The **Sun Inn** at Corfton is in just about every pub guide you can think of and has been voted best village pub in the county. It has a friendly atmosphere, a large garden with play area and its own brewery. It also acts as a useful tourist information point (a mini version of a tourist information centre).

⑤ Go through a gate, then a little way along the left-hand edge of another field until a gate gives access to parkland. Head in the direction indicated by the waymarker. **St Peter's Church** at Diddlebury soon comes into view, providing an infallible guide.

⑥ Cross two stiles at the far side of the park and go straight on down a slope, to the right of a fence. A footbridge gives access to **Diddlebury**. Turn right, then left by the church. Join a footpath which passes to the right of the village hall, then goes diagonally right past

the school, over two stiles and across fields to the road. Cross to the lane opposite, forking right after a few paces.

⑦ A footpath leaves the lane on the right, almost opposite **Chapel Cottage**. This is where you turn off for Walk 19. Otherwise, continue up the lane.

> ### WHAT TO LOOK FOR ⓘ
> **St Peter's Church** at Diddlebury has a Saxon nave, its north wall constructed of herringbone masonry, which was the style favoured by the Saxons. The north doorway is typically Saxon, and there is a Saxon window. The tower also seems to be partly Saxon, though even the experts are unsure. Do go inside – very few churches of this kind survive in England.

⑧ At a junction with a bridle track by a sign for Aston Top keep left, still on the lane. After a further ¾ mile (1.2km), branch left on a byway, **Dunstan's Lane** (no signpost or waymarker). Follow it to the Middlehope road and turn left. Keep straight on at a Y-junction. When a footpath crosses the road, turn left into woodland. The path is signposted on the right, but not the left – the left branch is a few paces further on. The path leads through the woods back to the picnic site.

> ### WHILE YOU'RE THERE ⓘ
> The **Dower House Garden** at Morville Hall, about 12 miles (19km) north east of Diddlebury, is a relatively new garden, begun only in 1989. Its ambitious aim is to tell the history of English gardens through a sequence of separate gardens in the style of different periods. It ranges from a turf maze through a medieval cloister garden and Elizabethan knot garden to a Victorian wilderness garden, to name but a few. Sweetly scented old roses are a particular speciality.

From the White House to Little London

You can extend your walk to the top of Middlehope Hill for great views towards Corve Dale.
See map and information panel for Walk 18

•DISTANCE•	8¼ miles (13.3km)
•MINIMUM TIME•	3hrs 30min
•ASCENT / GRADIENT•	1,099ft (335m) ▲▲▲
•LEVEL OF DIFFICULTY•	🚶 🚶 🚶

Walk 19 Directions (Walk 18 option)

Leave the main route at Point ⑦, joining a footpath roughly opposite **Chapel Cottage** and its neighbour. The path is easily followed across several fields and then through a copse to the village of **Aston Munslow**. On the way it also crosses a sunken lane and the access road to **Aston Hall**. Although you haven't climbed very high yet, you'll enjoy a beautiful view from this footpath, right across Corve Dale to the Clee Hills.

Meeting a lane at Aston Munslow (Point Ⓐ), turn left and keep straight on at a junction, along a no through road. Look out for the **White House**, on your left. This remarkable 14th-century hall of cruck construction has 16th- and 18th-century additions. (Crucks come in pairs – they are curved beams usually made by splitting an oak tree in half.) It is owned by the Landmark Trust which lets it as holiday accommodation, but it's open to visitors by prior appointment – to book, write to

the Director of the Landmark Trust, Shottesbrooke, Maidenhead, Berkshire, SL6 3SW.

The road climbs steadily to a junction where it turns sharp right, becoming a bridleway that leads to **Little London Farm**. The name is actually a fairly common one for farms in the Marches and Wales because cattle drovers had a habit of naming overnight stopping places after their final destination.

Turn off before you get to the farm, on a bridleway running uphill through bracken to the crest of **Middlehope Hill** (Point Ⓑ). Turn left at the top, with a strip of woodland on your right and fields on your left. Follow the bridleway down to join the lane at Point ⑧ on the main route, by **Aston Top**.

WHERE TO EAT AND DRINK ⓘ
The historic **Swan Inn** at Aston Munslow is an attractive timber-framed building with a good reputation for its home-cooked food. There's a cosy interior and a large beer garden outside. Dick Turpin is said to have stayed here once. At the nearby hamlet of Munslow, the **Crown** is also highly thought of and has its own micro-brewery.

Walk 20

A Walk on the Wild Side at Wilderhope

A walk from an Elizabethan manor house surrounded by conservation land on Wenlock Edge.

•DISTANCE•	3 miles (4.8km)
•MINIMUM TIME•	1hr
•ASCENT / GRADIENT•	410ft (125m) ▲ ▲ ▲
•LEVEL OF DIFFICULTY•	🚶🚶 🚶🚶 🚶🚶
•PATHS•	Excellent, need to ford shallow brook, 2 stiles
•LANDSCAPE•	Ridges and valleys at Hope Dale and Wenlock Edge
•SUGGESTED MAP•	aqua3 OS Explorer 217 The Long Mynd & Wenlock Edge
•START / FINISH•	Grid reference: SO 545928
•DOG FRIENDLINESS•	On lead in spring when ground-nesting birds have young, and near sheep
•PARKING•	National Trust car park at Wilderhope Manor
•PUBLIC TOILETS•	None on route

Walk 20 Directions

Wilderhope Manor belongs to the National Trust, but is leased to the Youth Hostels Association. It stands in Hope Dale between the twin ridges of Wenlock Edge and it's the best of several very fine houses in the area. It was built, around 1585, of the local limestone and has changed little in appearance since.

> ### WHAT TO LOOK FOR ⓘ
> The fields below Wilderhope Coppice are marked with a ridge-and-furrow pattern created by **medieval ploughing**. From the 9th century or so the open field system was developed, with the land divided into strips. Ploughing methods, using teams of oxen, shifted the soil to form a series of ridges, resulting in the pattern still visible today in many places. Where the open fields were later enclosed to form sheepwalk the pattern survived. Modern ploughing, however, destroys it.

With its gables and its projecting, conical-roofed, semicircular stair turret, it's an imposing sight. Lovely as it is, its setting is lovelier still. The Wilderhope Estate, which also belongs to the National Trust, is a glorious green jumble of wooded valleys, flower-rich meadows, ancient woodland and centuries-old hedgerows. The Trust has been acquiring sections of the Edge since 1982 and now cares for a fair-sized chunk of it. Management is aimed at maintaining its character and its wildlife interest, while improving access for walkers. It's encouraging to see what a difference a little sympathetic management can make as the Trust removes conifers to allow native trees to regenerate and pursues environment-friendly farming methods, which allow wild flora and fauna to flourish.

To see a little of this captivating landscape, walk back past the manor, cross the cattle grid and

---

WHERE TO EAT AND DRINK ℹ

There is nowhere en route, but the **Longville Arms** at Longville in the Dale is not far away. It's a friendly, relaxed place with an excellent reputation. There are two bars and a great choice of reasonably priced food. Or you can sit at picnic tables outside while the kids have fun in the play area.

---

turn right into a field. Go diagonally up to the top corner, then follow a hedge uphill to the crest of **Wenlock Edge**. Turn right at the top along the outer edge of **Longville Coppice** until you can access the coppice a little further on. Turn right to walk the length of it. The dominant species here are ash and hazel, but there are others too, including small-leaved lime. This native lime is a far more attractive species than the hybrid lime planted in parks and gardens. Pollen records show it was one of the commonest trees of the original wildwood, but it is nationally scarce today (though locally common in places), and nobody really knows why. It may be because it grows mostly on well-drained, easily worked soils – the sort which would have been first cleared of trees by the earliest farmers. But this argument could apply to other species that have not become scarce. Lime foliage is also readily eaten by grazing animals.

Go through a gate at the far end of the coppice on to **Pilgrims Lane**, a sunken track which quickly leads to a junction where you turn right. It seems logical to suppose that Pilgrims Lane took its name from the pilgrims who came to visit St Milburga's shrine at Much Wenlock, but another local tale links it with the occupants of some long-demolished cottages who are said to have been among the Pilgrim Fathers who sailed on the *Mayflower* to America in 1620.

Shortly before you reach **Pilgrim Cottage**, turn right to join the **Shropshire Way** and follow it towards **Wilderhope Manor**. As you approach the manor, turn left to go downhill on a wide green track. Ford a shallow brook and follow the path down through trees, then uphill across two fields towards the top of **View Edge** (the eastern ridge of Wenlock Edge, not to be confused with the other View Edge near Craven Arms). Go through a gate into **Wilderhope Coppice** and turn right, still climbing, on a path that leads past beech trees.

After about 300yds (274m) fork right, descending, then right again down steps to leave the coppice at a stile. Walk down two fields to a meadow at the bottom, which is known as **Pudding Bag**. Cross the brook and follow a track uphill, to the left of the hedge, to meet the Shropshire Way. Follow it to the right, passing **Wilderhope Farm** to return to the car park by the manor.

WHILE YOU'RE THERE ℹ

Acton Burnell Castle (English Heritage) is now just a shell, but it's well worth a look. It was built in the 13th century by Robert Burnell, Bishop of Bath and Wells and Lord Chancellor to Edward I. Close by are two stone gable-ends which are all that remain of a barn believed to have been the meeting place of the first English parliament at which the Commons were fully represented, summoned in 1283. It met in Shrewsbury but then transferred to Acton Burnell. St Mary's Church, also built by Robert Burnell, is said to be Shropshire's finest 13th-century building.

Paying Homage to St Milburga

Visit the destination of medieval pilgrims in this peaceful walk in the countryside around Much Wenlock.

•DISTANCE•	6¼ miles (10.1km)
•MINIMUM TIME•	2hrs 30min
•ASCENT / GRADIENT•	426ft (130m) ▲ ▲ ▲
•LEVEL OF DIFFICULTY•	🚶 🚶 🚶
•PATHS•	Field paths, couple of boggy patches, 16 stiles
•LANDSCAPE•	Peaceful, pastoral country between Wenlock Edge and Severn Gorge
•SUGGESTED MAP•	aqua3 OS Explorers 217 The Long Mynd & Wenlock Edge; 242 Telford, Ironbridge & The Wrekin
•START / FINISH•	Grid reference: SO 623998 (on Explorer 217)
•DOG FRIENDLINESS•	Keep under close control for much of walk
•PARKING•	Car park off St Mary's Lane in Much Wenlock
•PUBLIC TOILETS•	At car park and on Queen Street opposite main bus stop

BACKGROUND TO THE WALK

Much Wenlock has been a market town for at least 700 years. It is a delightful little place, with charming old houses and a real working farm just off the High Street. There's something to see round every corner, so do take the time to explore fully. The town museum is a model of its kind and in the adjoining tourist information centre you can pick up an excellent leaflet that guides you round the main sights.

Pilgrim's Shrine

The town's crowning glory is St Milburga's Priory, now an English Heritage property. Much Wenlock originally developed because of the presence of a religious house, and the name Wenlock may come from the Celtic 'gwyn-loc', meaning white monastery. The Cluniac priory is in ruins today, but it was once a prosperous and powerful religious centre. It was built in the 12th and 13th centuries, but the first religious house on this site was an abbey founded around AD 680 by Merewalh, the son of King Penda of Mercia. He placed his daughter Milburga in charge in 682. Under her guidance the foundation flourished and she was credited with miraculous works.

Milburga's abbey was destroyed around 874, possibly by a Danish raiding party, but in the 11th century Earl Leofric and Countess Godiva of Mercia built another religious house on the same site, which was in turn succeeded by a Cluniac priory founded by Roger de Montgomery after the Conquest. Many of the existing buildings are almost entirely Early English in style and represent a rebuilding by Prior Humbert in the 13th century. Only a little Norman work survives from Earl Roger's time, but what does remain is superb, especially the decorative arcading in the chapter house and the carvings in the lavatorium (wash room). The entire scene is dominated by the towering gable of the priory church. Such grand ruins testify to the prosperity of the priory, which flourished until the

Dissolution in 1540. It once drew wealth from a variety of interests, including a toll bridge on the Severn, coal and copper mines, iron works, forestry and vast agricultural holdings.

Holy Trinity Church on Wilmore Street is also connected with the priory. It was founded around AD 680 as a place of worship for the nuns of Wenlock Abbey and was enlarged between 800 and 1050. The present nave was built around 1150 by the Cluniac monks of what had become St Milburga's Priory. Abbess Milburga was originally buried in Holy Trinity, but in 1101 her bones were transferred to the priory and over the years many pilgrims came to worship at her shrine. A well bearing her name can still be found on Barrow Street, and people used to believe its water could cure eye diseases.

Walk 21 **Directions**

① Go down **Burgage Way**, left on **Mutton Shut** to **High Street**, right to **Barrow Street**, then left. Pass the church, then turn first right on **Bull Ring**. Continue past the **priory** and along a lane (Shropshire Way).

② Turn right along a track, which leads you to a footpath junction. Leave the **Shropshire Way** at this point, then follow the right-hand path. Cross a brook and continue along the left-hand hedge until you come to a waymarker that directs you diagonally towards a stile.

Walk 21

③ Cross the stile, then turn right along a field edge. Ignore a gate and stile in the corner; instead turn left, until another stile gives access to the adjacent field. Turn left to the far corner, then climb over a low fence and proceed along a narrow path.

WHERE TO EAT AND DRINK ⓘ

You'll be spoilt for choice in Much Wenlock. Possibilities on High Street include the **Talbot** and the **George and Dragon**, both deservedly popular. The Talbot, which has been offering refreshments since 1361, has a lovely flower-filled courtyard. Or try the inviting **Copper Kettle** across the road, an excellent tea room and antique shop.

---

④ Go through a gate at the end of the field and over a stile ahead, then straight on through a young wood. Emerging into a large field, keep straight on by the left-hand hedge before joining a track that runs to the left of a holly hedge. When the track bends right, keep straight on towards **Arlescott Farm**.

⑤ Two stiles give access to pasture to the right of the farm. Turn left, passing to the left of a pool and then to the right of **Arlescott Cottage** to intercept the **Jack Mytton Way**. Turn left to enter pasture. As you approach the far

---

WHAT TO LOOK FOR ⓘ

As you approach Arlescott Cottage you'll notice that the ground is marked by earthworks. These reveal the site of a deserted **medieval village**. Beyond the cottage, having joined the Jack Mytton Way, you'll see a ridge-and-furrow pattern, the result of medieval ploughing techniques. Beyond the ridge-and-furrow is a series of pronounced terraces. These are cultivation terraces, or strip lynchets, also the legacy of medieval (or possibly Celtic) farmers.

---

side, veer away from the hedge to find a gap in a lower hedge. Turn right, following the bridleway to a lane at **Wyke**.

⑥ Turn right, then left at a road junction. You're now back on the Shropshire Way, which passes **Audience Wood** before making a left turn, leading through woodland to fields. The path is clearly waymarked along field edges, then diagonally towards **Bradley Farm**.

⑦ Pass through the farmyard, turn left by the house, then right. Cross a lane and again take to the fields, going straight ahead until you enter pastureland. Head for the far right corner, cross a footbridge and turn left to the path junction near Much Wenlock, which you encountered earlier. Turn right to rejoin the lane from Much Wenlock.

WHILE YOU'RE THERE ⓘ

Despite its industrial past, **Broseley**, 4 miles (6.4km) north east of Much Wenlock, is another charming small town. For around 350 years it specialised in making clay pipes, which were known as Broseley Churchwardens. The wonderfully preserved Broseley Pipeworks is now a museum, which looks much as it did the day the last pipe-maker laid down his tools in 1957.

---

⑧ Turn right to the course of a dismantled railway, go left for a few paces, then right again at a sign for the Jack Mytton Way. Join a footpath on the left along the edge of **Gaskell Recreation Ground**. After passing a green shed, recross the old railway line and turn right on a fenced path. This passes the former station house, then turns left, soon emerging near the priory. Turn right and retrace your steps to the start of the walk.

Drama at Clive and Grinshill

Dramatic cliffs and views, and memories of a disreputable dramatist.

•DISTANCE•	5¼ miles (8.4km)
•MINIMUM TIME•	2hrs
•ASCENT / GRADIENT•	540ft (165m) ▲ ▲ ▲
•LEVEL OF DIFFICULTY•	🚶🚶 🚶🚶 🚶🚶
•PATHS•	Rocky, woodland and field paths, mostly well used, 5 stiles
•LANDSCAPE•	Sandstone outcrop, old quarries and gentle farmland
•SUGGESTED MAP•	aqua3 OS Explorer 241 Shrewsbury
•START / FINISH•	Grid reference: SJ 525237
•DOG FRIENDLINESS•	They'll love Grinshill Hill, but under close control elsewhere
•PARKING•	Car park in Corbet Wood, next to Grinshill Quarry
•PUBLIC TOILETS•	None on route

BACKGROUND TO THE WALK

The north Shropshire plain is broken at intervals by battered ridges of red sandstone rising dramatically above the sea of green lapping at their feet. Highest and finest of them all is Grinshill Hill, a craggy lump of rock held in the grip of gnarled Scots pines and graceful silver birches existing on the thinnest of soils. It's an exciting, almost Tolkienesque sort of place, with spectacular abandoned quarries and deeply sunken hollow ways.

On its slopes stand Clive and Grinshill, both built of Grinshill stone, which has been quarried since Roman times. The stone was used for some of the grandest Victorian building projects, including several railway stations, of which Shrewsbury is a superb example. It is still quarried today, but the modern workings don't impinge on this walk.

Clive is a particularly attractive village, with pretty cottages clustered below All Saints' Church. This is a Victorian rebuild, but is more than redeemed by the power of its setting in a steeply sloping churchyard, overflowing with daffodils in March and offering fine views. The tall spire is a landmark for miles around.

Dramatic Associations

I must admit to a personal interest in Clive. In the Second World War my father was sent from bomb-blasted Manchester to the safety of his Uncle Jack's farm at Wollerton, near Market Drayton. Nearly 50 years later, researching the family tree, he discovered that Jack Wycherley was a descendant of William Wycherley, the Restoration dramatist and satirist who entertained the court of Charles II with his plays. His most famous work is *The Country Wife* (1675). Wycherley was born at Clive Hall (it's on the main street) in 1640. By all accounts, he was a dissolute rogue who chased young girls and shared one of Charles II's mistresses, Barbara Villiers, the Duchess of Cleveland. Naturally we're all quite proud of him! He also married the Countess of Drogheda for her money and must have been gratified when she died a year later, leaving everything to him. But it didn't do him much good because the will was contested and the ensuing lawsuit bankrupted him. He was thrown into a debtors' prison which he endured for seven years until rescued by James II, who paid off his debts and gave him a pension. Wycherley married a young girl in 1716 when he was 75, but died 11 days later. His bones lie somewhere in the churchyard at Clive.

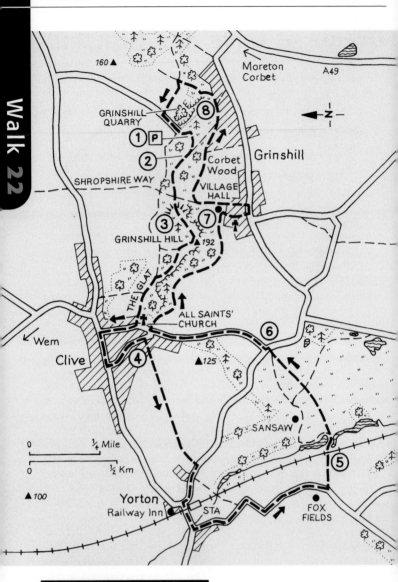

Walk 22 Directions

① On the east side of the car park a bridleway starts near a stone building. Join this and shortly fork right to pass below the car park. Go straight on at a junction, passing an old sycamore tree with an amazing exposed root system, then past a massive cliff-like slab of exposed rock.

② When you reach a junction by another slab, keep to the bridleway (marked with a blue arrow), descending until you come to a point where a wall rises on the right, at right angles to the bridleway. Follow the wall up to meet the **Shropshire Way**, but don't join it. Instead, turn left by a post with carvings of a butterfly and a toadstool, and keep climbing to reach a viewpoint.

Walk 22

③ Turn your back on the view and go uphill to join a wide path. Follow this to the left and keep left at a fork. Continue climbing to reach the summit. After enjoying the stunning view, turn your back on it again and take the left-hand path. Keep left at a fork. The path joins a walled track (**The Glat**), which leads to **All Saints' Church** at Clive. You could just turn left here, but to see more of **Clive**, and perhaps patronise the village shop, turn right instead, then soon left on the main street and left again on **Back Lane**.

④ Turn right on a footpath, which begins as a green lane, then crosses sheep pasture to meet a road. Turn right past **Yorton Station**, then left under the railway and left again. Soon after passing a house called **Fox Fields**, join a footpath on the left and cross an arable field and then the railway.

⑤ Push through trees to meet a track. Turn right for a few paces, then left between two pools to enter parkland. Follow the left-hand boundary, passing **Sansaw** and going through an iron kissing gate next to a wooden field gate. Sansaw's garden wall now turns left – don't follow it but keep straight on to another wooden field gate. Cross a driveway and continue across more parkland to a road.

⑥ Turn left, then immediately right, towards Clive. Turn right opposite **Back Lane** on a walled bridleway, which passes below the churchyard and contours round **Grinshill Hill** to the Jubilee Oak and **village hall** at Grinshill.

⑦ Turn right along a track, passing the church to meet the main street. Turn left, then left again on **Gooseberry Lane**. Pass the village hall again (the other side this time) and rejoin the walled bridleway. Ignore branching paths, staying on the bridleway, which climbs to meet a walled grassy track. Turn right past houses.

⑧ As the track forks, go left and then up steps to cross a stone step stile. Walk uphill through woodland, soon bearing right and climbing steeply until you come to a fenced area. Turn right on a broad path to reach a junction, then turn left on a track, and left again at the road, past **Grinshill Quarry** to the car park.

Here be Dragons

Explore Merrington's medieval common and a sandstone ridge at Webscott.

•DISTANCE•	5½ miles (8.8km)
•MINIMUM TIME•	2hrs 15min
•ASCENT / GRADIENT•	344ft (105m) ▲ ▲ ▲
•LEVEL OF DIFFICULTY•	🚶🚶 🚶 🚶🚶
•PATHS•	Field paths and bridleway, can be muddy, 6 stiles
•LANDSCAPE•	Farmland, medieval common, sandstone ridge with reclaimed quarries, panoramic views
•SUGGESTED MAP•	aqua3 OS Explorer 241 Shrewsbury
•START / FINISH•	Grid reference: SJ 465208
•DOG FRIENDLINESS•	Under control at Myddle, Merrington and Webscott
•PARKING•	Car park on north side of road at Merrington Green nature reserve
•PUBLIC TOILETS•	None on route

BACKGROUND TO THE WALK

The two main highlights of this walk are the former quarries at Webscott and the nature reserve managed by Shropshire Wildlife Trust at Merrington Green. It's a story of contrast. Webscott is a relatively new landscape, created by nature taking over a post-industrial site. Since quarrying ceased here, the holes so crudely gouged out of the sandstone have been colonised by mosses, ferns and trees. The effect is delightful. Merrington Green, on the other hand, is a very old landscape which can be maintained only by human management, otherwise nature will turn it into just another woodland.

Of course, it would have been woodland originally, but in the Middle Ages it was cleared. At that time, nearly every village would have had a similar patch of land where commoners could graze stock, collect firewood and dig marl or turf. Such a system results in a range of habitats, which is often more ecologically valuable than a uniform block of woodland. Merrington Green is still a registered common, but the commoners no longer exercise their rights, which means scrub is encroaching. It is controlled by hand as far as possible, but the reintroduction of grazing would be a better way. However, sheep would be at risk from traffic because the green is unfenced.

Spectacular Aerobatics

One of the most valuable aspects of the green is the presence of three pools which have formed in old marl pits. An incredible 17 species of dragonfly and damselfly have been recorded here, making this easily Shropshire Wildlife Trust's top dragonfly location. The easternmost pool is fringed by marsh horsetail, a descendant of the giant horsetails of the primeval swamps, where the first dragonflies evolved over 300 million years ago. The largest species of dragonfly ever known is preserved in the fossil record from this time – it had a wingspan the size of a sparrowhawk's. Modern dragonflies are much smaller and each is a miniature miracle of design. If you get to see a resting dragonfly it's worth studying it in detail to appreciate the lethal beauty of these precision-built killing machines. Typically, an adult dragonfly will live only a few weeks, but in that time it will consume large numbers of smaller insects, caught on the wing. Its aerial acrobatics can be spectacular and its wings beat 30 times a second, allowing a dazzling range of manoeuvres. It can even fly backwards. The adult stage is preceded by two or three years spent under water as a nymph, in which form the insect is also a consummate predator. When a nymph is ready to metamorphose, it climbs out of the water on to a suitable plant. The ugly larval skin splits and a jewel-coloured adult emerges, crumpled at first, until it dries off and its wings inflate.

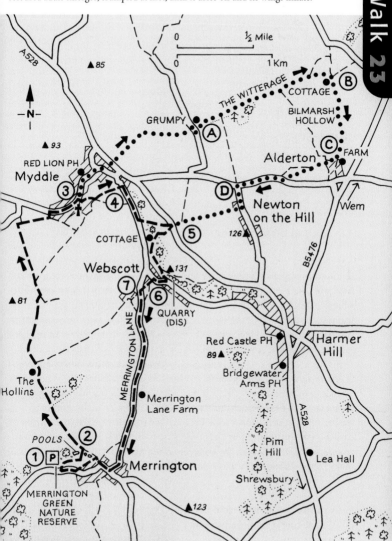

Walk 23 Directions

① There is a map of the reserve on one side of the car park and, on the other side, two footpaths: you can take either as they soon merge into one. Follow the path through grassland, then fork left into woodland. Turn right when you meet a pool. After passing one side of the pool, the path moves briefly away from it, then turns left to pass the end of it, with another pool on your right-hand side and a boardwalk underfoot.

② Turn left on a tree-bordered bridleway, which runs for nearly 2 miles (3.2km). As you approach a road, look for a stile on the right (at a bend) and walk across fields to meet the road on the edge of **Myddle**. Turn right into the village.

> ### WHILE YOU'RE THERE
> In 1403, Henry IV defeated the Yorkists at the Battle of Shrewsbury. The site is simply called **Battlefield**, and there's a church there, just to the north of Shrewsbury. It was built on the King's orders after the battle, and eight chaplains were installed to pray for the dead. It's very atmospheric, even when the church itself is closed.

③ After passing the **church**, turn right on a walled lane, then through a black gate on the left. Pass to the left of farm buildings, then cross two fields – you can see the path stretching ahead of you to a lane.

④ Turn right along the lane for 400yds (366m) until you can join a footpath on the left, which climbs a wooded slope. At the top a well-trodden path turns right by the woodland edge. However, the right of way goes diagonally across a field to a gate to the road.

⑤ Turn your back on the gate and go straight across the field, meeting the wood again at a corner. Go through a gate and descend through the trees, then through a garden (dogs on leads) and past a cottage towards the lane. Just before you reach it, join another path on the left that climbs back up the slope. As you approach a stile at the top,

> ### WHERE TO EAT AND DRINK
> Try the **Red Castle** or the **Bridgewater Arms**, or the exceptionally good organic café and farm shop at **Lea Hall** (no dogs allowed), all on the A528 at nearby Harmer Hill.

turn right, then left, descending through a former **quarry** and past a lovely house built into the rock. Turn right along the lane.

⑥ Join a footpath on the left and cross a narrow pasture. A right of way runs diagonally across the next field, but is currently impassable at the far side. If you suspect this may still be the case (new waymarkers might indicate improvements), play safe by taking another path, which follows the right-hand field edge.

⑦ Turn left along **Merrington Lane**, and eventually right at a T-junction at **Merrington**. When the road bends left, go straight on along the bridleway used earlier until you join a path that crosses the nature reserve to the car park.

> ### WHAT TO LOOK FOR
> You will notice some footpaths have waymarkers labelled 'Gough walk'. This is a millennium project, inspired by Richard Gough (1635–1723), who achieved fame through his book *The Antiquities and Memoirs of the Parish of Myddle*. Go in the church to find out more – it's fascinating stuff, and you can buy a pack of walk leaflets if you wish.

A House Called Grumpy at The Witterage

A longer walk full of interest, with marvellous views stretching north across the plain.

See map and information panel for Walk 23

•DISTANCE•	8 miles (12.9km)
•MINIMUM TIME•	3hrs
•ASCENT / GRADIENT•	262ft (80m) ▲▲ ▲ ▲
•LEVEL OF DIFFICULTY•	🚶🚶 🚶🚶 🚶

Walk 24 Directions (Walk 23 option)

Leave Walk 23 at Point ③ and continue along the street. As it bends right, join a path on the left, climbing some steps to the main road. Cross to a path opposite, which crosses a large field. Go through a gate at the far side and turn right by the ensuing field edge, but take care – it's ankle-twistingly uneven in places. At the far side go through woodland to meet a lane opposite a house with the unusual name of **Grumpy** (Point Ⓐ), which actually looks quite cheerful, with tubs of flowers everywhere.

Turn right, then immediately left on a bridleway known as **The Witterage**. It's easily followed until it enters a field where a notice explains that an existing footpath has been made into a concessionary bridleway under the Countryside Stewardship scheme. Follow this bridleway, looking for a couple of green arrows and ignoring the yellow arrows that direct you to the right. Basically, you just keep on in much the same direction, following the right-hand boundary through two fields.

Go through a gate in the corner of the second field, pass a cottage (Point Ⓑ) and turn right along an old track through lovely **Bilmarsh Hollow**. As you pass a farm on the edge of **Alderton** (Point Ⓒ), look for a signpost on the right that sends you along a green lane. As this bends right, cross a stile on the left into a field. Walk the length of the field, first heading for a solitary oak on the left, then continuing across the field from there. The oak marks the line of a grubbed-out hedge; soon you will come to what remains of the hedge, guarded by three more large oaks. Keep to the left of this hedge to find a stile at the far side, not far from the corner. Take care as you step off it. Go diagonally across the next field to a gate, then turn right along a road.

Turn left at a junction (Point Ⓓ) towards **Newton on the Hill**. After passing a couple of houses, cross a stile on the right and turn left to cross another stile into sheep pasture. Walk to the main road and cross to a path opposite to rejoin Walk 23 at Point ⑤.

Walk 25

Shrewsbury: Islanded in Severn Stream

An enjoyable riverside meander on the edge of one of Britain's finest towns.

•DISTANCE•	6 miles (9.7km)
•MINIMUM TIME•	2hrs
•ASCENT / GRADIENT•	Negligible
•LEVEL OF DIFFICULTY•	
•PATHS•	Riverside tow path, impassable in floods, 3 stiles
•LANDSCAPE•	Riverside meadows on edge of town
•SUGGESTED MAP•	aqua3 OS Explorer 241 Shrewsbury
•START / FINISH•	Grid reference: SJ 498123
•DOG FRIENDLINESS•	Lots of local dogs by river, some pavement pounding
•PARKING•	Abbey Foregate car park opposite Shrewsbury Abbey
•PUBLIC TOILETS•	At town end of Abbey Foregate, on north side

Walk 25 Directions

It was A E Housman who described Shrewsbury as 'islanded in Severn stream', and there has never been a better description. The Saxon town was built within the natural moat provided by a tight loop of the Severn, completely encircled except for a small gap, making a perfect defensive site. Even the gap was guarded by a ridge, on which a castle was later built. As it moves away from the town, the Severn continues its crazy meandering and the walk described here is contained within a series of loops to the east of the historic town centre.

Walk along **Abbey Foregate** away from town, passing the Abbey Church of St Peter and St Paul, founded in 1083 by Roger de Montgomery on the site of an earlier Saxon church, just outside the town walls. The most striking part of the present building is the great west tower, built in the 14th century during the reign of Edward III. Shrewsbury Abbey is the setting for the popular *Cadfael* novels by Ellis Peters (the pen name of the late Edith Pargeter). There are buildings from all periods along Abbey Foregate, but Georgian is the dominant style, with an abundance of beautiful brick town houses. Shrewsbury saw extraordinary

---

WHAT TO LOOK FOR
You can hardly miss **Shrewsbury Abbey**, but the Abbey Church that survives today was once part of a much larger complex, with a full range of monastic buildings. Following the dissolution of the monasteries (1536–9) by Henry VIII, the church survived for use as a parish church, and some of the other buildings continued in use until 1827, when Thomas Telford drove his Holyhead road through the site, proving that the vandalism of road builders is nothing new. Perhaps the saddest thing is the sight of the 14th-century refectory pulpit, which was spared but now sits pointlessly in the middle of the huge car park across the road.

growth in the second half of the 18th century and it was then that Abbey Foregate was developed as a desirable residential suburb.

Go as far as the **Shire Hall** (all too obviously a product of the 1960s) and **Lord Hill's Column**, a sky-high tower of Grinshill stone erected in 1816 to honour the military achievements of Viscount Hill who fought with Wellington at Waterloo. It is said to be the tallest Doric column in the world. Turn left by Lord Hill, past the Crown Courts on **Preston Street**.

WHERE TO EAT AND DRINK

Shrewsbury seems to have more enticing places to eat than almost any other town of its size. Even on the edge of town at Abbey Foregate there is an excellent choice. Pubs include the **Dun Cow**, the **Bricklayers Arms**, the **Crown Inn** and the **Bell**. **Mojo's Café and Sandwich Bar** is useful, there are at least two Indian restaurants and the **Peach Tree** café, bar and restaurant is open from 9AM for food.

When the road bends left into **Portland Crescent**, keep straight on along a stony track (signposted 'private road/public footpath'). When the track ends, the right of way remains well-defined, going straight across a field to the **River Severn**. Turn left on the **Severn Way**. Very soon you'll pass under an impressive railway bridge, cast at Coalbrookdale Foundry in 1848, the year Shrewsbury acquired its first train service.

A little further on, the path climbs to the edge of a housing estate and then runs along the edge of **Monkmoor Community Woodland**, where grassland has been newly planted with young native trees. At the far side of this, a tributary stream blocks the way forward. Go left until you can cross the stream, then return to the river in the next field.

Pass under two road bridges (both carrying the A49) and pass the suburb of **Monkmoor**, where the poet Wilfred Owen lived as a boy. He was born in Oswestry in 1893, the son of a railway worker, but the family moved to Monkmoor in 1907. They used to enjoy riverside walks most weekends, and on one occasion Wilfred noticed his brother's boots were covered in buttercup petals. He described them as 'blessed with gold', an image he used again during the First World War when portraying soldiers at the front in the Spring Offensive. Tragically, Owen was killed the week before the armistice in 1918.

When you come to a third road bridge, go up to cross the bridge then return to the riverbank on the far side and continue towards Shrewsbury. Cross the river again when you come to a foot/cycle bridge and go straight on at the far side, on the left-hand of two parallel paths. Turn right when you come to a road (**Holywell Street**); follow it back to **Abbey Foregate**.

WHILE YOU'RE THERE

Haughmond Abbey is just to the north of Haughmond Hill and in the care of English Heritage. There's lots to see, but the highlights include a 12th-century chapter house with richly decorated arches and a 14th-century abbot's hall. When the abbey was founded, probably in the 11th century, it was in a wild and isolated place. That's not the case today, with the horribly busy A49 not much more than a mile (1.6km) away, but it is still a pleasantly rural site.

Gone to Earth on Lovely Lyth Hill

Enjoy the glorious panoramic views that gave inspiration to the Shropshire novelist Mary Webb.

•DISTANCE•	8 miles (12.9km)
•MINIMUM TIME•	3hrs
•ASCENT / GRADIENT•	548ft (167m) ▲ ▲ ▲
•LEVEL OF DIFFICULTY•	🚶 🚶 🚶
•PATHS•	Cross-field paths, mostly well-maintained, about 30 stiles
•LANDSCAPE•	Rolling farmland and views from Lyth Hill's grassy top
•SUGGESTED MAP•	aqua3 OS Explorer 241 Shrewsbury
•START / FINISH•	Grid reference: SJ 473069
•DOG FRIENDLINESS•	Must be on leads near livestock, also at Exfords Green
•PARKING•	Car park in country park at top of Lyth Hill (signposted): OS map shows bus turning area, not car park
•PUBLIC TOILETS•	None on route

BACKGROUND TO THE WALK

Lyth Hill, which is included within a small country park, is of modest height, attaining only 557ft (169m). It's mainly grassland, with areas of scrub and woodland which support a variety of birds such as great spotted woodpecker, wood warbler and tree pipit. The country park is popular with local people, especially dog walkers, as it's within walking distance of Shrewsbury suburbs such as Bayston Hill and Meole Brace, and it's a good place for picnics or kite-flying. Most of all though, it's ideal for simply sitting back and enjoying the superb view, which is extraordinary, all the more so for coming as something of a surprise. It includes the Clee Hills, Wenlock Edge, The Wrekin, the Stretton Hills, Long Mynd and Stiperstones.

Novel Inspiration

This view inspired Mary Webb, or Mary Gladys Meredith as she was born in 1881 at Leighton, a small village south of Shrewsbury. In 1902 she moved with her family to Meole Brace, where she lived until her marriage to Henry Webb in 1912. Mary was a great walker and during the years spent at Meole Brace it was Lyth Hill that was her favourite destination. She was enchanted not only by the view, but also by the small wood called Spring Coppice. In 1917, after the publication of her first novel, the Webbs bought a plot of land on the hill and Spring Cottage was built for them. This was Mary's home, apart from a short spell in London, until her untimely death in 1927. The cottage is still there today, but much altered and extended.

Fame at Last

Mary wrote several novels at Spring Cottage, but she achieved very little fame in her lifetime. It was only after her death that posthumous praise from the prime minister, Stanley Baldwin, sparked off public interest and acclaim. Her best novels are considered to be

Precious Bane and *The Golden Arrow*, while *Gone to Earth* was made into a film, shot in Shropshire in 1950. The interest in Mary's work waned and her novels are not fashionable today. Indeed, they're all too easy to make fun of and Stella Gibbons's classic *Cold Comfort Farm* was actually a parody of one of Mary's books (*The House in Dormer Forest*). But they are worth reading if you love Shropshire. Each is richly imbued with a strong sense of the local landscape. Few writers have been so much in tune with their surroundings, or so able to convey its atmosphere. Mary adored Shropshire and it shows in her books. It's easy to see why she felt so passionate about it, as you gaze out at the view from Lyth Hill, which she knew so well.

Walk 26 Directions

① Head south on the **Shropshire Way**. Ignore a path branching right into Spring Coppice. The Way descends to a lane, where you turn left, then first right, on a track to **Exfords Green**.

② Cross two stiles to skirt a former **Primitive Methodist chapel**, which is currently being modernised. Leave the Shropshire Way, going diagonally right across a field, heading for the far right corner. Cross a stile quite close to the corner and go through a copse until you come to a lane.

Walk 26

WHILE YOU'RE THERE ⓘ
Take a look at the craggy rocks near the viewpoint, at the top of the hill, near the car park. At first glance they look a little like concrete, but a closer inspection reveals that they are actually formed from **conglomerate**, which is composed of rounded pebbles embedded in a sandy matrix. This is a Precambrian sedimentary rock dating from around 650 million years ago.

③ Cross to a path almost opposite, following the left-hand edge of a field until a stile gives access to another. Head diagonally across to a point close to the far right corner. Cross a wobbly stile and continue across another field, past two oak trees. A worn path goes obliquely right across the next two fields to meet a lane.

④ Turn right, then right again at the main road, to pass through **Longden**, and right again on **School Lane**. This descends very slightly to cross a brook, after which you go through a gate on the left and diagonally right across a field corner to a stile.

⑤ A yellow arrow directs you diagonally across the next field to a stile under an oak tree to the left of a telegraph post. Cross another field to reach a road. The path continues opposite, crossing two further fields until it meets a lane at **Great Lyth**. Turn right, keeping straight on at a junction, then turn left at the next.

⑥ Turn right on the access track to **Lower Lythwood Hall** and **Holly Ash**. At the latter, turn left as the track becomes a green lane leading to a field. Cross the field, passing a row of three oak trees, then keeping to the right of a pond to reach a

stile by two oaks at the far side. In the next field go diagonally right, then through a gate and continue along a track for a few paces until you can cross a stile on the right.

⑦ Walk straight up a sloping field and turn left at the top. Cross a stile in the corner and keep going on along a worn path until you come to a waymarker, which directs you to the left, descending beside a brook to meet the road at **Hook-a-gate**.

WHERE TO EAT AND DRINK ⓘ
The flower-bedecked **Tankerville Arms**, at Longden, has hand-pulled traditional ales, which you can enjoy indoors or in the beer garden. A useful **village shop** stands close by, for stocking up on chocolate and crisps. **Cygnets** at Hook-a-gate offers a warm welcome to families. It serves cask ales and has a large garden, suitable for dogs.

⑧ Turn right for 200yds (183m), then right again on a footpath that climbs to join **Hanley Lane** at **Bayston Hill**. Continue to **Overdale Road** and turn right until you intercept the Shropshire Way at **Lythwood Road**. Turn right, following the Way to **Lythwood Farm** and then across fields to **Lyth Hill**, where you turn right to your starting point.

WHAT TO LOOK FOR ⓘ
If you'd like to know more about Mary Webb, you might enjoy the excellent **museum** at the tourist information centre in Much Wenlock. Naturally, the focus is on Wenlock itself, but there is also lots about the Shropshire novelist, including a fascinating display of photographs of the filming of *Gone to Earth* in 1950. Kids needn't despair at the idea of a museum – there's plenty for them too.

Meres, Mosses and Moraines at Ellesmere

A wonderful watery walk through Shropshire's lake district.

•DISTANCE•	7¼ miles (11.7km)
•MINIMUM TIME•	3hrs
•ASCENT / GRADIENT•	180ft (55m) ▲ ▲ ▲
•LEVEL OF DIFFICULTY•	𝟇 𝟇 𝟇
•PATHS•	Field paths and canal tow path, 8 stiles
•LANDSCAPE•	Pastoral hills with glacial hollows containing small lakes
•SUGGESTED MAP•	aqua3 OS Explorer 241 Shrewsbury
•START / FINISH•	Grid reference: SJ 407344
•DOG FRIENDLINESS•	Can run free on tow path, but under tight control elsewhere
•PARKING•	Castlefields car park opposite The Mere
•PUBLIC TOILETS•	Next to The Mere, almost opposite car park

BACKGROUND TO THE WALK

Ellesmere is another of those delightful little towns in which Shropshire specialises. It's well worth devoting some time to exploring it. But Ellesmere's biggest asset must be The Mere, the largest of all the meres that grace north Shropshire and south Cheshire. It attracts good numbers of water birds and is especially important for winter migrants such as wigeon, pochard, goosander and teal. It also has a large heronry occupied by breeding birds in spring and early summer.

On this walk you will explore about half of The Mere's shoreline and follow the tow path of the Llangollen Canal past Cole Mere and Blake Mere. Cole Mere is included within a country park and there is access from the tow path at Yell Bridge (54). If you want to explore Cole Mere, you can walk all the way round it. Blake Mere is particularly lovely; it's separated from the tow path only by a narrow strip of woodland, but there is no other access to it.

Glacial Formations

The word mere is an Anglo-Saxon term for a lake. Unlike a normal lake, however, these meres have no stream flowing in or out of them. So how were they formed? It's a complex story but the Meres Visitor Centre has lots of information. What follows here is a simplified version. During the last ice age, the landscape was scoured by glaciers and when they retreated between 10,000 to 12,000 years ago, they left clay-lined hollows which retained melting ice, forming some of the meres. Others filled up later because they lay below the level of the water table. Water levels are maintained by natural drainage (groundwater percolation) from the surrounding countryside.

The landscape is composed of gentle hills that, combined with the meres, form a very pleasing scene. Technically, it consists of glacial drift, a mixture of clays, sands and gravels originally scoured from rocks by the glaciers as they moved south and east across Britain and then deposited in banks and mounds known as moraines as the glaciers retreated. In places, you can identify the origins of the glacial drift. Blue-black pebbles are slates from Snowdonia or Cumbria, and pale, speckled stones are granites from Cumbria or Scotland, while pink pebbles are from the local sandstone. These glacial meres are unique in this country and rare in global terms.

North Shropshire is also renowned for its mosses, which were created by the glaciers too, but they are filled with peat rather than water. If you've done Walk 2 you'll be familiar with the wonderful moss at Whixall, but there are several small mosses around Ellesmere too, though none with public access. The meres and mosses together form a wetland complex which, ecologically, is of national, if not international, significance.

Walk 27 Directions

① Cross to **The Mere** and turn left. Pass **The Boathouse** and **Meres** **Visitor Centre** and walk towards town, until you come to **Cremorne Gardens**. Join a path that runs through trees close by the water's edge for about ¾ mile (1.2km).

② Leave the trees for a field and turn left, signposted 'Welshampton'. The path soon joins a track, which leads to **Crimps Farm**. Turn right past the farm buildings to cross a stile on the right of the track. Continue along another track.

③ The track leads into sheep pasture where you go straight on, guided by waymarkers and stiles. When you come to a field with a **trig pillar** in it, the waymarker is slightly misleading – ignore it and go straight across. In the next field you should aim for three prominent trees close together at the far side. As you approach them, turn left into the field corner.

> **WHERE TO EAT AND DRINK** ⓘ
>
> There is plenty of choice in Ellesmere. Special mention goes to **Vermuelen's** bakery/deli where you can buy the ingredients for a picnic. Or there's **The Boathouse** by The Mere, an unusual oak-beamed 1930s restaurant/tea room. There's a good range of snacks and drinks on offer, and dogs are welcome in the garden, which borders The Mere.

④ Go through a gate and descend by the right-hand hedge. When it turns a corner, go with it, to the right. Skirt a pool and keep going in the same direction on a grassy track, passing another pool. The track soon becomes much better defined and leads to a farm where you join a road.

⑤ Turn left and go straight on at a junction into **Welshampton**. Turn right on **Lyneal Lane** and follow it to a bridge over the **Llangollen Canal**. Descend steps to the tow path and turn right, passing under the bridge. Pass Lyneal Wharf, Cole Mere, Yell Wood and Blake Mere, then through **Ellesmere Tunnel**.

Beyond this are three footpaths signposted to The Mere. Take any of these short cuts if you wish, but to see a bit more of the canal, including the visitor moorings and marina, stay on the tow path.

> **WHAT TO LOOK FOR** ⓘ
>
> Many bird species can be seen, but one of the most endearing is the **great crested grebe**. This distinctive diving bird is nearly always present on the larger meres. You can recognise it by the crest on top of its head. In spring it has cute, stripy chicks which it sometimes carries on its back to give them a rest from all that paddling.

⑥ Arriving at **bridge 58**, further choices present themselves. You could extend this walk to include the signposted Wharf Circular Walk (recommended) or to explore the town (also recommended): just follow the signs. To return directly to The Mere, however, go up to the road and turn left.

⑦ Fork right on a road by **Blackwater Cottage**. Turn right at the top, then soon left at **Rose Bank**, up steps. Walk across the earthworks of the long-gone **Ellesmere Castle** and follow signs for The Mere or the car park.

> **WHILE YOU'RE THERE** ⓘ
>
> While The Mere is the highlight of **Ellesmere**, it would be a shame not to explore the town, especially the refurbished canal wharves and basin. There's lots to see, including the offices from which Thomas Telford directed the construction of the canal. Ellesmere was the headquarters of the Llangollen Canal (originally called the Ellesmere Canal) and so there are former workshops, warehouses and dry docks, while British Waterways still has an office and maintenance depot here.

From Castle to Canal

Follow the Llangollen branch of the Shroppie through pastoral countryside.

•DISTANCE•	6 miles (9.7km)
•MINIMUM TIME•	2hrs 30min
•ASCENT / GRADIENT•	Negligible
•LEVEL OF DIFFICULTY•	
•PATHS•	Tow path, lanes and field paths, very overgrown, 19 stiles
•LANDSCAPE•	Low-lying farmland, pastoral and arable, attractive canal
•SUGGESTED MAP•	aqua3 OS Explorer 240 Oswestry
•START / FINISH•	Grid reference: SJ 325312
•DOG FRIENDLINESS•	Can run free on tow path, but probably nowhere else
•PARKING•	Car park next to Whittington Castle – honesty box
•PUBLIC TOILETS•	At castle when open

BACKGROUND TO THE WALK

This walk, and Walks 29 and 31, explore sections of the Montgomery Canal (the Monty). Read about the history of it here, then turn to Walk 31 to learn about recent restoration work. The waterway that we now call the Montgomery Canal runs for 35 miles (56km) from the Llangollen (formerly Ellesmere) Canal at Frankton Junction to Newtown, Powys. Originally, it was three canals – the Ellesmere, and the eastern and western branches of the Montgomery – built by three different companies over 25 years. The Ellesmere (Frankton to Llanymynech) section opened first, in 1796. It met the Montgomery Canal's eastern branch at Carreghofa, but the Monty was completed only as far as Garthmyl (near Welshpool) before the money ran out in 1797. Work ceased for years until a Newtown entrepreneur, William Pugh, put up the cash. By 1819 it was finally finished, right through to Newtown.

A Long Time Coming

Frankton Junction became the hub of the Ellesmere system. There were actually two junctions, forming an H-shape, from which waterways radiated out to Weston Lullingfields, Ellesmere, Pontcysyllte and Llanymynech. The limestone quarries at Llanymynech provided one of the canal's most valuable cargoes. The Weston branch was intended to continue to Shrewsbury, but was never completed. It's derelict today.

Many renowned engineers were involved with the Monty, including father-and-son teams William and Josias Jessop and John and Thomas Dadford, as well as Thomas Telford. In engineering terms it's an unusual canal; it first descends by 11 locks from Frankton to the Severn, then climbs again, with 14 locks taking it up the Severn Valley to Newtown.

By 1850, the Monty had become part of the Shropshire Union Railway and Canal Company (the Shroppie), but was subsequently taken over by the London and North Western Railway Company. In 1923, it came into the ownership of the London, Midland and Scottish Railway Company (LMS). In 1936, the canal burst its banks by the River Perry below Frankton Locks. The LMS made no effort to repair it; the canal was simply left to its fate. Legal abandonment came in 1944 with the LMS Act of Parliament, which closed many miles of waterway. Under the 1948 Transport Act, the Monty passed into the ownership of British Waterways. Restoration work began in 1968; turn to Walk 31 for more on that.

Walk 28 **Directions**

① Turn right by the Shrewsbury road (**B5009**), using a footway on the left. After about ½ mile (800m), cross a stile and follow a waymarked path across three fields to the far right corner of the third.

② Walk along the edge of the next field, with a wood on your left. Cross a stile in the corner, then go obliquely across another field as indicated by a waymarker. A prominent oak tree is a useful guide. There is a stile near the tree, but you may have to wade through nettles to get to it. Continue in the same direction across the next field to a lane and turn left.

> ### WHAT TO LOOK FOR ⓘ
> The village of Whittington is dominated by its 13th-century **castle**, built by Fulke FitzWarine on the site of an earlier timber castle. What remains of his stronghold is mostly earthworks because the castle fell into disuse after the Civil War and its stone was plundered for road repairs. However, the handsome gatehouse survives intact, its twin circular towers reflected in the moat.

③ Keep left when you come to a fork and continue to the **A495**. Turn right for a few paces, then cross to the other side. Join a footpath that runs along the left-hand edge of a field to a stile and footbridge. Beyond these, keep going along the field edge until a gap in the hedge. Go through, but continue in the same direction as before, soon going up a bank.

④ Meet the canal at **Pollett's Bridge** (No 6). Don't cross it – go under to join the tow path. Follow this to **Hindford Bridge** (No 11), then go up to a lane. Turn right past the **Jack Mytton Inn**, then right again, signposted 'Iron Mills and Gobowen'.

> ### WHILE YOU'RE THERE ⓘ
> Oswestry was once the headquarters of the Cambrian Railway and a hub for services to North Wales. One of the former engine sheds now houses the **Cambrian Museum of Transport**, which chronicles Oswestry's railway history. The Cambrian Railway Society regularly steams up one of its locos on site and there is plenty of railway memorabilia.

⑤ Take a footpath on the left. Walk down a long, narrow paddock to the far end, then cross a stile on the right. Follow a fence to a foot-bridge, then continue across the next pasture to another footbridge and keep straight on to a stile ahead. Go up to the far right corner of the next field, through a gate and then left by a field edge.

> ### WHERE TO EAT AND DRINK ⓘ
> There is a **tea room** at the castle, a **Spar** shop near by and two pubs, **Ye Olde Boote** and the **White Lion**. The **Jack Mytton Inn** at Hindford is an appealing place with a large canalside garden in a very pleasant location. Children are welcome and there is a vegetarian menu.

⑥ Join a track that soon bends right beside the course of a dismantled railway. Look out for a stile giving access to the railway. Turn right on the former trackbed for a few paces, then up the bank on the left – watch out for steps concealed in the undergrowth here. Cross a stile to a field, turn right to the far side and cross another stile. Bear left to a large oak tree, then continue to a lane. Follow it to **Top Street** and turn right, then left to **Whittington Castle**.

Round the Waterways at Frankton

Two branches of the Shroppie add canalside colour to this quiet countryside walk.
See map and information panel for Walk 28

•DISTANCE•	8 miles (12.9km)
•MINIMUM TIME•	3hrs
•ASCENT / GRADIENT•	Negligible
•LEVEL OF DIFFICULTY•	
•PATHS•	Some electric fences, one section narrow and eroded

Walk 29 Directions
(Walk 28 option)

Leave Walk 28 at Point ③, to branch right along a no through road to **Berghill**. Keep left at a fork, then left again on a track (Point Ⓐ). Soon you'll notice there's a small area of woodland on your right. When this comes to an end, the right of way should continue a little further along the track and then branch right across the adjacent field.

However, unfortunately the line of the right of way is currently blocked. Until this is remedied you will need to turn right into the field just after the end of the wood. You may need to negotiate an electric fence here.

Follow the left-hand hedge until you come to an obstructed gate, bringing you back on the right of way now. Turn your back on the gate and go straight across the field, initially using a cottage with two prominent chimney stacks as a rough directional guide. Go

through a gate at the far side and across another field. As you proceed you'll see a brick footbridge over a ditch ahead. This takes you to the tow path of the **Montgomery Canal** (Point Ⓑ).

Turn left, passing under **Lockgate Bridge**, after which the tow path swings left past **Frankton Locks**, where a replica milepost (erected in 1981) indicates 'Newtown 35 Welsh Frankton 0'.

The tow path swings left again, beside the **Llangollen Canal**. It changes sides at **bridge 3** (Point Ⓒ), after which it is quite narrow and eroded in places. At **Pollett's Bridge** (No 6), change sides again to rejoin the route of Walk 28 at Point ④.

WHERE TO EAT AND DRINK
Go up to the road at bridge No 5 to find the **Narrowboat Inn** and **Maestermyn Marina**. There's a shop at the marina selling drinks and ice creams. The Narrowboat Inn is a 19th-century canalside cottage, which was converted into a pub in the 1980s. There's a very good choice of food and a beer garden overlooking the canal.

Place Your Bets at Oswestry

The going is good from Racecourse Common to Offa's Dyke.

•DISTANCE•	4 miles (6.4km)
•MINIMUM TIME•	1hr 15min
•ASCENT / GRADIENT•	459ft (140m) ▲▲ ▲
•LEVEL OF DIFFICULTY•	🚶🚶 🚶🚶 🚶🚶
•PATHS•	Brambly section at Sheep Walk, otherwise fine, 11 stiles
•LANDSCAPE•	Woods, commons and pasture
•SUGGESTED MAP•	aqua3 OS Explorer 240 Oswestry
•START / FINISH•	Grid reference: SJ 258305
•DOG FRIENDLINESS•	Can run free on common, but not in sheep pastures
•PARKING•	Car park/picnic site on southern part of Racecourse Common, off B4580 west of Oswestry
•PUBLIC TOILETS•	None on route

Walk 30 Directions

Its Welsh name is Cyrn y Bwch (Horns of the Buck) which sounds less prosaic than Racecourse Common, but there really was a racecourse here where the local squirearchy, from both sides of the border, held race meetings from the early 1700s until 1848. Apparently, the main event was the impressive-sounding Sir Watkin Williams Wynn Cup. You can still see traces of the course, which was returfed by French prisoners during the Napoleonic wars.

WHAT TO LOOK FOR ⓘ

Racecourse Common is basically acid grassland, but on the north common there are areas of relict heath, which still support heather and whinberry. Look for drifts of beautiful blue **harebells** in the late summer. The south common has some magnificent **rowan** trees. These are at their best in October, when the vivid red berries look especially striking against the russet tones of the dying leaves.

There are grandstand views across Wales, so do take the time to explore the common as well as doing this walk. When you're ready to go, have a look at the skyline map which identifies the Shropshire, Cheshire and Derbyshire hills visible to the east. Look at the actual view too, of course, of which perhaps the most striking aspect is the contrast between the north Shropshire plain and the south Shropshire Hills.

Turn your back on the skyline map and turn right on a path that runs close to the edge of the common. Cross the **B4580** to access the northern part of the common and go to the right when the path forks. As you approach the far end of the common, take a worn path on the right. There are several other paths but only this one actually goes anywhere – you should recognise it because it's much more heavily trodden than the others. There's bracken to the right of it and gorse bushes and rowan trees to the left. It soon leaves the common and

Walk 30

continues as a grassy track. Follow it only for a very short distance, keeping your eyes open for a path branching off to the right at a stile.

Follow the path across a gorse-studded, brackeny pasture, heading for the far left corner. Cross a stile, continue to another and then go straight on to the **B4580**. Turn left on the footway then first right on a quiet lane. Follow it to a junction, where you turn right, then immediately left. Pass the turning to Cwmsychtyn and continue to another junction, where you take a footpath that uses the driveway of **The Old Farm**, then crosses a lawned area to a stile. Cross a track to enter a field and go diagonally to the far corner. Cross to the next field and head towards the far left corner, then into **Gwalia Wood**.

Follow a path through the wood and into a field. Go diagonally towards the far corner, guided by a group of tall sycamore trees, and then across the next field to a stile giving access to woodland at **Sheep Walk**. Turn left, soon crossing a track and going straight on as indicated by a waymarker. The path is overgrown by brambles, but stick as close to the line of it as you can and you'll soon come to another waymarker, sending you left by a laurel hedge to meet a grassy path. Turn right, right again shortly, still by the hedge, then right once more to join **Offa's Dyke Path** (you will recognise it by the acorn logo that signifies a national trail).

Follow the path beside the prominent earthwork of Offa's Dyke through beautiful **Candy Wood**, above the steep slopes of Craig Forda. The wood is dominated by oaks, but there are some superb beech trees too, which must have been planted, as beech is not native this far north. The beechwoods of the Cotswolds are generally believed to be growing at the beech's natural northern limit, but it does well when planted, not just here in the Marches, but as far north as Scotland. Ignore branching paths and continue through the adjacent **Racecourse Wood** until a stile gives access to **Racecourse Common**. Turn right, leaving Offa's Dyke Path, and follow a waymarked path close by the edge of the common. Ignore branching paths and you will soon find yourself back at the car park.

The Full Monty at Queen's Head

A 19th-century canal village is one of the highlights along the restored Monty.

•DISTANCE•	6½ miles (10.4km)
•MINIMUM TIME•	2hrs 30min
•ASCENT / GRADIENT•	92ft (28m)
•LEVEL OF DIFFICULTY•	
•PATHS•	Tow path, quiet lanes and field paths, 5 stiles
•LANDSCAPE•	Level, low-lying farmland by Montgomery Canal
•SUGGESTED MAP•	aqua3 OS Explorer 240 Oswestry
•START / FINISH•	Grid reference: SJ 338268
•DOG FRIENDLINESS•	Good, but keep close at heel along Woolston Road
•PARKING•	Car park at Queen's Head, between A5 and B5009
•PUBLIC TOILETS•	None on route

BACKGROUND TO THE WALK

Comedians sometimes joke about the bizarre British propensity for grim roadside picnics. I always thought this was a little unfair, until I got off the bus at Queen's Head one day and saw that an official picnic site had been provided, ear-shatteringly sandwiched between Holyhead Road and the truly horrible A5 Oswestry bypass. And disturbingly, it was full of cars and picnickers! But despite this testament to some travellers' poor imaginations, at least Queen's Head is a convenient place to begin this delightful walk along the Montgomery Canal.

Clearing the Way

If you've read Walk 28 you'll know a little about the history of the Monty. This walk explores a recently restored section, so it's worth saying a few words about the restoration work, which was started by the Shropshire Union Canal Society in 1968. One of the most remarkable things is that most of the work has been done by volunteers. The Welshpool stretch was the first to benefit, followed by the locks at Carreghofa (near Llanymynech), while the Inland Waterways Association's Waterway Recovery Group restored the four locks at Frankton Junction, with the aid of volunteer groups from all over the country.

Frankton Locks reopened in 1987. Since then, restoration has continued apace. South of Frankton, a new lock and aqueduct had to be built, but by 1996 the canal was open all the way from Frankton to Queen's Head, where a new bridge was also required. South of Queen's Head, volunteers restored Aston Locks and developed a nature reserve, on the opposite bank to the tow path, as some small compensation for the valuable wildlife habitat that is lost when an overgrown canal is restored. However, from a conservation point of view, the restoration has been disappointing in many ways, despite an agreement in 1984 between British Waterways and the Nature Conservancy Council on the need for careful conservation and sensitive management.

The section south of Queen's Head was reopened in the late 1990s and a highlight of this stretch is Maesbury Marsh, the best surviving canal village on the Monty. It's hard to imagine that this quiet place was once a busy port, but it was the nearest wharf to Oswestry, so trade was brisk. There used to be a factory, warehouse, coal and grain stores and flour mill, as well as workshops and offices. Most of the buildings remain, though converted to other uses. The Navigation Inn still stands by the canal, with the former tow horses' stables round the back, and boatmen's cottages survive too, though now modernised. A crane stands evocatively, if somewhat forlornly, by the wharf.

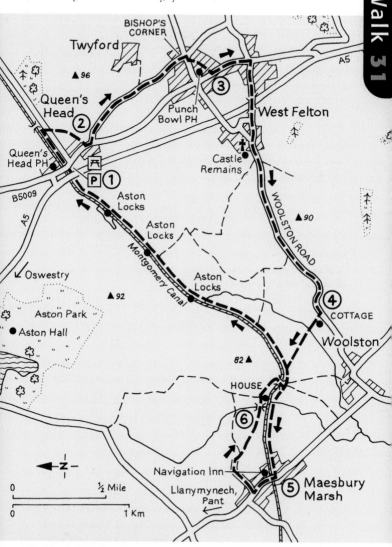

Walk 31 Directions

① Begin by heading north on the tow path: make two right turns to descend to it, then go right again

under **Queen's Head Bridge**. Within a few minutes you will approach another bridge and should look out for a signpost directing you to a footpath across the adjacent road. Climb a stile, then cross a narrow field to another stile, a little to the right. Go diagonally right up a bank and down the other side, to pass through a gappy hawthorn hedge, then continue in the same direction to the far corner of a field. Cross into another field and turn right to the road.

② Turn left, then left again, signposted 'Twyford'. Ignore the Twyford turn a little further on and instead continue to a crossroads (**Bishop's Corner**). Turn right on **School Road**, then immediately left on a grassy path, called **Hicksons Lane**.

> ### WHERE TO EAT AND DRINK ⓘ
> You can choose from the **Queen's Head** at the start, the **Punch Bowl** at West Felton or the attractive **Navigation Inn** right by the canal at Maesbury Marsh. All do food, offer veggie options and welcome children. The first two have large gardens, with a play area at the Punch Bowl.

③ Turn left on **Old Holyhead Road**, then right at a crossroads on **Fox Lane**, soon crossing the main A5 road on a footbridge. Go straight on through **West Felton**, then left on **Woolston Road**. The OS map shows plenty of footpaths, but many are hopelessly obstructed so it is better to stick to the road until such time as things improve.

> ### WHAT TO LOOK FOR ⓘ
> Go to the rear of the churchyard at West Felton and look across a track to the tree-covered mound rising above a moat. This is the remains of a Norman **motte and bailey castle**, typical of hundreds that were built in the borders. The castle would have been built of timber and stood on top of the motte, with wooden bailey walls surrounding the site.

④ Climb a stile in a hedge just before you come to a small stone cottage on the right. Walk across a cattle pasture and go into the next field. You can see a wooden canal bridge now at the far side, near the far left corner. Head towards it and as you get nearer you'll see a stile to the right of the bridge. This gives on to the tow path, where you should turn left.

> ### WHILE YOU'RE THERE ⓘ
> Visit **Llanymynech** and **Pant**, neighbouring border villages with a wealth of industrial remains beside the Monty, particularly a lime processing works at Llanymynech, where you can see the old bottle kilns and a rare rotary kiln. Best of all is the Shropshire Wildlife Trust reserve at Llanymynech Rocks, with its spectacular disused quarries, wonderful views, Offa's Dyke Path and profusion of lime-loving wild flowers in the spring and summer.

⑤ Leave the tow path at **Maesbury Marsh** and walk through the village before taking the first turn right, along **Waen Lane**. This becomes a public bridleway at a cattle grid. A few paces further on, take the footpath that leaves the bridleway at a gate on the right. Head diagonally across a large field to the furthest corner, guided by waymarkers and a vehicle track.

⑥ Cross a footbridge and continue over the next field, then across a stile to join a bridleway. Keep straight on, passing to the left of a house and along field edges until an unsigned but trodden path goes right, to cross the canal at the wooden bridge you saw earlier (► Point ④). Descend some steps on the right and go under the bridge to join the tow path. Follow it back to **Queen's Head**.

Hope for the Dormouse

Stunning countryside in the shadow of Stiperstones.

•DISTANCE•	9½ miles (15.3km)
•MINIMUM TIME•	3hrs 30min
•ASCENT / GRADIENT•	1,279ft (390m) ▲▲▲
•LEVEL OF DIFFICULTY•	👫 👫 👫
•PATHS•	Some boggy areas, streams to ford, route-finding skills required, 38 stiles
•LANDSCAPE•	Pastoral scene of hills and valleys on Welsh border
•SUGGESTED MAP•	aqua3 OS Explorer 216 Welshpool & Montgomery
•START / FINISH•	Grid reference: SJ 350017
•DOG FRIENDLINESS•	Mostly on lead, particularly in nature reserves
•PARKING•	Hope Valley Nature Reserve, signposted from A488
•PUBLIC TOILETS•	None on route

BACKGROUND TO THE WALK

Hope Valley is an ancient woodland of sessile oak, but in the 1960s much of it was felled and replanted with conifers. However, the oaks regenerated from their mossy stumps and Shropshire Wildlife Trust, recognising the potential for restoration, bought the wood in 1981. Most of the conifers have now been removed and Hope Valley is recovering beautifully.

Back from the Brink

The Trust installed nest boxes for birds and in the 1980s a naturalist checking one of them was startled to discover a dormouse. This was an exciting find because dormice were known to be in serious decline nationally, and there had been speculation that they might have gone altogether from Shropshire. Since then much research has been done to find out exactly where dormice do occur in the county. One way to detect their presence is to look for discarded hazelnut shells. Dormice nibble them in a unique style, leaving a perfectly smooth oval hole with an inner rim.

The good news is that over 30 dormouse colonies have been discovered, several of them in the valleys round Stiperstones. The bad news is that coniferisation, hedge removal, flail cutting and other modern practices have left these colonies isolated and vulnerable. The Trust is working with local landowners to restore hedgerows linking woods, to maintain mature hedgerows and to carry out appropriate woodland management. You're not likely to see any of Hope Valley's dormice, shy and famously sleepy as these endearing mammals are, but it's good to know they're there.

Walk 32 Directions

① Follow a bridleway through the reserve. Ignore all branching paths and eventually meet a lane. Turn left. After passing the **Stables Inn** you'll see two footpaths on the right. Take the right-hand path, going forward to a hedge corner and then following the hedge to the field corner.

② Follow the left-hand edge of the next field until a pair of stiles gives access to a terraced path going down a pasture. Cross a brook by a large oak and follow a track towards a farm. Cross a stile, turn left and follow the waymarkers to a lane.

③ Turn left, then first right on a track as far as a stile. Turn right along a field edge, and past a cottage, until the hedge turns a corner. Carry on across the field,

climbing to a stile/gate. The path continues across a track and two more fields, then through a copse to a driveway. Turn left to a lane, then right, keeping straight on along a track 'unsuitable for motors'.

④ Cross a lane and climb up **Bromlow Callow**, aiming left of the fenced Scots pines on the summit. Follow the fence round to a stile and descend to a lane. Turn left, then left again on a footpath,

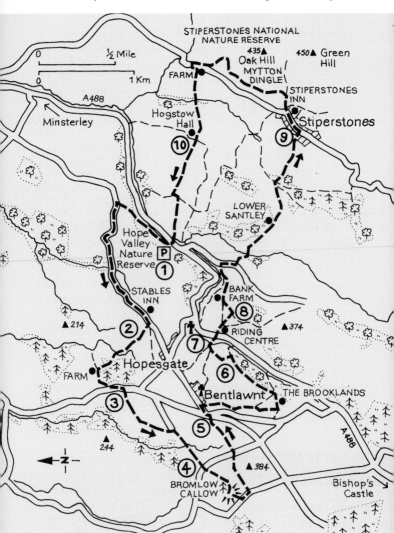

WHERE TO EAT AND DRINK ℹ

The **Stables Inn** is homely and welcoming. Home-cooked meals and bar snacks are available. You can't take your dog inside, but there is a garden. There are well-stocked and very characterful shops at Bentlawnt and Stiperstones (which also act as tourist information points), and the excellent **Stiperstones Inn** (► Walk 33).

gradually veering away from the dry-stone wall to a stile at the far side. Cross another field to a lane and continue opposite, along field edges to a driveway.

⑤ Turn right to a lane, then left through a crossroads, towards **Hopesgate**. Turn first right on a bridleway and follow it to a T-junction, then go left. After passing **The Brooklands** it bears left along the edge of a field, then straight on across more fields.

⑥ When you come to an old quarry turn left down a bank (the ground is uneven), past a fallen birch tree and across a field. At the far side a muddy path descends right to a brook. Turn right until you see a stile at the other side, then ford the brook. Cross the stile and turn right to reach a footbridge across the brook.

⑦ Walk to the **A488** and cross to a path opposite. Go past a riding centre, then into a field. Follow the

WHILE YOU'RE THERE ℹ

From Bromlow Callow, two hills dominate the view to the south. The big one is **Corndon**, just over the border. The smaller one is **Stapeley Hill**, well worth a visit for Mitchell's Fold, an impressive stone circle erected in the Bronze Age. Cairns, standing stones and pillar mounds also dot this atmospheric hilltop.

left-hand edge to a stile. Turn left to a fence end, then climb a wooded slope to a stile. Bear left uphill to another stile (some trial and error may be necessary here) and on through dense bracken to another.

⑧ Turn left until the fence ends and climb the bank on your right. Descend to a track to the right of **Bank Farm** and follow it down to a lane. Turn right, then first left on a bridleway. Bear slightly right across a field to enter a wood. Descend to cross a brook and then climb up to another field. Bear right, with woodland on your left, cross a bridge, skirt **Lower Santley farm** and keep to the field edge until the way enters a wood. Turn second right on a path to **Stiperstones**.

WHAT TO LOOK FOR ℹ

Wild flowers struggle to survive in conifer woods because insufficient light gets to the floor in spring. Now that the conifers have mostly been removed, Hope Valley overflows with bluebells in spring, as well as species considered indicative of ancient woodland, such as yellow archangel and early purple orchid.

⑨ Turn left, past the pub and shop, then right at **Mytton Dingle**. After passing through a gate, turn left into **Stiperstones National Nature Reserve**. Follow the path round Oak Hill, then down to a road. Cross to a bridleway and turn left. Turn right at a T-junction, through a farmyard, then along a track.

⑩ Reaching a junction, turn left for a few paces, then right on a footpath. Cross four fields, then go left on a track. Pass through a gateway, then turn right, following the right-hand hedge to a gate. Turn left to the **A488** and cross to the **Hope Valley Nature Reserve**.

Back to Purple

From the mining village of Snailbeach to the dragon's crest of Stiperstones.

•DISTANCE•	4½ miles (7.2km)
•MINIMUM TIME•	2hrs
•ASCENT / GRADIENT•	951ft (290m) ▲▲ ▲
•LEVEL OF DIFFICULTY•	🏃🏃 🏃🏃 🏃🏃
•PATHS•	Good paths across pasture, moorland and woodland, 1 stile
•LANDSCAPE•	Shropshire's second highest hill, with great views
•SUGGESTED MAP•	aqua3 OS Explorer 216 Welshpool & Montgomery
•START / FINISH•	Grid reference: SJ 373022
•DOG FRIENDLINESS•	On lead in nature reserve and near livestock
•PARKING•	Car park at Snailbeach
•PUBLIC TOILETS•	At car park

BACKGROUND TO THE WALK

At first sight it looks as though this walk will be all about industrial archaeology, for it begins at Snailbeach, formerly one of the most important lead mines in Britain. Mining ceased long ago and the derelict landscape has been transformed into one of the most fascinating post-industrial sites in the Midlands, complete with engine houses, loco sheds, compressors, crushers and tramways.

But there's another sort of transformation going on near by, on the rugged moorland ridge of Stiperstones. This is the Back to Purple project which aims to restore Stiperstones to its full glory. The quartzite ridge was formed 480 million years ago. During the last ice age it stood out above the glaciers and was subjected to constant freezing and thawing, which shattered much of the quartzite into a mass of scree surrounding several residual tors and leaving the top of the ridge jagged as a dragon's or dinosaur's crest. Subsequent soil formation has been so slow that much of the scree remains on the surface, largely unvegetated. Where soil has formed, it is thin, acidic and nutrient-poor, sufficient only to support a limited range of plants. Over much of the summit area the vegetation is dominated by heather and whinberry, with some crowberry and cowberry. At one time, this meant that in summer most of Stiperstones, except the very crest, turned a glorious purple.

Part of Stiperstones is protected, but modern agriculture and silviculture have encroached, fragmenting the ridge with areas of improved grassland and conifers so that it no longer turns nearly so purple. But things are changing. For several years it has been the subject of the ambitious Back to Purple initiative, managed by a partnership of English Nature, Forest Enterprise and Shropshire Wildlife Trust. Thousands of conifers have been felled, including the unsightly Gatten Plantation, which lay just below the summit ridge (and is still shown on OS maps). On the southern part of the ridge, further conifers have been cleared to reveal the jagged outline of Nipstone Rock, hidden for many years. Thousands of heather seedlings have been planted in these areas to supplement natural regeneration.

Work is also being undertaken to restore and protect other habitats which lie below the summit ridge such as herb-rich grasslands, hay meadows, wet flushes and woodland. The flora of these areas includes bog cotton, heath bedstraw and the increasingly scarce mountain pansy.

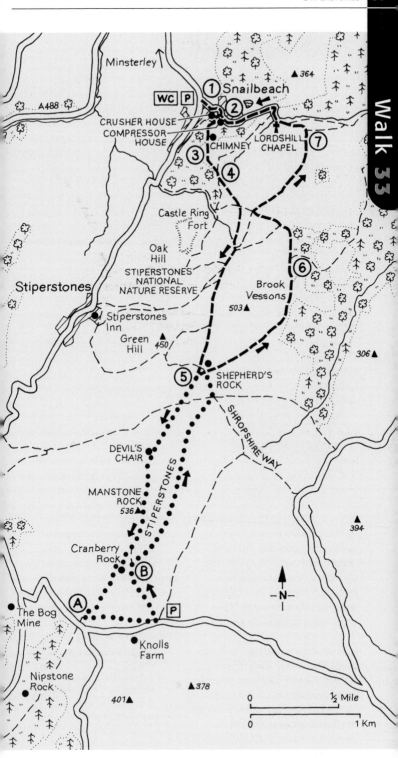

Walk 33 Directions

① Take the **Lordshill lane** opposite the car park, then join a parallel footpath on the left. Rejoining the lane, cross to the site of the locomotive shed, then continue up the lane, noticing the green arrows directing you to the main sites.

② Turn right on a track between the **crusher house** and the **compressor house**. A few paces past the compressor house, turn left up steps. At the top, turn right, then soon left up more steps. Turn left to the Cornish engine house, then right and continue through woodland. A short detour leads to the smelter chimney, otherwise it's uphill all the way.

> **WHERE TO EAT AND DRINK** ⓘ
> There is nothing along the way, but you are not far from the **Stiperstones Inn**, open for food and drink from 8 in the morning until 10 at night. It also acts as a tourist information point, sells maps and walks leaflets and offers B&B. Dogs are allowed in the bar, but not the lounge bar. There are also shops and pubs in **Minsterley**, north of Snailbeach.

③ A sign indicates that you're entering **Stiperstones National Nature Reserve** (NNR). The woods give way to bracken, broom and bramble before you cross a stile to the open hill. A path climbs the slope ahead to a stile/gate at the top.

④ Two paths are waymarked. Take the left-hand one, which runs between a fence and the rim of the spectacular dingle on your right. The path then climbs away from the dingle and meets a rutted track. Turn right. As the path climbs you can see the rock tors on the summit. There's also one much closer to hand, isolated from the rest. This is **Shepherd's Rock**.

⑤ Just beyond Shepherd's Rock is a junction marked by a cairn. Turn right here, then fork left to go round the other side of the rock. Leave the NNR at a gate/stile. The path runs to the left, shortly bordered by a hawthorn hedge. You'll soon see that this is an old green lane, lined at various points by either hedges/trees on both sides, one line of trees or a tumbledown stone wall.

> **WHILE YOU'RE THERE** ⓘ
> Explore the Snailbeach site, then visit **The Bog Mine**, a little further south. There's a seasonal visitor centre, waymarked walks and mine workings. Be there at dusk if you'd like to see some bats – they live in one of the mine tunnels (known as The Somme) which has been blocked by a grid for their protection.

⑥ At a junction take the left-hand path back into the NNR. At the next junction, fork right to leave the NNR at a gate by a plantation. Go diagonally across a field to a track; turn right, going back across the field, through the plantation, then across pasture on a bridleway.

⑦ Fork left at a bridleway junction and continue past **Lordshill chapel** to a lane. Turn right and stay with it as it swings left to **Snailbeach**.

> **WHAT TO LOOK FOR** ⓘ
> **Lordshill Baptist chapel**, built in 1833 and enlarged in 1873, was in regular use until recently. After a period of disuse it was restored and Sunday meetings are held here most summers. It also appeared in the film of Mary Webb's *Gone to Earth*, which was set on Stiperstones (▶ Walk 26).

Sitting in the Devil's Chair at Stiperstones

Extend your walk on Stiperstones to include the exciting rocky tors on the summit of Shropshire's second highest hill.

See map and information panel for Walk 33

•DISTANCE•	3½ miles (5.7km)
•MINIMUM TIME•	1hr 15min
•ASCENT / GRADIENT•	429ft (131m) ▲ ▲ ▲
•LEVEL OF DIFFICULTY•	🚶 🚶 🚶

Walk 34 Directions (Walk 33 option)

You could do this loop as a walk in its own right by starting at the car park next to the road bisecting Stiperstones (grid ref SJ 369976), but it would be a great shame to miss out on the main route. Doing the two together is a much better way of fully appreciating these dramatic quartzite outcrops.

Assuming you are doing the main walk, leave it at Point ⑤ and carry straight on towards the line of tors along the Stiperstones crest. The most striking of the tors is the **Devil's Chair**, while the highest, topped by a trig pillar, is **Manstone Rock**. All sorts of myths have been inspired by these rocks, many of them concerning Wild Edric, a Saxon nobleman who briefly, but fiercely, resisted the Normans before capitulating in 1070.

The path is to the left of the tors at first, but eventually you will find it easier to change to the other side. When you come to the NNR boundary (Point Ⓐ), turn left on a path that runs close to the perimeter. It leads to a staggered cross tracks near a car park.

Turn left and climb back up towards the ridge until you come to a junction marked by a large cairn (Point Ⓑ). Turn right, ignore a path forking left and stay on the main track by a stone wall. The land to your right was conifer plantation until recently, but is now being restored to heathland.

Continue to a junction with two paths – the Shropshire Way and another one going to **Shepherd's Rock**. Take the Shepherd's Rock path to return to Point ⑤ of Walk 33.

WHAT TO LOOK FOR

Legend has it that if you visit Stiperstones on a dark night you will see the Devil and his cronies gathered at the **Devil's Chair**, while witches congregate at **Manstone Rock** on the longest night each year. And if you should see an army on the move you will know England is in danger, for that is when Wild Edric and his men will emerge from the lead mines to tackle the enemy, in a very Arthurian twist to Edric's story (so where were they in 1940?).

Walk 35

The Lion of Pontesbury

A short but spectacular walk that includes a wonderful nature reserve at Earl's Hill.

•DISTANCE•	4 miles (6.4km)
•MINIMUM TIME•	2hrs
•ASCENT / GRADIENT•	984ft (300m) ▲▲▲
•LEVEL OF DIFFICULTY•	👫 👫 👫
•PATHS•	Easily followed, may be boggy by Habberley Brook, 7 stiles
•LANDSCAPE•	Hills, oakwoods and plantation above deeply cut valley
•SUGGESTED MAP•	aqua3 OS Explorer 241 Shrewsbury
•START / FINISH•	Grid reference: SJ 408056
•DOG FRIENDLINESS•	Can run free in forests, but keep under close control around livestock and in nature reserve
•PARKING•	Forestry Commission car park at Pontesford Hill – turn off A488 at Pontesford, by Rea Valley Tractors
•PUBLIC TOILETS•	None on route

Walk 35 Directions

Earl's Hill was created in the Precambrian period, about 650 million years ago, and is volcanic in origin. Iron-Age people built a fort on top in about 600 BC, and there are intriguing local legends and customs attached to the hill, one of them involving a search each Palm Sunday for a golden arrow, a story that was the inspiration behind Mary Webb's novel *The Golden Arrow* (► Walk 26). Mary lived in nearby Pontesbury for a time and made long walks into the hills.

Earl's Hill is often said to resemble a sleeping dragon or lion and, from certain angles, you can just about see the lion. More prosaically, it is both a Scheduled Ancient Monument (because of the Iron-Age fort) and a Site of Special Scientific Interest (SSSI) for its wildlife value. It became Shropshire Wildlife Trust's first nature reserve

back in 1964; an auspicious start, given the quality of the site. The adjoining Pontesford Hill, where the walk begins, is leased and managed by Forest Enterprise.

Take a bridleway, which runs beyond the timber vehicle barrier. Go left at a fork and shortly cross a stile half-hidden below the bank on your left. Turn right across a field to join a bridle track. Turn right, following the bridleway through farmland and then into a wood. Keep left, descending through

WHILE YOU'RE THERE
Wroxeter is a hamlet by the Severn, south east of Shrewsbury, which would be unremarkable but for its superb Roman remains. It was the site of Viroconium, the fourth largest city in Roman Britain. English Heritage looks after the site, which includes a high basilica wall and the excavated remains of municipal baths, an exercise hall, market hall and forum. There's a small on-site museum too.

oakwoods above the steep valley of **Habberley Brook** and soon branching right to cross the brook at a footbridge. Bear right uphill, eventually leaving woodland for plantation. Ignore any minor paths and climb to a junction with a wide path. Keep left, staying on the bridleway, which leaves the trees and continues as a hedged track towards the hamlet of **Oaks**.

WHERE TO EAT AND DRINK

You will find plenty of choice in Pontesbury, such as the **Horseshoes Inn**, the **Nags Head**, the **Railway Inn** and the **Red Lion**, which is very attractive, with masses of flowers brightening the front. The **Plough** on Habberley Road has a quiet, pleasant location and almost all the pubs have gardens. Pontesbury also has shops, a chippy and a Chinese restaurant.

Don't join the lane at Oaks, but turn right, still on the bridleway which skirts round tree-crowned **Church Hill** before descending into plantation once more. Soon after the bridleway passes some buildings and makes a sharp left turn, start looking for a footpath on the right. Follow it diagonally left down two fields to the far corner of the second and then into forest again.

Turn right to find a footbridge and cross **Habberley Brook**. Go up a slope to a bridleway junction at a gate/stile; keep straight on towards the south end of **Earl's Hill**. Go through a gate by a dead oak tree and follow the right-hand hedge, then continue along the edge of a wood until a gate gives access to it.

Go straight on to pass through another gate, then turn right and start climbing across the southern end of the hill. Take the second path

on the left, which climbs very steeply to the top of the hill, passing through the Iron-Age fort to reach the summit. Ecologically, Earl's Hill is most valuable for its great variety of habitats, and you can see most of them from here, ranging from fast-flowing Habberley Brook through mixed woodland, anthill meadows, scrub, scree and cliffs to the acid grassland that surrounds you on the summit. The anthills, made by yellow hill ants, are composed of well-drained, sandy soil which heats up quickly in the first sunny days of spring, supporting flowers which appreciate a little extra warmth, such as wild thyme, heath bedstraw and heath speedwell. In this way, each anthill forms a distinct micro-habitat with a different range of flowers than the surrounding meadowland.

Descend from the top in a northerly direction, across the top of **Pontesford Hill** (with more prehistoric earthworks on your left – outworks of the main fort) and down through the conifers to meet a path by another prehistoric fort at the northern end of the hill. Turn right, then left to rejoin the bridleway by which you originally left the hill. The car park can be found to the left.

WHAT TO LOOK FOR

Earl's Hill and Habberley Brook are rich in all kinds of wildlife. Rarer species include the **grayling butterfly**, which inhabits the bare top, and the **common lizard**, which is no longer at all common. A good place to see a lizard is the exposed scree below the summit to the east, but you would have to approach very slowly and quietly to have any chance of sighting one. **Dormice** live in the woods on the west side of the hill, but they're even more elusive than lizards.

Life and Death in Bishop's Castle

A quirky, colourful border town on the edge of Clun Forest and the glorious green hills that enfold it.

•DISTANCE•	7 miles (11.3km)
•MINIMUM TIME•	2hrs 30min
•ASCENT / GRADIENT•	738ft (225m) ▲ ▲ ▲
•LEVEL OF DIFFICULTY•	🚶 🚶 🚶
•PATHS•	Waymarking can be patchy, path near Woodbatch cropped over, some gates to climb, about 10 stiles
•LANDSCAPE•	Gently hilly and mostly pastoral, with great views
•SUGGESTED MAP•	aqua3 OS Explorer 216 Welshpool & Montgomery
•START / FINISH•	Grid reference: SO 324886
•DOG FRIENDLINESS•	Can run free on track between Bankshead and Shepherdswhim, livestock elsewhere
•PARKING•	Car park off Station Street
•PUBLIC TOILETS•	At car park and by Market Square

BACKGROUND TO THE WALK

Bishop's Castle is one of the smallest towns in the country. If it was in the south east, it would be smaller than many a neighbouring village. But a town it is, and one of enormous charm and fascination. There is nothing ordinary about Bishop's Castle. Its documented history began in Saxon times when Egwin Shakehead, grateful for having been miraculously cured of the palsy at St Ethelbert's tomb in Hereford Cathedral, gave what is now Bishop's Castle to the Bishop of Hereford. The castle was built around 1100 by another Bishop of Hereford, but very little remains of it today. What does survive can be viewed from Castle Street.

From Rotten Borough to Colourful Town

In the early Middle Ages, the parish of Bishop's Castle was partly in England, partly in Wales, so territorial dispute was a way of life. In later years, after peace came to the Marches, Bishop's Castle acquired notoriety as the smallest and rottenest of rotten boroughs, a term which denoted electoral corruption. From 1585 this tiny town returned two MPs to Parliament. Local landowners (including Robert Clive, better known as Clive of India) expended vast sums of money on buying voters and seats to increase their power. In 1726, one rejected candidate was able to prove that of the 52 people voting for his rival, 51 had received bribes. The Reform Act of 1832 put an end to this kind of thing, and Bishop's Castle was disenfranchised.

More recently, it has attracted artists, writers, musicians and craftspeople and has reinvented itself as a town of fairs, festivals and fêtes. Dozens of colourful, hand-painted banners are hung along the main street for events such as the Michaelmas Fair. It must surely be the most colourful place in Shropshire, with buildings painted in all the colours of the rainbow. The Six Bells Inn looks magnificent in yellow, and the violin maker's house at the top of the town is a delightful bluey-purple. Rather more eccentric is the house painted white with green circles – but after a while it starts to look almost normal, such is the effect of Bishop's Castle. High Street boasts the entertaining Purple Funeral Company, with purple and gold paintwork and vividly painted coffins in the window. The Tutankhamen style is particularly striking, and the seascapes are lovely too, though you can have whatever you want on your coffin, including football colours. They are the work of funerary artist Carol Aston, who says Bishop's Castle is a 'very accepting place'.

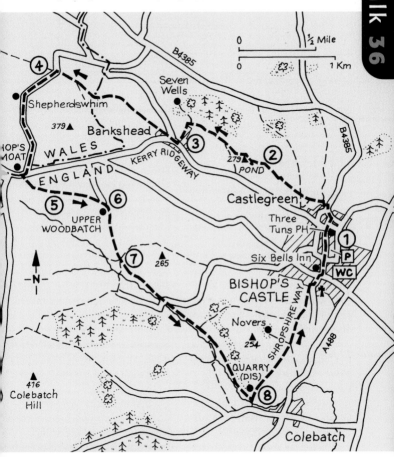

Walk 36 Directions

① Walk up **Church Street**, High Street and Bull Street, then go left along **Bull Lane** to **Castlegreen**. Turn right, then left after No 11 on a footpath which leads to a stile and a choice of routes. Take the left-hand path, crossing two fields, then going straight on along a green

lane. When it ends, go through a gate and along a field edge to a stile.

② Turn right in the next field, cross a stile at the top and go obliquely left over another field to a fence corner. Follow the fence/hedge past a pond to a stile. Go obliquely left across the highest point of the next field, then down to a gate halfway along the far hedge. Go diagonally right across another field to meet a hedge, next to a line of crab apple trees. Follow the hedge to a track and turn left to meet a road.

③ Turn right, immediately right again and then left on to a lane, which soon becomes a track. It descends into woodland, crosses the border into Wales and eventually meets a lane.

> **WHILE YOU'RE THERE** ⓘ
> Learn about local history at the **House on Crutches Museum**, the timber-framed building overhanging the cobbles at the top of High Street. Or find out about the Bishop's Castle Railway at the **Rail and Transport Museum**. The **Beer and Brewing Museum** at the Three Tuns is a must for real ale enthusiasts.

④ Turn left and walk up to meet a road, the **Kerry Ridgeway**, at **Bishop's Moat**, where you cross back into England. Turn right, then through the first gate on the left (take care: it hangs from one hinge only). Go diagonally left to the end of a line of hawthorn trees, then continue in the same direction over another field to meet the far hedge where there's a kink in it.

⑤ Go diagonally across a third field to meet a line of trees which leads to a gate. Continue down the next field to the far right corner, walking through one of those scrap-metal collections that many farmers seem to love so much.

> **WHAT TO LOOK FOR** ⓘ
> The tree-covered mound at Bishop's Moat is all that remains of a Norman **motte and bailey castle** which was a more important defence than the castle at Bishop's Castle. It was originally called Bishop's Motte and was probably built between 1085 and 1100. It commands an extensive view of the Welsh Camlad Valley from its border position on the Kerry Ridgeway, once a prehistoric trading route and later a drove road.

⑥ Meeting a farm lane, turn right through the farmyard at **Upper Woodbatch**, going past a collection of barns. As you approach the final group, you can see the track descending by a fence – the right of way, however, is on the other side of the fence, so go through a gate to join it and follow it down through two fields towards a brook.

⑦ About 120yds (110m) before you reach the brook, turn left across the field. Go through a gate at the far side and continue across two more fields to meet a lane. Join the **Shropshire Way** opposite, following it along the bottom of several fields, quite close to the brook.

⑧ After passing an abandoned quarry, turn left uphill and head for **Bishop's Castle**, soon joining a track that leads to **Field Lane**. Follow this to Church Lane, which leads to **Church Street** and the beginning of the walk.

> **WHERE TO EAT AND DRINK** ⓘ
> The **Six Bells** and the **Three Tuns** are both famous for their on-site breweries producing traditional ales. The food sounds interesting too, from Shropshire fidget pie to Big Nev's bangers (sausages made with ale) at the Six Bells. There are several other pubs, and a range of coffee houses, such as the wonderful **Yarborough House**, where they also sell second-hand books, records, CDs and fair trade goods, such as tea, coffee, chocolate and a range of gifts, cards and clothes. **Poppy House** and the new **Pickled Onion** are great too, each with an art gallery and a garden.

Sheep Shape the Mynd

Upland heath, prehistoric remains and magnificent views.

•DISTANCE•	7½ miles (12.1km)
•MINIMUM TIME•	3hrs
•ASCENT / GRADIENT•	1,545ft (471m) ▲▲▲
•LEVEL OF DIFFICULTY•	🚶🚶 🚶🚶 🚶🚶
•PATHS•	Mostly moorland paths and tracks, 3 stiles
•LANDSCAPE•	Moorland plateau with extensive views
•SUGGESTED MAP•	aqua3 OS Explorer 217 The Long Mynd & Wenlock Edge
•START / FINISH•	Grid reference: SO 453936
•DOG FRIENDLINESS•	On lead between March and July on the Long Mynd
•PARKING•	Easthope Road car park, Church Stretton
•PUBLIC TOILETS•	At car park

BACKGROUND TO THE WALK

The Long Mynd derives its name from 'mynydd', a Welsh word for mountain. It's not a mountain though, but an undulating plateau cut by steep-sided valleys known as batches or hollows, forming one of the most distinctive and individual upland ranges in Britain. Clothed in heather, whinberry, bracken and wiry moorland grasses, with a scattering of stunted, wind-contorted hawthorns and the occasional holly or rowan, it constitutes our most southerly grouse moor, though active management for grouse ceased in 1989. While the grouse skulk in the heather, exploding into a frenzy of alarm calls and occasional flight if you venture too close, the skies above are regally patrolled by species such as raven, buzzard and kestrel.

Ancient Settlement

The Mynd is a wonderful place, which is sometimes referred to as the last wilderness in the Midlands. In truth, however, this is no wilderness. It has been subject to human use and, to some extent, human occupation, since the earliest times. It is liberally dotted with prehistoric remains, including Bronze-Age tumuli and dykes, with an Iron-Age fort on Bodbury Hill. An ancient road, the Port Way, runs along the top of the Long Mynd and has been in use for at least 4,000 years. There are more than 40 tumuli beside it or close to it, while the occasional stone tool has also been found. It was probably a trading route (port means market) and the southern section of it was later used by cattle drovers coming from mid-Wales.

The Mynd is an upland heath today and this may be how it was when neolithic people first came here. During the Bronze Age, upland oak forest spread across the plateau, but this had been cleared by the Iron Age, when the Mynd was the home of a pastoral community practising transhumance – the movement of stock into the hills for the summer months. By the Middle Ages, parts of the Mynd had become permanent sheepwalk and this pattern of land use persists. Most of it is common land, owned by the National Trust, and farmers in surrounding villages retain rights of common, allowing them to graze sheep and ponies on the hill. Nowadays, there are few ponies, but very many sheep. The Mynd is seriously overgrazed, which means the glorious mosaic of heather, whinberry and other heathland plants is in retreat before a rampant tide of bracken. The Trust, long concerned about this, has finally secured what may be a solution. In 2002, the government announced grant assistance to compensate farmers for reducing the numbers of sheep on the Long Mynd. The Trust has also closed car parks, which shouldn't have been allowed in the first place, and is helping to fund shuttle bus services. The former car parks are already returning to heath.

Walk 37 Directions

① Walk up **Lion Meadow** to **High Street** and turn right. Turn left at **The Square**, go past the church and straight on into **Rectory Field**. Walk

to the top left corner, then turn right by the edge, soon entering **Old Rectory Wood**. The path descends to a junction, where you turn left, soon crossing **Town Brook**, then climbing again to a gate on to the **Long Mynd**.

② Go forward beside the brook to meet iron railings, then continue in the same direction with the brook on your left. After an almost imperceptible height gain, the path begins to climb more steeply and heads away from the brook. Eventually the path and brook meet up again near the head of the latter.

WHERE TO EAT AND DRINK ⓘ
Both the **Green Dragon** and the **Ragleth Inn** at Little Stretton are very popular. The Dragon is a free house with a beer garden, and does food daily, including a children's menu and veggie dishes. The Ragleth Inn welcomes grubby boots and wellingtons, children under 14 and dogs of the well-behaved variety in the bar. It does snacks and meals, and has a large garden and children's play area. There's also a village shop.

---

③ The path crosses the brook. Proceed a further 50yds (46m) to a junction marked by the first in a succession of pink-banded posts. Just follow these posts now, gaining height very gradually again. Ignore branching paths and, after ascending a slight rise, you'll see the summit ahead on the left.

④ Meet an unfenced road about 100yds (91m) left of a junction. Turn left, ignore a path to Little Stretton and go straight on when the road bends left, joining a bridleway. At the next junction, turn left to the summit, then keep straight on to the **Port Way**. Turn right past the site of **Pole Cottage**.

⑤ Turn left on a footpath, signposted to Little Stretton. It's a wide rutted track and when it forks go left – you can see the path ahead, cutting a green swath over the shoulder of **Round Hill**. Go straight on at a junction, then descend to

Cross Dyke (a Bronze-Age earthwork). After the dyke the path ascends briefly, but soon levels out, then begins its descent, eventually following a brook to **Little Stretton**.

⑥ Cross at a footbridge by a ford and turn right on a lane, but only for a few paces. Look out for a footpath on the left. It climbs by a field edge to the top corner, then turns left, following the top of a steep slope to a pasture. Follow the right-hand edge of this until the path enters woodland. Descend to **Ludlow Road**.

WHILE YOU'RE THERE ⓘ
The walk bypasses the village of **Little Stretton**, but it's worth a detour if you like period architecture. There are several charming buildings, including the picturesque Manor House, built around 1600. Don't be fooled by the pretty, timber-framed, thatched church though – it was built in 1903.

---

⑦ Immediately join a bridleway next to the footpath. It climbs into woodland, emerging at the far side to meet a track, which soon becomes a road. As it bends to the right there's access left to **Rectory Field**. Descend to **The Square**, turn right on **High Street** and left on **Lion Meadow** to the car park.

WHAT TO LOOK FOR ⓘ
The **ring ouzel**, or mountain blackbird, occurs on the Long Mynd. It is similar to a blackbird, but with a white half-moon just below the throat. Fewer than 1,000 pairs breed nationally and it is in rapid decline. The Long Mynd Breeding Bird Project is assessing breeding success and habitat requirements. If you see a ring ouzel, please note the location and report it – contact details are given on a notice next to the shuttle bus stop at Pole Cottage.

Shapely Seductive Strettons

If you like proper pointy hills, the enticing Strettons will make your day.

•DISTANCE•	6 miles (9.7km)
•MINIMUM TIME•	3hrs
•ASCENT / GRADIENT•	1,060ft (323m) ▲▲ ▲▲ ▲
•LEVEL OF DIFFICULTY•	🚶🚶 🚶🚶 🚶
•PATHS•	Good paths through pasture and woodland, 14 stiles
•LANDSCAPE•	Beautiful range of hills overlooking the Stretton Gap
•SUGGESTED MAP•	aqua3 OS Explorer 217 The Long Mynd & Wenlock Edge
•START / FINISH•	Grid reference: SO 453936
•DOG FRIENDLINESS•	Under close control near livestock
•PARKING•	Easthope Road car park, Church Stretton
•PUBLIC TOILETS•	At car park

BACKGROUND TO THE WALK

Squeezed between the heathery bulk of the Long Mynd and the enticing Stretton Hills lies Church Stretton. This small market town makes an ideal base for a few days of quality walking. If you've done Walk 37, you'll be familiar with the Long Mynd and you may have looked across the Stretton Gap at Caer Caradoc and its neighbours and thought you'd like to know them better. If you consulted an OS map you might have been disappointed at the relative scarcity of footpaths across the tops. Fortunately, that's not a problem as there has been permissive access to these hills for many years. Please bear in mind, though, that it's a privilege, not a right, and don't endanger it by letting your dog roam loose around sheep.

Geological Fault

The Strettons may well be the shapeliest hills in the county. Or, at least, three of them are: Ragleth Hill, Caer Caradoc and The Lawley, which run in a north–south alignment to the east of Church Stretton. Basically, they are hog's-backs, very much like The Wrekin (► Walk 1). But, also like The Wrekin, catch them from the right angle (end-on is best, or check out Caer Caradoc from The Cwms) and they look almost conical, with an alluring mini-mountain shape that screams 'Climb me'. If you do climb one of them, for instance Caer Caradoc, and look north, you will see The Wrekin, lying on exactly the same alignment, and taking much the same form as Caer Caradoc and The Lawley.

The Strettons are also of volcanic origin, like The Wrekin; long, narrow ridges of resistant Precambrian rock, which was thrust up from the earth's core by movements along the Church Stretton fault. This break in the earth's crust has been traced from Staffordshire to South Wales, but it is here in Shropshire that its effects are most noticeable, where the hard Precambrian rocks are brought up against much softer rocks, such as limestones. If you look at the OS map you will notice a line of springs marked along the western slopes of Caer Caradoc. This marks the line of the fault. If you walked along the footpath that runs below the springs, you would see some small quarries where earlier generations of farmers dug out the soft limestone to make agricultural lime to sweeten the acidic soils that prevail in the area.

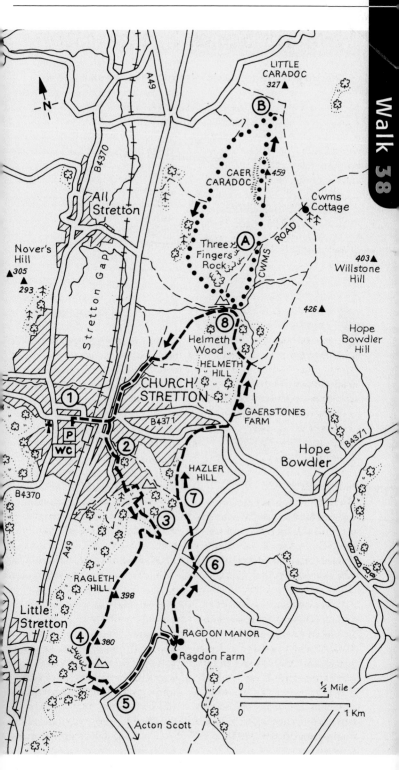

N

LITTLE
CARADOC
327 ▲

Ⓑ

CAER
CARADOC
459 ▲

Cwms
Cottage

Ⓐ

Three
Fingers
Rock

CWMS ROAD

403 ▲
Willstone
Hill

426 ▲

Hope
Bowdler
Hill

Nover's
Hill
▲305

293

A49

B4370

All
Stretton

Stretton Gap

Ⓐ

Ⓑ

Helmeth
Wood

HELMETH
HILL

CHURCH
STRETTON

GAERSTONES
FARM

Hope
Bowdler

B4371

Ⓐ1

P

WC

B4371

Ⓐ2

Ⓐ3

HAZLER
HILL

Ⓐ7

B4370

A49

RAGLETH
HILL
398 ▲

Ⓐ6

Little
Stretton

Ⓐ4
▲380

RAGDON MANOR

Ragdon Farm

Ⓐ5

Acton Scott

0   1/2 Mile

0   1 Km

Walk 38 | **Walk 38 Directions**

① Walk along **Easthope Road** to **Sandford Avenue** and turn right past the train station. Cross the **A49**, proceed along Sandford Avenue, then turn right on **Watling Street South**. Turn left by a post box, fork right on **Clive Avenue**, and shortly left on **Ragleth Road**.

② Turn right into a Woodland Trust reserve, **Philla's Grove**. Keep left at a fork, climbing by the edge of the wood, and left again at the next junction. Leave the wood at a stile and turn right on a footpath. After a level section, the path climbs steeply to a stile. Turn right for a few paces, then fork left to follow a higher path, which goes by the left-hand fence through woodland.

> **WHILE YOU'RE THERE** ⓘ
> Take the kids to **Acton Scott Historic Working Farm**, south of Church Stretton, which re-creates daily life on an upland farm in the late 19th century. There are rare breeds too, such as longhorn cattle, Tamworth pigs and Shropshire sheep.

③ When the path emerges on to the open hillside, keep straight on as far as a stile, but don't cross it. Turn your back on it and follow a trodden path up **Ragleth Hill**, then walk along the spine of the hill.

④ A pole marks the southern summit (the smaller of two), but the way down isn't obvious. Go left, across a rocky area to the far fence, then follow it down to the corner where a stile gives access to a field. Turn left across the field corner, cross another stile and climb to the top left corner of the next field. Go straight on to the far left corner of another field and join a lane.

⑤ Turn left, then first right to **Ragdon Manor**, where you take a footpath on the left through the farmyard. Cross a stile and go straight across a field to a gap at the far side. Keep on along the edges of two more fields.

> **WHAT TO LOOK FOR** ⓘ
> If you are unconvinced by the power of sheep to shape a landscape, take a look at **Helmeth Wood**. It's easy to visit from the bridleway round Helmeth Hill. While the other Strettons are mainly covered in short, springy turf, this one is entirely wooded, and there's only one reason for that – the fence that keeps sheep out.

⑥ Turn left on a lane and go across a junction to a footpath on the right. The path goes diagonally across a field to the far corner, crosses a lane and continues opposite. Walk through gorse and bracken to a gate, beyond which the path continues through woodland.

⑦ Approaching a second gate, don't go through, but turn right to contour round **Hazler Hill**. Turn right at a lane, walk to a junction and cross to a bridleway opposite, which passes **Gaerstones Farm**. After Caer Caradoc comes into view, look for a bridleway branching left to a gate/stile about 40yds (37m) away. The bridleway descends past **Helmeth Hill** to meet another bridleway at the point where this is crossed by a brook.

⑧ Turn left, soon emerging from woodland into pasture. Keep on in much the same direction, a fence on your left. The path leads to a lane where you turn left to return to **Church Stretton**. Turn right at **Sandford Avenue**, cross the main road, pass the station and go left on **Easthope Road** to the car park.

From Cwms to Caer Caradoc

A short, sharp climb brings the highest of the Strettons within reach.
See map and information panel for Walk 38

•DISTANCE•	2½ miles (4km)
•MINIMUM TIME•	1hr
•ASCENT / GRADIENT•	767ft (234m) ▲▲ ▲▲ ▲
•LEVEL OF DIFFICULTY•	🚶🚶 🚶 🚶

Walk 39 Directions
(Walk 38 option)

Leave the main walk at Point ⑧. Instead of turning left, turn right along the track, which follows a brook through **Cwms**, a narrow valley penetrating the hills. The track is known as Cwms Road and is part of a former drovers' route from mid-Wales to Shrewsbury.

After about 650yds (594m), a stile on the left (Point Ⓐ) lets you join the grassy slopes of **Caer Caradoc**. Just bear right towards the top. You can see the path rising ahead of you, passing to the left of a rock outcrop, though the summit is not visible from this point. Once you have passed the outcrop, go through a break in the ramparts of the Iron-Age fort that encircles the summit. After a short climb you reach the summit itself, and the full magnificence of the view can be appreciated. Wenlock Edge and the

Clee Hills dominate the view to the east, with The Wrekin to the north and the Malverns a dark smudge in the south. The Long Mynd broods just across the Stretton Gap, backed by Stiperstones and the Welsh hills.

From the summit, descend through the northern ramparts of the hill fort down to a saddle separating Caer Caradoc from Little Caradoc (Point Ⓑ). Turn left before a pool to meet a path that contours round the lower slopes. Turn left and keep going to a stile. Descend very steeply from this point to rejoin the main route at Point ⑧.

> **WHERE TO EAT AND DRINK** ⓘ
> Try **Flinders** in Church Stretton, a coffee and tea shop and continental-style café. It's welcoming and the jacket potatoes with garlic mushrooms are wicked. Well-behaved dogs accepted. The **Buck's Head Hotel** is recommended in the *Ramblers' Yearbook*. Children are welcome and so are dogs, but not in the bar when food is being served – there's a beer garden outside.

> **WHAT TO LOOK FOR** ⓘ
> How do we know that Cwms Road was once a **drove road**? Apart from the documentary evidence, there are various other clues. Here, it's trees: if you look down from Caer Caradoc into Cwms you will see Cwms Cottage, readily identifiable because it stands next to a clump of Scots pines. It was customary for people offering drovers an overnight stop or refreshments to indicate this by planting two or three Scots pines, and this may well explain the presence of these trees here. They don't occur naturally in the Stretton Hills.

Walk 40

Breadwalk to Bone Bed

Take a peek 400 million years into the past on Whitcliffe Common.

•DISTANCE•	5¼ miles (8.4km)
•MINIMUM TIME•	2hrs
•ASCENT / GRADIENT•	820ft (250m) ▲▲ ▲▲ ▲▲
•LEVEL OF DIFFICULTY•	🚶 🚶 🚶
•PATHS•	Good but one sometimes turns to shallow stream, 2 stiles
•LANDSCAPE•	High pasture land above River Teme, some woodland
•SUGGESTED MAP•	aqua3 OS Explorer 203 Ludlow
•START / FINISH•	Grid reference: SO 510746
•DOG FRIENDLINESS•	Ideal for dogs, but must be on lead between Priors Halton and Mortimer Forest
•PARKING•	Car park off Castle Street, Ludlow
•PUBLIC TOILETS•	At car park

Walk 40 Directions

Turn right through **Castle Square**, then follow **Dinham** down to the **River Teme**. Look out for Dinham House, an imposing brick mansion with a long list of illustrious past residents, including Lucien Bonaparte, banished to England by his brother Napoleon for making an 'unsuitable' marriage. Further down Dinham is the 12th-century Chapel of St Thomas of Canterbury, one of Ludlow's two oldest buildings (the other is the castle).

Cross **Dinham Bridge** to **Whitcliffe**. This is an ancient common over which Ludlovians have held common rights since at least 1240. They no longer exercise their grazing rights, nor do they quarry stone, and probably very few even bother to gather firewood. But they do come here to walk their dogs and admire the view from the top of the cliff of their incomparable town, set against its backdrop of the Clee Hills.

Follow the lane round to the right. At a junction go straight on along a no through road signposted to Priors Halton. When you reach **Priors Halton farm**, take the footpath on the left. Ignore another path branching right after 230yds (210m) and proceed along a track towards Mortimer Forest. When the track gives out just keep straight on across the field. Meeting a road, turn right for 650yds (594m), then left on a bridleway at a signpost.

Go straight up sheep pasture, then through a gate into **Lower Whitcliffe** (Mortimer Forest). Keep climbing, soon crossing a forest track, after which the gradient eases

WHILE YOU'RE THERE ℹ

Spend a few hours in **Ludlow**. Many people think it is Britain's loveliest small town. Not only is it beautifully situated, but it has a total of 469 listed buildings, an astonishing number for such a small place. One of the oldest is the 11th-century castle, built on a superb defensive site high above the confluence of the rivers Corve and Teme.

as you continue up to a road. Turn right for 100yds (91m), then cross to a bridleway. Go forward along a track, then turn left past a barn, following blue arrows. Once you leave the farm behind, the bridleway continues as a sunken track along the county border.

WHERE TO EAT AND DRINK ⓘ

Ludlow has a great choice of places, from humble chippies to Michelin-starred restaurants. The beautiful **Feathers Hotel** is one of the most photographed buildings in Britain, and may just tempt you in. The 13th-century **Charlton Arms** by Ludford Bridge is a very friendly place with a riverside patio – hard to beat on a sunny day. Dogs and children are welcome on the patio and in the bar, and locally brewed ales and home-cooked food are available.

It soon plunges back into the forest, where you keep straight on, ignoring branching paths, including the colour-coded forest trails. The path is high-banked and stone-paved in places, and obviously an ancient highway, so unlike the bland, modern forest paths. When you come to a junction with a forest road, take the middle path of three directly ahead. Mossy, ferny and often very wet in winter, it continues towards Ludlow,

---

WHAT TO LOOK FOR ⓘ

Many of the larger trees that grace Whitcliffe's slopes are **hornbeam**, an uncommon species this far north. You can recognise hornbeam by its distinctive smooth, fluted trunk and winged seeds. Hornbeam mast (the fruit of the tree) is a favourite food of the **hawfinch**, the largest of the British finches, but a shy, wary bird which is little known. Flocks of these elusive birds visit the woodlands at Whitcliffe nearly every winter to feast on the mast.

---

eventually running along the edge of the forest and descending to meet a track. Turn right to a road and turn left, then shortly right on a half-hidden footpath descending through the trees. You're on the **Mortimer Trail** now, which links Ludlow with Kington. Join a road and go straight on at a junction on the higher of two roads, still on the Mortimer Trail, then take a path on to **Whitcliffe Common**.

Fork left to a viewpoint with a good view of the castle. Descend towards **Dinham Bridge**, but only cross the Teme here if you want a short cut. Otherwise, turn right beside the Teme, along a path known as the **Breadwalk**, which was laid out in 1850, the previously unemployed workmen being paid in bread. Eventually you'll be forced to climb uphill, but continue in the same direction to **Ludford Corner**, where you'll see an ordinary-looking cliff marked by a plaque. This small chunk of Ludlow rock is an internationally significant Site of Special Scientific Interest (SSSI), which geologists refer to as **Ludlow Bone Bed**. It's packed not only with bones, but also fish scales, spores, plant debris and tiny mites – fossil evidence of the first plants and animals to colonise the land. These rocks were laid down as sediments in a shallow tropical sea about 400 million years ago and Whitcliffian is now a term used worldwide for rocks of this age.

Across the main road a lane leads into the lovely little hamlet of Ludford, which is well worth a visit before you walk past the **Charlton Arms Hotel** and over **Ludford Bridge**. Go up **Lower Broad Street** and **Broad Street** to **King Street**, then turn left to **Castle Street**.

Over the Edge at Stokesay

A spectacular 13th-century house with gorgeous hills overlooking it.

•DISTANCE•	6¼ miles (10.1km)
•MINIMUM TIME•	2hrs 30min
•ASCENT / GRADIENT•	909ft (277m) ▲▲ ▲
•LEVEL OF DIFFICULTY•	🚶🚶 🚶🚶 🚶
•PATHS•	Mostly excellent, short stretch eroded and uneven, byway from Aldon to Stoke Wood occasionally floods, 12 stiles
•LANDSCAPE•	Woods and pasture in unspoilt hills above River Onny
•SUGGESTED MAP•	aqua3 OS Explorers 203 Ludlow; 217 The Long Mynd & Wenlock Edge
•START / FINISH•	Grid reference: SO 437819 (on Explorer 217)
•DOG FRIENDLINESS•	Under control around Brandhill, Aldon and livestock
•PARKING•	Lay-by on A49 immediately north of Stokesay turn
•PUBLIC TOILETS•	None on route

BACKGROUND TO THE WALK

This is an exquisite walk, with the most wonderful views from the aptly named View Edge, mostly west to Clun Forest, but also east and south to the Clee Hills, Wenlock Edge, Mortimer Forest and Ludlow. Brandhill Gutter and Aldon Gutter are highlights of the walk, and considerably more salubrious than they sound – a gutter is a local name for the sort of narrow, steep-sided valley more commonly known in Shropshire as a dingle.

Medieval Fashion Statement

But, however gorgeous the landscape, it has a rival for once, in the shape of the almost impossibly picturesque Stokesay Castle, which isn't really a castle at all. It's a fortified manor house, which might sound like a pedantic distinction, but isn't. A true castle was defensive in purpose, and therefore strictly practical. Stokesay Castle, however, could not have resisted prolonged assault. It was part fashion statement, part status symbol, and is today the best preserved and probably the oldest example of its kind in England.

In the mid-10th century, the manor of Stoke was held by Wild Edric, a Saxon nobleman (► Walk 34), but after the Norman Conquest it was given by William I to Picot de Say – hence the name Stokesay. (The word stoke, a common English place name, means enclosure.) Picot built a house and a church some time after 1068, but in 1280 Stokesay was sold to a wealthy wool merchant, Laurence of Ludlow, who set about rebuilding and fortifying the house, once he had obtained a licence to crenellate from Edward I. Ten generations of Laurence's descendants lived at Stokesay, but in the reign of Charles I it came into the ownership of the Craven family and was used as a supply base for the King's forces when they were based at Ludlow in the early stages of the Civil War. It was surrendered to the Roundheads, without a siege, when it came under attack, which is fortunate for us, as it would have been destroyed otherwise. By the 19th century it had fallen into decay, and was being used as a barn. Happily, in 1869 it was sold to John Darby Allcroft, a Worcester glove manufacturer and MP, who set about restoring it. Today, Stokesay Castle is in the care of English Heritage.

Though everything about Stokesay is special, the great hall is a particularly rare survival, almost untouched since medieval times and containing its original staircase, open octagonal hearth and innovative timber roof. There is also a fine solar (an upper living room in a medieval house), containing Elizabethan panelling and a sumptuous fireplace, accessible only by an exterior stair. Across the courtyard is a picture-book structure added in the 16th century, a timber-framed gatehouse decorated with wonderful carvings.

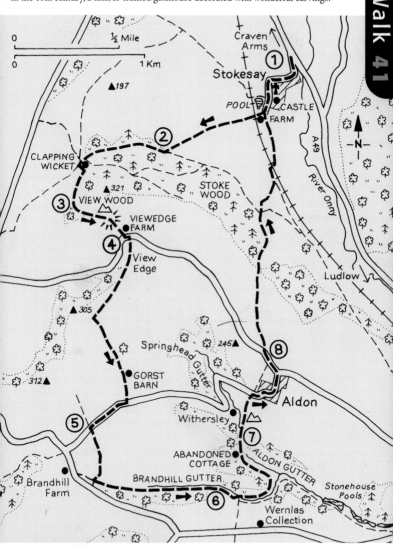

Walk 41 **Directions**

① Take the footway from the lay-by to the lane that leads to **Stokesay Castle**. Walk past the castle and take the second footpath on the right, at the far side of a pool. It skirts a farm, then crosses the railway. Keep straight on through three meadows on a worn path, with a succession of stiles providing further guidance.

Walk 41

② Enter **Stoke Wood**, proceed to a track and turn right. Leave the wood at a stile at the far end and walk past a house (**Clapping Wicket**) before turning sharp left up the field in front of the house. Turn right at the top, walking by the edge of **View Wood**.

③ Join a track that leads into the wood, then emerges from it to run alongside the edge. It soon plunges back into the trees, climbing quite steeply, then levelling out to reach a lane by **Viewedge Farm**.

④ Turn left for a few paces, then join a footpath on the right. Turn right by a field edge and walk to the top of a knoll, continuing in the same direction across fields until you come to a waymarker that sends you sharp left across an adjacent field. Join a track at the far side and continue past **Gorst Barn** to a lane. Turn right.

> ### WHILE YOU'RE THERE ⓘ
> Did you know that over 220 breeds of chicken are now extinct? Find out more at the **Wernlas Collection**, near Onibury Gutter, where they breed rare and traditional poultry. They've got all sorts of exotic birds, from the cute to the downright weird, and about 10,000 chicks are hatched each season. Kids (and adults) can cuddle and stroke many of them, along with donkeys and rare breeds of goats, sheep and pigs.

⑤ Turn left on a footpath, crossing three pastures to a concealed stile, which gives on to a bridleway. Turn left down **Brandhill Gutter**. Eventually you have to go through a gate on the right, but you should immediately turn left to continue in the same direction. Keep close to the stream (or, very often, dry streambed) on your left.

⑥ After passing through a gate, the bridleway becomes narrow, uneven and eroded for a while but soon improves. It eventually crosses the stream (next to a stile) and starts to swing northwards, into **Aldon Gutter**. Beyond an abandoned cottage, the bridleway passes to the right of pheasant pens – watch carefully for the waymarkers here.

> ### WHERE TO EAT AND DRINK ⓘ
> Though there is nothing along the walk route, you're only a short way from the café at **Secret Hills** (► Walk 43), which has indoor and outdoor tables overlooking a meadow. The adjacent **Stokesay Castle Inn** is open all day and serves home-cooked food, tea and coffee. It's pleasant and traditional, with a garden, a children's play area and a good reputation.

⑦ About 200yds (183m) after the cottage, the bridleway bears right, climbing the steep valley side to meet a lane at the top. Turn right to pass through the hamlet of **Aldon**, then left at a T-junction.

⑧ Join a byway on the right at a slight bend in the lane (no sign or waymarker). This lovely hedged track leads between fields, then through **Stoke Wood**, beyond which it descends to **Stokesay** and the start of the walk.

> ### WHAT TO LOOK FOR ⓘ
> The view of Stokesay Castle from the adjacent churchyard is superb, and **St John's Church** is a rare example of Commonwealth style. The original Norman church was badly damaged during the Civil War and rebuilt between 1654 and 1664 under Cromwell's Commonwealth (also known as the Interregnum), a time when very few churches were built.

Steaming up Wart Hill

Great views from the hills, with reminders of the age of steam.

•DISTANCE•	6 miles (9.7km)
•MINIMUM TIME•	3hrs
•ASCENT / GRADIENT•	918ft (280m) ▲▲▲
•LEVEL OF DIFFICULTY•	🚶 🚶 🚶
•PATHS•	Generally good, some muddy patches, steep, sometimes slippery descent from Wart Hill, about 20 stiles
•LANDSCAPE•	Wooded hills, pastureland and varied terrain by River Onny
•SUGGESTED MAP•	aqua3 OS Explorer 217 The Long Mynd & Wenlock Edge
•START / FINISH•	Grid reference: SO 430843
•DOG FRIENDLINESS•	Mostly permissive paths so keep on leads
•PARKING•	Car park for Onny Trail, next to railway bridge on unclassified road from A49 to Cheney Longville
•PUBLIC TOILETS•	None on route

BACKGROUND TO THE WALK

Craven Arms is a young town, though possibly a very old settlement. It owes its present form to the coming of the railways, before which it was little more than a huddle of cottages at the hamlet of Newton, near the Craven Arms Hotel. The Shrewsbury and Hereford railway was built through Craven Arms in the 1840s, followed by the Knighton line to Wales, the Buildwas line to the coalfields and the Bishop's Castle line, making The Arms, as it was known, a major railway junction. The cattle and sheep that had formerly travelled the drove roads now came by train, and other business opportunities were opened up. Local landowner Lord Craven recognised the potential and built a new town. For a while it seemed as though it might mushroom, but it never quite happened. Two of the railway lines have gone, but the Shrewsbury-to-Hereford line is still busy. The Knighton line is now part of the Heart of Wales line and runs through gloriously remote countryside to Swansea.

Doomed Line

The line that inspired most affection has long gone. This was the Bishop's Castle line, authorised in 1861. The plan was for a link from the Shrewsbury and Hereford line to the Oswestry and Newtown (later Cambrian) line near Montgomery, with short branches to Montgomery and Bishop's Castle. Financial problems dogged the railway company from the start, but they went ahead with an official opening in 1865, using a borrowed locomotive hauling borrowed coaches. Regular traffic started the next year, but only from Craven Arms to Bishop's Castle, via a junction at Lydham Heath. The rest of the line was never finished. There was meant to be a double junction at Lydham, but they completed only part of it, and that faced in the wrong direction for trains from Craven Arms. Throughout the railway's life, it was necessary for locomotives to uncouple at Lydham and run around their carriages to recouple in reverse for the last few miles. Not surprisingly, the railway was never profitable. It is said it was so slow that people would get off to pick blackberries or mushrooms, then stroll along the line to reboard. When rural bus services started soon after 1900, the Bishop's Castle line was doomed, though it hung on until 1935.

The easternmost stretch of the line has now been turned into the Onny Trail, which is open for public access under the Countryside Stewardship scheme. It makes a delightful walk along the banks of the River Onny, giving an idea of what immensely scenic countryside was traversed by the old Bishop's Castle Railway. It also forms the return leg of this beautiful walk.

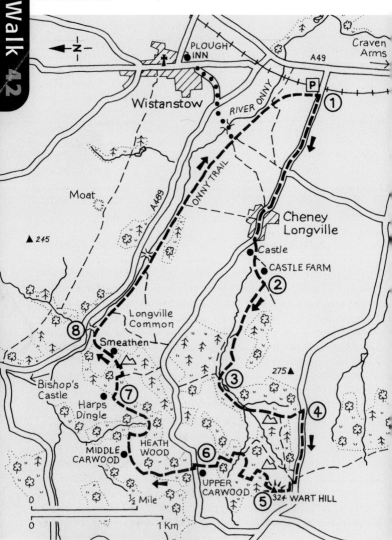

Walk 42 Directions

① Walk to the lane and turn right. Keep straight on at a junction and pass through **Cheney Longville**. At the far side of the village, fork left at

a sign for **Castle Farm**. A stony track passes the farm and enters cattle pasture.

② Walk along the right-hand field edge. In the next field, go straight on up a slope. The path soon levels

Walk **42**

out and, a little further on, a waymarker sends you diagonally to the bottom right field corner.

③ Climb a stile into woodland, walk to a T-junction and turn left. Look for a concealed stile on the left, or use the nearby gate, and take a waymarked path which runs past a pool, then continues through plantation, soon swinging left then climbing. Go straight on at a junction with a permissive path, climbing steeply to a lane.

④ Turn right, then right again after 500yds (457m) at a sign for the Wart Hill Wander (a waymarked trail from Secret Hills – ▶ Walk 43). A few paces further on, turn left at another signpost. A steep climb now takes you through woodland to the top of **Wart Hill**, covered in bracken, gorse and a scattering of pines.

⑤ Keep going in the same direction, past the trig point, then follow the waymarkers on a steep descent, first through conifers and then through birch woods. The path rises and falls, twists and turns before eventually turning left on a stony track.

⑥ Go past **Upper Carwood** to a lane, turn left, then immediately right on another track into **Heath Wood**. At the far side of the wood, cross a stile at a junction and turn right. The track passes **Middle Carwood**, swings right and then left into woodland. Emerging from the trees, it follows the woodland edge, then goes sharp right at a T-junction near a house.

⑦ A brief climb through woods leads to a junction. Turn left, descending steeply. Leaving the trees, take a narrow path through bracken to pass to the left of a house, then keep going down, turning right where indicated. The path then hairpins down through hazel coppice to meet up with the **Onny Trail**.

⑧ Turn right, following the waymarked trail. You'll pass three bridges spanning the Onny; the third provides the opportunity for a short detour to the **Plough Inn** at Wistanstow, if you wish. Otherwise, just keep going to the car park.

Folly on Wenlock Edge

Tackle steep Callow Hill for a closer look at a tower visible for miles around.

•DISTANCE•	6½ miles (10.4km)
•MINIMUM TIME•	2hrs 30min
•ASCENT / GRADIENT•	817ft (249m) ▲▲▲
•LEVEL OF DIFFICULTY•	🚶 🚶 🚶
•PATHS•	Mostly good, not always clear between Quinny Brook and Halford, muddy in places, 18 stiles
•LANDSCAPE•	Pasture and woodland on scarp slope of Wenlock Edge
•SUGGESTED MAP•	aqua3 OS Explorer 217 The Long Mynd & Wenlock Edge
•START / FINISH•	Grid reference: SO 433828
•DOG FRIENDLINESS•	Off lead in woodland, under close control in sheep pasture
•PARKING•	Car park off B4368 Corvedale Road, Craven Arms
•PUBLIC TOILETS•	None on route

BACKGROUND TO THE WALK

In the 18th and 19th centuries, follies were the height of fashion. The focal point of this walk is Flounder's Folly, a stone tower which stands on top of Callow Hill, the highest point of Wenlock Edge. Like so many follies, it has an entertaining tale behind it, which may or may not be true. The story goes that a wealthy merchant called Benjamin Flounder ordered the tower to be built in 1838 so he could admire the view across Corve Dale to his fine house at Ludlow. But he got a nasty surprise when he first climbed to the top of the newly completed tower. His mansion was not to be seen – there was a hill in the way. 'Take it down' he roared, and it's unclear if he meant the hill or the tower. Both were spared, however, when a watery gleam on the horizon was pointed out to him. Benjamin (who must have been extraordinarily stupid) was placated by the suggestion that it was the Mersey, and that he would be able to watch his ships leaving Liverpool. The initials BF are carved into the stonework and, as more than one person has observed, perhaps that says it all.

But why did he have the tower built? It may have been for the view, or perhaps Benjamin was just a fashion victim. He might even have had more altruistic motives. Several British follies have been built purely because a generous landowner wished to provide work at a time of high unemployment – and 1838 would fit the bill in that respect.

Fashionable Follies

The first follies appeared in the 16th century, but it wasn't until the 18th century that the craze took off, partly reflecting a new enthusiasm for all things classical. Wealthy young men were educated in the classics, then sent off on the Grand Tour. They came back full of the glory that was Greece and Rome and set about building temples on their country estates. This developed into a romantic search for the ideal landscape and people would enhance, as they thought, the view from their country seats with all manner of purpose-built towers and castles, preferably ruined. At least there is nothing pretentious about Flounder's Folly. A tall plain tower built from local stone, it looks well enough from a distance, but is dilapidated at close quarters. It has been neglected in recent years and efforts are being made to raise money for its restoration.

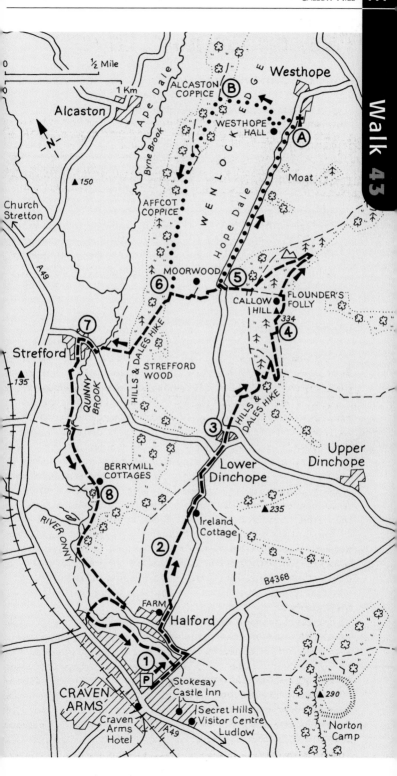

Walk 43

Walk 43 Directions

① Walk down **Corvedale Road**, cross the **River Onny** and turn left towards **Halford**. Reaching the hamlet, turn right towards Dinchope. Pass a farm, then take a footpath on the left. It climbs to the far corner of a field, then along the left-hand edge of another.

② When the hedge turns a corner, continue across the field to a stile by a telegraph pole, then up the next field to a concealed stile, near the top left corner. Turn left along a lane and ignore all turnings, following signs for Lower Dinchope and Westhope. Pass through **Lower Dinchope** to a junction.

> **WHAT TO LOOK FOR** ⓘ
> In the 1960s and 1970s, our **buzzard** population plummeted because of pesticide poisoning. Since the banning of the worst poisons, it has staged a successful comeback. For years it was confined to Scotland, Wales and the West Country, but is now moving steadily eastwards across England, and is very common in Shropshire, especially round Craven Arms.

③ Take a path almost opposite, where a sign indicates that you're joining the **Hills and Dales Hike**, (which begins at Secret Hills). Just follow the frequent waymarkers, which guide you across fields and into woodland, before sending you zig-zagging up graded and stepped paths to the top of **Callow Hill**.

④ Turn left at the top, skirting round **Flounder's Folly**, then returning to the edge until you are forced to descend sharp left into conifers. The path plunges steeply down to a clearing. Join a track which continues more gently, soon passing a barrier to meet the Dinchope–Westhope road.

⑤ Turn right, then immediately left on a track, where the road bends sharply right. Go left again at the turning for **Moorwood farm**.

⑥ Enter **Strefford Wood** and descend left on a bridleway. At the bottom of the wood the Hills and Dales Hike goes to the left. Stay with the bridleway, which leaves Strefford Wood and descends to a lane. Turn left, then right, crossing **Quinny Brook** into **Strefford**.

⑦ Turn first left on a no through road, which becomes a footpath running through fields to a footbridge over Quinny Brook. Cross the bridge and proceed to another. Cross this too and keep going to a stile just beyond three large oaks. Again, keep straight on, past **Berrymill Cottages** and through a copse into a field.

⑧ Walk the length of the field to a stile at the far side, close to the top left corner. Go through a wood, then across fields towards Halford. Watch for a concealed stile as you reach the village. Go along a track to a junction, then turn right on another track which crosses the River Onny. A permissive path on the left runs into **Craven Arms**.

> **WHILE YOU'RE THERE** ⓘ
> **Secret Hills** is part of an initiative to attract more visitors to Craven Arms. There are interactive displays (including a simulated balloon flight) inside a grass-roofed building, a shop, café and riverside meadows to explore. It's the starting point for several waymarked walks, including the Hills and Dales Hike, which overlaps with this walk.

Land of Hope and Glory

A brief foray into Hope Dale to extend your exploration of Wenlock Edge.
See map and information panel for Walk 43

•DISTANCE•	8¼ miles (13.3km)
•MINIMUM TIME•	3hrs
•ASCENT / GRADIENT•	1,030ft (314m) ▲▲▲
•LEVEL OF DIFFICULTY•	👥 👥 👥

Walk 44 Directions
(Walk 43 option)

This walk will give a slightly better idea of the complex structure of Wenlock Edge because it provides a glimpse of Hope Dale, which lies between the two main ridges. Hope is a local word for a valley and is a common place name in Shropshire.

Leave the main route at Point ⑤, turning sharp right along the lane instead of taking the track to Moorwood. After about a mile (1.6km) you'll see **Westhope church** on the right. Just before

---

WHERE TO EAT AND DRINK ⓘ

There is a fair choice in Craven Arms. Why not try the **Flowers Coffee Shop**, where you can also buy collectables and curiosities or hire a mountain bike? It has outside tables for sunny days. So does the café at **Secret Hills**. The **Craven Arms Hotel** and **Stokesay Castle Inn** are both very pleasant.

---

you reach it, turn left on a farm lane (Point Ⓐ). Follow it round to the left, into the farmyard at **Westhope Hall**, then turn right to join a waymarked track. When it enters a field turn left on another track leading to **Alcaston Coppice** (Point Ⓑ).

Go straight ahead into the coppice for 100yds (91m) to meet another path at a T-junction. Turn left, keep straight on when you come to a junction, then go left at the next, to continue close to the left-hand edge of the adjoining wood, **Affcot Coppice** (Forestry Commission).

The path does drift away from the edge at times, but is easy enough to follow – basically just go straight on. You're not likely to move far off course because there are fields to your left and a very steep slope to your right as Wenlock Edge plunges down to Ape Dale. Eventually you come to a sign for Strefford Wood, and a fingerpost. Go straight on to rejoin Walk 43 at Point ⑥.

WHAT TO LOOK FOR ⓘ

The **yew tree** by Westhope church is thought to be at least 800 years old. Because it is so strongly associated with churches, many people don't realise that yew is a native and you can find it growing in the wild. It loves the chalk soils of the south, but also thrives on limestone further north, including Wenlock Edge. You should see a scattering of yews as you walk through the woods along the top of the scarp slope. In September it produces attractive red berries, but don't be tempted by them as they are toxic.

And So to Bedstone

A walk on Hopton Titterhill, with dramatic views and charming villages.

•DISTANCE•	5 miles (8km)
•MINIMUM TIME•	2hrs
•ASCENT / GRADIENT•	892ft (272m) ▲▲▲
•LEVEL OF DIFFICULTY•	🚶🚶 🚶🚶 🚶🚶
•PATHS•	Forest tracks and quiet lanes, some field paths, no stiles
•LANDSCAPE•	Steep-sided hills between rivers Clun and Redlake
•SUGGESTED MAP•	aqua3 OS Explorer 201 Knighton & Presteigne
•START / FINISH•	Grid reference: SO 348777
•DOG FRIENDLINESS•	Will love Hopton Forest, take care on road
•PARKING•	Forestry Commission car park in Hopton Forest, off minor road west from Hopton Castle to Llanbrook and Obley
•PUBLIC TOILETS•	None on route

Walk 45 Directions

This walk takes you across the top of a hill called Hopton Titterhill, but most people know it as Hopton Forest now because it has been almost completely afforested with conifers. Don't let that put you off, because there are also patches of beechwood, fantastic views, a Norman castle and two charming villages to enjoy. But it's important to realise that Hopton is a magnet for mountain bikers. There are trails here aimed at all abilities, from beginners to the most adventurous downhill racers. If that puts you off, avoid weekends. I've never met a cyclist on a weekday at Hopton.

From the car park, return to the access track and take another stony track opposite, beyond a timber barrier and to the right of an information board. There are various numbered posts in the forest, marking points on the cycle trails. Ignore a path branching left at **post 3** and continue along the

main path to **post 7**. Take the second left, going uphill through beech trees and on along an initially grassy path through mixed woodland and plantation. Turn left at a T-junction, then right at the next junction, by **post 10**.

Fork left to climb the small, stony, conical summit, carpeted with heather and whinberry – the natural ground cover on the hill before afforestation shaded out most of it. Enjoy the marvellous view, then return to the main path, using one of several paths that radiate out in all directions from the summit. Continue in the same direction as before, descending now

---

WHERE TO EAT AND DRINK ⓘ

You'll find nothing along the route, but you're not that far from the **Crown Inn** at Clunton (► Walk 50). Or you could try the **Kangaroo Inn** at Aston on Clun, where there's also a useful village shop, the **Hundred House Inn** at Purslow, the **Engine and Tender** near Broome Station or the gorgeous **Bird on a Rock Tearoom** at Abcott.

to meet a stony track by a pool. Turn left and ignore the very steep path (labelled 'downhill racing') which descends right. A little further on you'll come to a major junction. Ignore two paths branching left and continue along the stony track. When the track bends left keep straight on instead, down a grassy track, enjoying fantastic views ahead. Keep straight on at all junctions, then go through a gate at the edge of the forest.

Bear left to follow an intermittent hedge of hawthorn trees (and one oak) across a field. Go through a gate at the far side, to the right of another oak. Cross a cattle pasture, again to a gate at the far side. Turn left along the edge of the next field, on a track that becomes increasingly well defined as it descends to **Bedstone**. When you reach the village you need to turn left to return to Hopton, but it's worth having a look round first as there are some lovely houses here. There's a Norman church too, with a timber-framed bellcote and a shingled spire. It was subject to 19th-century restoration, but retains some original windows and a Norman font. Near by stand a few thatched cottages and a Victorian schoolhouse, while Manor Farm is a splendid timber-framed house, partly faced in stone in 1775. To the south of the village is Bedstone Court, a flamboyant black-and-white mansion of 1884. It was

designed by Thomas Harris for Sir Henry Ripley MP and is said to be a calendar house, with 365 windows, 52 rooms and 12 chimneys.

WHILE YOU'RE THERE

Just over the Herefordshire border is Lingen, where there is an interesting garden to visit. **Lingen Garden** has cottage favourites, alpines, a bog garden, scree beds, the national collection of *Iris sibirica* and much more, including a tea room. It's a nursery too, so you can buy plants for your own garden.

Take the **Hopton Castle road** and you'll reach the castle itself before the village. Only the keep survives, but it's solid and substantial and enjoys a fine setting. It was built by the de Hopton family in the 11th century and rebuilt in the 14th century. During the Civil War it was held for Parliament, but taken by the Royalists after a three-week siege. Most of the defending garrison was killed and the bodies dumped in the moat.

Turn left at a junction by the castle, passing through the attractive little village. It has only a handful of houses, most notably the timber-framed former rectory. The church is Victorian, built between 1870 and 1871, by the architect T Nicholson. Keep straight on towards **Obley**, then turn left when you come to the Forestry Commission sign for **Hopton**, following the access track to the car park.

WHAT TO LOOK FOR

Look under the conifers in the forest and you will see that for most of the year almost nothing grows there because the shade is simply too dense. But for a couple of months in the autumn you should see fair numbers of different types of **fungi**. The most striking species is the fly agaric, the traditional toadstool of children's picture books – bright red with white spots. If you see one don't be tempted to take it home for a fry-up because it is highly toxic. The harvesting of wild fungi has become popular recently, but you really do need to know what you're doing.

Follow the Buzzard to Bury Ditches

Enjoy the magnificent views from a dramatic hill fort, rising above plantations on Sunnyhill.

•DISTANCE•	5½ miles (8.8km)
•MINIMUM TIME•	2hrs
•ASCENT / GRADIENT•	804ft (245m) ▲▲▲
•LEVEL OF DIFFICULTY•	👫 👫 👫
•PATHS•	Field and woodland paths, one boggy and overgrown, fence and gates to climb at Acton Bank, 8 stiles
•LANDSCAPE•	Hilltop woodland and plantation, mixed farmland in valley
•SUGGESTED MAP•	aqua3 OS Explorer 216 Welshpool & Montgomery
•START / FINISH•	Grid reference: SO 334839
•DOG FRIENDLINESS•	Off lead for much of way, but not round Acton
•PARKING•	Forestry Commission car park at Sunnyhill off minor road north from Clunton
•PUBLIC TOILETS•	None on route

BACKGROUND TO THE WALK

It is impossible to spend much time in Shropshire without becoming aware of the hill forts that have been imposed on the landscape. The south west corner of the county is particularly rich in these impressive monuments, with one of the highest concentrations in England and Wales. The same is true of the neighbouring parts of Herefordshire and Montgomeryshire, so that there is hardly a hilltop in the area that doesn't provide a view of several forts. Some were built in the late Bronze Age, but most were constructed in the Iron Age; that is, after around 600 BC. They were built in stages, often over very long periods of time, possibly as much as 1,000 years in some cases.

Following the Lie of the Land

This walk takes you to one of the finest of all, Bury Ditches, which crowns Sunnyhill (also called Tangley Hill), above the valleys of the Clun and the Kemp. Elliptical in shape, Bury Ditches is an example of a contour fort, which means that its Celtic builders took advantage of the topography, making the ramparts follow the natural contours of the landscape. Such construction wasn't always possible, but where the natural slope was sufficiently steep, it enabled them to get away with fewer ramparts, or even none at all. On the relatively gentle northern slope of Sunnyhill summit, three substantial ramparts were considered necessary, but there are only two on the south side, below which the slope plunges down with a daunting steepness.

It's possible for archaeologists to tell approximately when a fort was built by the design of the ramparts. Bury Ditches' construction suggests a date somewhere around the 6th century BC (ie early Iron Age). All the local community would have been involved, including young children. Trees would have to be cleared first, using axes made from flint, stone or bronze, and then the ramparts and ditches would be dug with deer-antler picks and shovels

Walk 46

made from the shoulder blades of cattle. Earth, turf and stones would have been carried away in hand baskets. It's a task of almost unimaginable proportions, especially when you consider that Bury Ditches covers a larger area than most hamlets and many villages in Shropshire.

It was once believed that hill forts were used only for defence at times of danger, but excavation and other archaeological techniques have revealed that the larger ones were more like defended villages, where people lived and farmed. Did they also appreciate the view, in a purely aesthetic sense, one wonders? The immense panorama visible from the top of Bury Ditches is one of the finest in Shropshire, but it was lost for several years, after the Forestry Commission planted conifers on top of the fort. Fortunately, a timely gale in 1978 flattened many of the alien trees and the Commission took the hint, removing the rest.

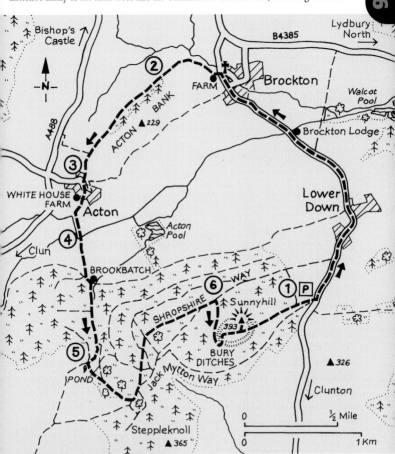

Walk 46 Directions

① From the car park at **Sunnyhill**, walk back to the lane and turn left. Descend through the hamlet of **Lower Down** and continue to

Brockton. Turn left on a track shortly before you come to a ford. Pass a collection of semi-derelict buses behind a farm, then go through a gate on the left and walk along the right-hand edges of three fields, parallel with the track.

Walk 46

② Climb over a fence into a wood and continue in the same direction, contouring round the base of **Acton Bank**. After leaving the wood the path continues through scrub, then through pasture below some old quarries, before it meets a lane at the hamlet of **Acton**.

③ Turn left, pass to the right of a triangular green and join a path running past **White House Farm**. Frequent waymarkers guide you past the house, across a field, then left over a stile and along the right-hand edge of another field.

④ Cross a footbridge and continue straight across the ensuing field towards a building at the far side. Cross a stile in the hedge, turn left for a few paces and then right on a track which passes by a house called **Brookbatch** and rises into woodland. When the track eventually bends to the left, go forward over a stile instead and continue climbing.

⑤ Emerging on to a track, turn left past a pond. Cross a cattle grid into Forestry Commission property and leave the track, turning right on a footpath leading through beechwoods. It winds through the trees to meet the **Shropshire Way** (waymarked with a buzzard logo). Turn left, then soon right at a

junction. Ignoring a right turn, stay on the Shropshire Way, which soon forks left off the main track.

⑥ You now have a choice of two buzzards to follow: the main route of the Shropshire Way goes straight on, but you should choose the alternative route which branches right. The path leads to **Bury Ditches** hill fort, then cuts through a gap in the ramparts and crosses the interior. At a colour-banded post (red, blue and green), a path branches left to allow a visit to the summit, with its toposcope and incredible views. Bear right to return to the main path and turn left to follow it to the car park.

On Offa at Knighton

A terrific stretch of Offa's Dyke, passing high above the Teme Valley on the Welsh border.

•DISTANCE•	8 miles (12.9km)
•MINIMUM TIME•	3hrs
•ASCENT / GRADIENT•	1,542ft (470m) ▲▲▲
•LEVEL OF DIFFICULTY•	🚶 🚶 🚶
•PATHS•	Excellent, mostly across short turf, 8 stiles
•LANDSCAPE•	Steep hills overlooking the broad Teme Valley
•SUGGESTED MAP•	aqua3 OS Explorer 201 Knighton & Presteigne
•START / FINISH•	Grid reference: SO 287734
•DOG FRIENDLINESS•	Can run free in Kinsley Wood, but sheep present elsewhere
•PARKING•	Informal car parking in Kinsley Wood, accessed by forest road from A488 (or park in Knighton, next to bus station or near Offa's Dyke Centre)
•PUBLIC TOILETS•	In Knighton, off Broad Street, and Offa's Dyke Centre

BACKGROUND TO THE WALK

Knighton straddles the border, nine toes in Radnorshire and one in Shropshire. Its Welsh name is Tref-y-clawdd, which translates as town on the dyke, a reference to its position on the great earthwork known as Offa's Dyke. Offa was ruler of the English kingdom of Mercia between AD 757 and 796, and the eponymous dyke is the longest archaeological monument in Britain, an impressive structure consisting mainly of a bank, with a ditch on the Welsh side.

Ancient Earthworks

Nobody is certain why Offa ordered its construction. It used to be thought it was an agreed frontier, a way of defining the border or maybe even regulating trade. It's now thought that a period of instability, with constant cross-border raiding, led to Offa's decision to secure his frontier with a defensive boundary. It was formerly believed to have run all the way from Treuddyn (north of Wrexham) to Chepstow, but current thinking is that it may have been shorter than that. Recent work in Gloucestershire has suggested that the earthwork in the lower Wye Valley, previously accepted as part of Offa's Dyke, actually dates from a different period. The Shropshire earthwork is certainly part of Offa's Dyke, however. Most of the best preserved sections are in Shropshire, particularly on remote Llanfair Hill, a little to the north of this walk, which is also the dyke's highest point (1,410ft/430m).

To date, nearly 200 archaeological digs have been carried out on the dyke system. As far as its purpose is concerned, the only thing that has been concluded with any reasonable certainty is that it was built in such a way as to defend Mercia from the raiding Welsh. It was probably not simply an agreed frontier or a boundary marker. But, then again, if it was defensive, why have no traces of fortifications or palisading been discovered? Clearly, there is still much to learn.

Offa's Dyke National Trail, opened in 1971, is a splendid walk that runs for 177 miles (285km) from Prestatyn to Chepstow, following the earthwork for 30 miles (48km). The dyke has survived for 1,300 years, but has never been under such pressure as it is today. It's damaged by agriculture, undermined by rabbits, threatened by development and now eroded by walkers. So please walk alongside it where the route has been realigned to allow this, rather than on top. Encouragingly, a conservation scheme has recently been initiated involving a partnership between the Offa's Dyke Path Management Service (based in Knighton), local farmers and various interested bodies.

Walk 47 Directions

① Adjacent to the car park, at the northern end of **Kinsley Wood**, is a meadow with a barn in it. Join a bridleway which runs along the left-hand edge of this meadow. After about 200yds (183m), veer slightly away from the field edge and descend through a group of oak trees to **Offa's Dyke Path** (ODP).

② Turn right and follow the ODP for about 2½ miles (4km). The path runs just above a steep slope falling away to the west and just below the top of **Panpunton Hill**, and follows the dyke all the way. After climbing around the head of a combe, it gains the top of **Cwm-sanaham Hill** (1,328ft/406m), then continues northwards, soon descending very steeply past a house called **Brynorgan**.

Walk 47

③ Meeting a road, leave the ODP, turning left, then left again at **Selley Cross**. After ½ mile (800m) or so, just beyond **Selley Hall Cottage**, join a footpath on the right. Follow the path to the far side of a field, then turn right, heading to the top right corner. Cross a stile, then continue straight across several fields, until you meet a lane at **Monaughty Poeth**.

> **WHERE TO EAT AND DRINK** ⓘ
> Prince and Pugh's is an excellent tea shop and only one of several in Knighton. There are plenty of pubs too, such as the **George and Dragon**, a 17th-century free house with home-made food and a beer garden. The medieval, flower-bedecked **Horse and Jockey** near the station looks attractive, and the **Knighton Hotel** has a choice of bars and a coffee shop.

④ Turn left for ¾ mile (1.2km) to a junction at **Skyborry Green**. Turn left again, then immediately right, joining a bridleway that climbs to **Bryney farm**. Turn right on a footpath, which is waymarked at regular intervals as it contours round the hill, before descending to the road again at **Nether Skyborry**.

⑤ Turn left for ½ mile (800m), then right on to the ODP just before **Panpwnton farm**. The path crosses the railway and the **River Teme**, then follows the Teme towards

> **WHAT TO LOOK FOR** ⓘ
> The 13-arched **Knucklas** (Cnwclas) **Viaduct** is an impressive piece of railway engineering – you'll get a good view of it as you approach Monaughty Poeth. Its battlemented style was inspired by the ruins of the 12th-century castle on the adjacent hill. The Heart of Wales rail line is hugely scenic and the best way to arrive in Knighton.

> **WHILE YOU'RE THERE** ⓘ
> The **Offa's Dyke Centre** is a must. There are interesting displays and a good range of tourist information. Behind the centre is a stretch of the dyke and an inscribed stone commemorating the opening of the National Trail by Lord Hunt (of Everest fame), who lived at nearby Llanfair Waterdine until his recent death.

Knighton, soon crossing the border and turning right to the **Offa's Dyke Centre**.

⑥ Leaving the centre, turn left through **Knighton**, then left again on **Station Road**. After passing the station, turn left on **Kinsley Road**. Join the first path on the right into **Kinsley Wood**, opposite Kinsley Villa and Gillow. Fork left after a few paces, then embark on a climb so steep it's almost vertical. The gradient eases a little before the path emerges from the trees to continue through scrub and across a forest road. Keep straight on to the top of the ridge, then turn left to walk across the summit. The path descends to a track where you turn right to return to the parking area.

Walk 48

Under the Sun at Clun

A stunning walk from the tranquil Clun Valley into the surrounding hills.

•DISTANCE•	5½ miles (8.8km)
•MINIMUM TIME•	2hrs 30min
•ASCENT / GRADIENT•	1,066ft (325m) ▲▲▲
•LEVEL OF DIFFICULTY•	🏃🏃 🏃🏃 🏃
•PATHS•	Excellent, through mixed farmland (mainly pasture) and woodland, 3 stiles
•LANDSCAPE•	Steep-sided, round-topped hills above valley of River Clun
•SUGGESTED MAP•	aqua3 OS Explorer 201 Knighton & Presteigne
•START / FINISH•	Grid reference: SO 302811
•DOG FRIENDLINESS•	Keep under close control near sheep and cattle
•PARKING•	Car park at Clun community area, signed from High Street
•PUBLIC TOILETS•	At short-stay car park by castle and off High Street

BACKGROUND TO THE WALK

Clun is enfolded by enticing green hills on all sides. It may have been settled as early as the Bronze Age; certainly by the Iron Age there was some sort of community there. But it was the Saxons who first settled in any numbers. Later, the Norman Picot de Say built a castle here around 1099 and laid out a new town in a regular grid pattern, which still survives. Clun was granted its town charter in the 14th century and is still, strictly speaking, a town, but it looks and feels more like a village. There is lots to see, including the substantial castle ruins, 12th-century church, 15th-century packhorse bridge, 17th-century almshouses, 18th-century town hall and any number of charming cottages.

Literary Hotspot

Equally interesting, but not so well known, are the literary connections that abound in Clun. E M Forster visited the town, which subsequently featured as Oniton in his novel *Howard's Way*, published in 1910. One of his key characters, Margaret Schlegel, is totally captivated by the romance and magic of this corner of the Marches, and it's not hard to see why. Clun is easily recognisable from Forster's descriptions and it's clear that he spent some time here.

The castle, with its great keep and commanding site, is said to have been the inspiration for Garde Doloureuse in Sir Walter Scott's novel *The Betrothed*, published jointly with *The Talisman* as *Tales of the Crusaders* in 1825. Scott is believed to have stayed at the Buffalo Inn while working on the book. More recently, playwright John Osborne lived near Clun and now lies buried in the churchyard. The best known literary link is with A E Housman, the author of a timeless collection of poems called *A Shropshire Lad*. Housman famously described Clunton and Clunbury, Clungunford and Clun as 'the quietest places under the sun', though it seems he was only appropriating a traditional rhyme, in which the adjective was infinitely variable.

Clun also featured in *Valley With a Bright Cloud*, a ghost story written by Gareth Lovatt Jones in 1980, while nearby Clunbury became the adopted home of Ida Gandy in 1930. A writer and the wife of a country doctor, Gandy set out in an old Baby Austin to see rural

England. On arriving in Clunbury she was so captivated that she decided to stay. The family settled in the village and Ida continued to write, and to broadcast too, with most of her work inspired by Shropshire. Her most famous book is *An Idler on the Shropshire Borders*, written in 1970, around 25 years after the Gandys had left Shropshire for retirement in Dorset.

Walk 48 Directions

① Walk down **Hospital Lane** to **High Street** and turn right to **The Square**. Pass the **Buffalo Inn**, turn left on **Buffalo Lane** and cross **Clun Bridge**. Go up **Church Street**, turn

right on the Knighton road, then left on **Hand Causeway**, signposted to Churchbank and Hobarris.

② After ¾ mile (1.2km), take a bridleway on the right, which leaves the lane on a bend by **Glebe Cottage** and immediately goes left into a field. Walk up the field, through a gate at the top, then straight on through two more fields to meet a lane running across the top of **Clun Hill** (part of the prehistoric Clun–Clee Ridgeway).

③ The path continues opposite, along the right-hand edges of two fields. At the end of the second one, go through a gate on the right and diagonally to the far corner of another field, then in much the same direction down the next – towards a pool in the valley below.

> **WHERE TO EAT AND DRINK** ⓘ
> The 15th-century **Sun Inn** (also known as the Sun at Clun) is inviting, but so are the **Buffalo Inn** (where Sir Walter Scott stayed) and the **White Horse**. All three welcome children, are highly thought of by people who know about beer, and have gardens, so dogs should be no problem. There are tea shops too – **Clun Bridge Tea Room** is in several guide books, but **The Maltings** and **Bridge Crafts and Coffee Shop** are just as good.

④ Go through a gate and turn left on a byway, then right when you come to a T-junction. At **Hobarris** go left on to a track, just before the main farm buildings. Soon after crossing a brook, branch left along a hollow way. When this bends right, go straight on instead, over a stile into a field. Go straight uphill, joining a field-edge track. To your left, three Scots pines and a prehistoric cairn mark the summit of **Pen-y-wern Hill**. Turn left when you come to a lane.

⑤ At a crossroads, keep straight on, descending to the second of two bends in the lane. Ignore a signposted path on the right; instead take an unsignposted one a few paces further on. It leads into

plantation and soon bends right. About 200yds (183m) after this, branch left on a descending path.

> **WHILE YOU'RE THERE** ⓘ
> Take a peek into the beautiful gardens of **Trinity Hospital**, in Hospital Lane, which are open to the public, but do respect the residents' privacy. The hospital comprises almshouses founded in 1614 by Henry Howard, Earl of Northampton, for 12 poor men, who were summoned to prayer by a bell and subject to a curfew. Today, the almshouses accommodate 15 residents of both sexes, under more liberal conditions.

⑥ After a further 200yds (183m) branch left again, descending through a beautiful oakwood, with scattered rowans and a ground cover of whinberries. Keep going down to meet a path at the bottom of the wood.

⑦ Turn left on the path, which almost immediately swings left, plunges back into the wood and winds through the trees to meet the lane. Turn right towards Clun.

⑧ Turn left at a junction with two tracks. Keep going along the lane until a stile on the right gives access to a field. Go diagonally left towards Clun. Join a lane, then turn right and cross a footbridge by a ford. Turn right to **High Street** and **Hospital Lane**.

> **WHAT TO LOOK FOR** ⓘ
> The wood on Black Hill has a ground cover of **whinberry**, or bilberry as it is called elsewhere. It produces delicious summer fruits which used to be picked on a large scale by Shropshire people, who would sell them to traders for a few pennies a pound. Some pubs and restaurants in south west Shropshire still offer the local speciality, whinberry pie.

Over Black Hill to the Valley of Cwm

Descend from conifer-covered hills into the secret world of Cwm.
See map and information panel for Walk 48

•DISTANCE•	9½ miles (15.3km)
•MINIMUM TIME•	4hrs
•ASCENT / GRADIENT•	1,850ft (564m) ▲▲▲
•LEVEL OF DIFFICULTY•	🚶 🚶 🚶

Walk 49 Directions (Walk 48 option)

Leave the main route at Point ⑤, turning right at the crossroads along a byway that takes you into the plantations clothing **Black Hill**. Keep straight on until a sign sends you to the right. Emerging from the trees (Point Ⓐ) into a clear-felled area, turn right on a bridle track. Ignore branch paths and stay on the waymarked bridleway, turning left at a Y-junction, then shortly left at a T-junction.

Stay on this track for ¾ mile (1.2km), around the summit of **Black Hill**, enjoying wonderful views down into Cwm, a secluded valley in a setting of great beauty. Arriving at a waymarked junction (Point Ⓑ), turn right, then very soon fork left. Descend to a T-junction, turn right and soon left, going very steeply down to a field. Turn left to a lane. Turn left again and walk through the tiny hamlet of **Cwm.**

At a sharp bend in the lane (Point Ⓒ), by the entrance to **Cwm Farm**, take a footpath that climbs diagonally up two pastures to meet the lane again. Don't join the lane, but turn left on a byway (signposted 'public right of way'). This grassy track, bordered by beech trees at first, gives lovely views of Cwm and the hills beyond. Ignore a bridleway branching right and stay on the byway, which eventually leads into Black Hill's conifers.

Turn right on another track when you see a signpost for a footpath (Point Ⓓ). Pass a mast, then turn left. Keep straight on at two cross paths. At the next junction turn right downhill. Descend to a T-junction and turn left on a bridleway. This soon leaves the trees behind and runs on to a junction. Turn left here to walk to a road junction where you rejoin the main route at Point ⑧.

WHAT TO LOOK FOR ⓘ

Generally speaking, conifer woods are too dark for wild flowers to flourish, but on Black Hill the delicate **wood sorrel** proves an exception to the rule. Blooming in considerable numbers in very early spring, mostly on mossy logs or banks, its lovely flowers are white with mauve or pink veins and its bright green leaves, distinctively shamrock-shaped, are nearly as pretty.

The Wood Colliers' Legacy at Clunton

A leafy walk from Clunton Coppice to Purslow Wood.

•DISTANCE•	3¾ miles (6km)
•MINIMUM TIME•	1hr 15min
•ASCENT / GRADIENT•	574ft (17m)
•LEVEL OF DIFFICULTY•	
•PATHS•	Woodland paths, grassy track, quiet lanes and Forestry Commission paths, some overgrown, no stiles
•LANDSCAPE•	Woodland and plantation on steep valley sides
•SUGGESTED MAP•	aqua3 OS Explorer 201 Knighton & Presteigne
•START / FINISH•	Grid reference: SO 338805
•DOG FRIENDLINESS•	Great walk for dogs
•PARKING•	Small car park near nature reserve sign at Clunton Coppice on Cwm Lane, which runs south from Clunton
•PUBLIC TOILETS•	None on route

Walk 50 Directions

Half a century ago the dominant woodland type in south west Shropshire was sessile oak. Not much remains today, so it's fortunate that one of the largest surviving woods, Clunton Coppice, is owned by Shropshire Wildlife Trust. In the distant past it was managed for charcoal production, which involved coppicing. This is a system of woodland management in which trees are cut close to the ground, then left to grow again. The cut stools quickly put out new shoots which can be harvested for small timber or left to grow on. Where coppicing is still carried out it is usually for wildlife rather than commercial purposes.

Leaving the car park, carry on along the lane until a footpath leaves it on the left. Follow it through **Clunton Coppice**, noticing the variety of species. Sessile oak is dominant, but small-leaved lime, yew and hornbeam also occur, while the shrub layer includes hazel, holly and rowan. Some hazel or oak is coppiced every year and the brash (the stuff too small to be used as firewood) is piled on the slow-growing oak stools to prevent deer nibbling the tender regrowth. The charcoal burners (or wood colliers, as they were often known in the Marches) who worked Clunton

> ### WHILE YOU'RE THERE ⓘ
> **Shropshire Wildlife Trust** has 37 reserves altogether and welcomes the public to almost all of them. Why not visit the Trust's centre on Abbey Foregate in Shrewsbury? The centre itself is a nature reserve, with many birds breeding in the garden, which is a re-creation of a medieval physic garden. The Trust inherited this when it took up residence in 2001 and intends to save the most interesting plants, while also making it a true wildlife garden.

Walk 50

Coppice in the past would have lived in the wood all summer, sleeping under simple shelters, because it was important to keep the charcoal kilns continuously alight and closely regulated to avoid flare-ups.

WHAT TO LOOK FOR ⓘ

Damp oak woods are good places to find **non-flowering plants** such as mosses, ferns and fungi. Clunton Coppice is no exception and the luxuriant growth of vivid green mosses is one of its most attractive attributes. Ferns and fungi are plentiful too, but can you find *Phellinus robustus*, a bracket fungus which lives high up in the branches? This is so scarce that it has been recorded in only two British locations – Windsor Great Park and Clunton Coppice.

The path becomes a track, which descends past **Badgers Croft** to a lane. Continue straight on for about 50yds (46m) until you've passed **The Meadows**. Go through a gate on the right into a field and diagonally left up the slope into **Purslow Wood**, a Forestry Commission plantation. Follow a track uphill, soon emerging from the trees into a felled area. Keep climbing, shortly crossing a forestry track. Pick the best way up through scrub, dodging fallen trees and brash (you can avoid this if you wish by staying on the track, turning right, then left) to rejoin the forestry track. Turn left, climb to a junction and go left for a few paces. Leave the forestry track, going across a turning area to join a bridleway that climbs slightly. When a fence blocks your way, turn left to rejoin the forestry track.

Turn right for 20yds (18m), then go downhill on a bridleway, which is overgrown with bracken and bramble. Turn left when you meet a lane. If you prefer to avoid the overgrown bridleway you can do so by continuing along the forestry track for a further 350yds (320m), then turning sharp left on a path which descends to the lane. Bear in mind that it's only by actually using overgrown paths that we can most easily keep these routes open.

Follow the lane back to the point at which you met it earlier, when descending from Clunton Coppice. Instead of returning up the track the same way, join a green lane which starts just before a field gate. Follow it past a house and garden, then along the northern edge of Clunton Coppice and ultimately past **Bush Farm**, where it becomes a paved lane leading to a junction on the edge of **Clunton**. Turn left up **Cwm Lane** to return to **Clunton Coppice**. Just as you reach the coppice, look for a group of hornbeam trees on the left. Hornbeam is superficially a little like beech, but is distinguished from it by its smooth fluted trunk and winged fruits. It's an uncommon tree this far north (► Walk 40).

WHERE TO EAT AND DRINK ⓘ

In 1994 the **Crown Inn** at Clunton was threatened with closure, like so many country pubs. However, the locals knew just how to save it. They clubbed together and bought it, and happily it is still going strong today. The present couple running it took over in 2002 and are keen to attract more walkers, so you can be sure of a warm welcome, and not just from the woodburning stove. Food is served from noon, children and well-behaved dogs are welcome (dogs on leads), and the landlord specifically points out that walkers do not have to remove their boots.

Walking in Safety

All these walks are suitable for any reasonably fit person, but less experienced walkers should try the easier walks first. Route finding is usually straightforward, but you will find that an Ordnance Survey map is a useful addition to the route maps and descriptions.

Risks

Although each walk here has been researched with a view to minimising the risks to the walkers who follow its route, no walk in the countryside can be considered to be completely free from risk. Walking in the outdoors will always require a degree of common sense and judgement to ensure that it is as safe as possible.

- Be particularly careful on cliff paths and in upland terrain, where the consequences of a slip can be very serious.

- Remember to check tidal conditions before walking on the seashore.

- Some sections of route are by, or cross, busy roads. Take care and remember traffic is a danger even on minor country lanes.

- Be careful around farmyard machinery and livestock, especially if you have children with you.

- Be aware of the consequences of changes in the weather and check the forecast before you set out. Carry spare clothing and a torch if you are walking in the winter months. Remember the weather can change very quickly at any time of the year, and in moorland and heathland areas, mist and fog can make route finding much harder. Don't set out in these conditions unless you are confident of your navigation skills in poor visibility. In summer remember to take account of the heat and sun; wear a hat and carry spare water.

- On walks away from centres of population you should carry a whistle and survival bag. If you do have an accident requiring the emergency services, make a note of your position as accurately as possible and dial 999.

Acknowledgements

Thanks are due to Mum for encouragement and for understanding when pressure of work meant cancelling a planned trip. Thanks also to Nick and Jo for advice. A great many miles were walked in preparing this book so apologies to Shaun for never being home when he came round and to Rosie the cat for all those evenings she had to wait until far too late for her tea. Thanks are also due to Chris for coping so patiently with the inadequacies of my prehistoric word processor and my own lack of computer literacy.

AQUA3 AA Publishing and Outcrop Publishing Services would like to thank Chartech for supplying aqua3 maps for this book.
For more information visit their website: www.aqua3.com.

Series management: Outcrop Publishing Services Limited, Cumbria
Series editor: Chris Bagshaw
Front cover: www.BritainonView.com **Back cover:** AA Photo Library/J Martin